TEACHING WORD MEANINGS

The Literacy Teaching Series

Anders and Guzzetti • Literacy and Development in the Content Areas, Second Edition

Au • Multicultural Issues and Literacy Achievement

Stahl and Nagy • Teaching Word Meanings

Wolf • Interpreting Literature With Children

For a complete list of other titles in LEA's Literacy Teaching Series, please contact Lawrence Erlbaum Associates, Publishers.

TEACHING WORD MEANINGS

Steven A. Stahl
University of Illinois

William E. Nagy
Seattle Pacific University

LAWRENCE ERLBAUM ASSOCIATES, PUBLISHERS
2006   Mahwah, New Jersey   London

Lawrence Erlbaum Associates, Inc., Publishers
10 Industrial Avenue
Mahwah, New Jersey 07430

Cover design by Kathryn Houghtaling Lacey

Library of Congress Cataloging-in-Publication Data

Stahl, Steven A.
    Teaching word meanings / Steven A. Stahl & William E. Nagy.
        p. cm.
Includes bibliographical references and index.
ISBN 0-8058-4363-9 (cloth : alk. paper)
ISBN 0-8058-4364-7 (pbk. : alk. paper)

1. Vocabulary—Study and teaching (Elementary).   2. Reading compre-
    hension.   I. Nagy, William E.   II. Title.
LB1574.5.S72   2005
372.61—dc22

                                            2004054188
                                            CIP

Books published by Lawrence Erlbaum Associates are printed on acid-free paper, and their bindings are chosen for strength and durability.

Printed in the United States of America
10 9 8 7 6 5 4 3 2 1

Contents

Preface   **vii**

Part I: The Lay of the Land

1   The Importance of Vocabulary   **3**

2   Vocabulary Knowledge, Reading Comprehension, and Readability   **9**

3   Problems and Complexities   **26**

4   A Comprehensive Approach to Vocabulary Learning   **47**

Part II: Teaching Specific Words

5   Teaching Words for Ownership   **61**

6   Teaching Concepts   **77**

7   Teaching High-Frequency Words   **97**

8   Talking About Words   **109**

Part III: Independent Word Learning

9   Exposure to Rich Language   **125**

10 Promoting Word Consciousness   **137**

11 Teaching Word Learning Strategies: Word Parts   **157**

12 Teaching Word Learning Strategies: Context   **173**

13 Teaching Word Learning Strategies: Definitions   **182**

14 Conclusion: Matching Instructional Approaches to Students   **195**
     and Words

References   **199**

Author Index   **211**

Subject Index   **215**

Preface

This book is about how children learn—and how teachers can help them learn—the meanings of new words. Learning new words is foundational to success in school. Researchers have known for years that how many word meanings a student knows is one of the single strongest predictors of how well that student will understand text. Knowing the meanings of words, and being able to use them, is essential for effective writing. As well, knowing the concepts in a domain is intimately tied in with knowing the words that convey them. Hence, having a large vocabulary is both a powerful tool for a variety of academic and life goals, and an end in itself. One of the things that effective teachers must be able to do is support and increase the vocabulary growth of their students.

Thus, this is a book about vocabulary instruction. Both of us are proud to have devoted much of our professional lives to studying how children learn words, and how teachers can help them learn even more. However, the word *vocabulary* carries with it a variety of images and connotations, some of which have little to do with the goals of this book. That's one of the reasons we didn't use the word *vocabulary* in the book's title. Let us start by telling you a few things that we're not trying to do in this book, which this word might seem to imply.

First of all, we're not primarily interested in the processes by which children develop their *sight vocabularies*. The phrase *sight vocabulary* refers to those words whose printed form the child can recognize easily and quickly. Helping children develop large sight vocabularies is indeed an important part of early reading instruction, but for the most part this process involves words that are already part of children's oral vocabularies. In this book, on the other hand, we're interested in helping children learn new word *meanings*.

Because early reading instruction is often focused on decoding, some might think that vocabulary should start in earnest only after children have mastered the mechanics of reading. We disagree. In fact, it has been argued that the "fourth-grade slump" experienced by some students is the result of a general neglect of vocabulary development in the primary grades. Of course, the methods for promoting vocabulary growth in primary-grade students will look a lot different from those used with older students, and will take place primarily through the medium of the spoken language.

Another problem with the word *vocabulary* is that it may call up images of traditional instructional activities that run the danger of being lethally boring, as well as being ineffective. However, to have the desired impact, vocabulary instruction must not only teach words, but also help students develop an interest in words.

One more thing we would like to make clear from the outset is that our purpose is not to get teachers to spend large amounts of time doing vocabulary activities. We do, of course, present some means of teaching word meanings that are effective and, we hope, interesting for both teachers and students. However, our goal is not to increase the amount of time you spend on "vocabulary," but rather to increase the extent to which you are intentional about improving the reading vocabularies of your students. Sometimes this will involve activities in which you help students learn the meanings of specific words. However, there are a variety of things you need to do to help students develop large vocabularies—many of which you want to be doing for other reasons as well. Our goal, then, is to give you a variety of tools that will all contribute to your students' vocabulary growth.

This book is divided into three parts. (Any of you old enough to have studied Latin may recognize the allusion the introduction of Caesar's *Gallic Wars*.)

Part I, "The Lay of the Land," addresses the big picture, trying to make sure that you have a good grasp on the *whys* before we move to the *how tos*. In chapter 1 we remind you of several reasons why vocabulary is such an important part of a child's education. In chapter 2, we talk about the relationship between vocabulary and reading comprehension. This relationship is more complex than one might expect; the complexities give us some important clues about what an effective approach to vocabulary instruction must look like. Chapter 3 presents the obstacles to vocabulary growth—reasons why setting out to help children develop large vocabularies is a challenging task. In chapter 4, we outline the response to the complexities and problems raised in the preceding two chapters—a multifaceted approach to promoting long-term, large-scale vocabulary growth in schoolchildren.

Part II, "Teaching Specific Words," covers the variety of instructional techniques that can be used to help children learn the meanings of individual words. There are various techniques because there are different kinds of words to learn, and different reasons for learning them. In chapter 5, we talk about the kind of intensive instruction that is necessary for those words that you want children to be able to use effectively for understanding, as well as in their own writing. Chapter 6 is about teaching concepts. Often, the meanings of words—that is, the concepts they represent—*are* the content being taught. When these concepts are new or difficult, instruction must ensure that students achieve a thorough understanding of these concepts. Chapter 7 addresses high-frequency words—the core words of the language that occur in every genre and every topic, which you are tempted to assume that your students already know. Most of them do, but as the students in our classrooms come to represent an ever-increasing diversity of cultural and linguistic backgrounds, we cannot afford to take anything for granted.

Chapters 5 through 7 examine instruction focused specifically on teaching word meanings. Chapter 8, on the other hand, deals with the kind of explanations about words that teachers must be ready to provide throughout the curriculum. Only a small part of the schoolday need be devoted to vocabulary per se, but teachers must capitalize on the myriad of opportunities that arise throughout the day for adding to students' store of word knowledge.

Part III, "Independent Word Learning," talks about what we can do to promote vocabulary growth besides teaching or explaining individual words. Although teaching children specific words is essential, it is even more important that we increase children's rate of learning words that are not covered in instruction. In chapter 9, we talk about exposure to rich language, the essential raw material for independent word learning. Chapter 10 deals with word consciousness—the interest in words and motivation to learn them that drive independent word learning. In chapters 11 through 13, we discuss specific word learning strategies—use of word parts, context, and dictionaries.

In the conclusion, chapter 14, we provide a simple framework—seven basic categories of words—to sum up one of the main themes of the book: Because there are different kinds of words, and different reasons for learning them, teachers need to be strategic in deciding which words to teach, how to teach them, and which words not to teach at all.

—Steven A. Stahl
—William E. Nagy

I

The Lay of the Land

Part I of this book is called "The Lay of the Land." The goal of this book is to help teachers promote large-scale, long-term vocabulary growth in their students. Like most other aspects of teaching, this is a difficult and complex task. Success depends on understanding as well as on effort. This part of the book aims to provide the big picture.

Chapter 1 is called "The Importance of Vocabulary." One reason that vocabulary is important is because of its role in reading comprehension, which in turn is essential for the rest of students' learning. To be academically successful, students must have large reading vocabularies. The other main reason for the importance of vocabulary is that the students who need your help the most—whether because of family resources, or the use of a different language at home, or any other factors—are very likely going to also have challenges mastering the vocabulary that is essential for success in school.

Chapter 2, "Vocabulary Knowledge, Reading Comprehension, and Readability," explores the reasons why children who know more words also understand text better. It may sound obvious why this is the case, but there are actually a rather complex set of connections between vocabulary and reading ability. Each of these connections tells us something about what an effective approach to promoting vocabulary growth must look like.

Chapter 3, "Problems and Complexities," gives the bad news. Helping students develop large reading vocabularies is a difficult task, for a number of reasons. If you don't know the nature, and the severity, of the problems facing the students, it may be hard to see the need for the solutions, or to devote the energy necessary to make them work.

Chapter 4 presents "A Comprehensive Approach to Vocabulary Learning." We can't offer some simple magic bullet to solve students' vocabulary problems, but we can provide a coherent plan. This chapter is, in effect, an overview of the rest of the book, which presents the various components of a comprehensive, multifaceted approach to helping students learn the thousands of words they need to know to be successful in school and beyond.

1

The Importance of Vocabulary

Polonius: What's that you read, m'lord?
Hamlet: Words, words, words.

(Shakespeare, 1600–01, *Hamlet*, Act II, Scene ii)

Words, words. They're all we have to go on.

(Stoppard, 1967, *Rosencrantz and Guildenstern are Dead*, p. 41)

Words are so pervasive in our life, so central to being human, that we do not often stop to reflect on their value and power. Like the proverbial fish that is unaware of the water in which it swims, we are seldom conscious of how much of our experience is in terms of language.

The words that we use both express and shape who we are. Our vocabulary, even more than our accent, gives away our social and educational background. As a major factor in determining what we can understand, it opens or closes access to sources of information that will impact our future.

This is a book about vocabulary—about how schoolchildren learn words, and about how teachers can help them learn more. We need to make it clear at the outset, that by *vocabulary* we will be referring to students' knowledge of word *meanings*. We distinguish this from *word recognition*, which involves recognizing the written form of words. Likewise, we are not talking about *sight vocabulary*, which is recognition of words "by sight" or automatically. Word recognition, sight vocabulary, and decoding are important topics in their own right, but in this book we are concerned with how students acquire new *meanings*—that is, how they learn new concepts, and how they learn new words for familiar concepts.

Why a book about vocabulary? Because words are the tools we use to access our background knowledge, express ideas, and learn new concepts. The words children know will determine how well they can comprehend texts, in the upper elementary grades, in middle and high school, and in college. Reading is far more than recognizing words and remembering their meanings, but if the reader does not know the meanings of a sufficient proportion of the words in the text, comprehension is impossible.

The importance of vocabulary knowledge for reading comprehension would seem self-evident to anyone who has ever read a jargon-filled text and was left scratching his or her head. Here is an example from an early draft of a paper written by one of us with a colleague:

> The findings of our study also reveal that there is nothing especially difficult about setting up a mental representation for a new lexical item as presumably children would have to do for unknown words. For example, for localist versions of connectionist viewpoints, it seems probable that one would first have to create a new lexical node before orthographic, phonological, and semantic information could become connected with it. (reference withheld because of embarrassment)

To understand this paragraph, one needs to know the meanings of words like *connectionist, lexical, node,* and so on. Without that knowledge, this paragraph is gibberish. This passage illustrates one of the oldest findings in educational research—the strong relationship between vocabulary knowledge and reading comprehension. Correlational studies, readability research, and experimental studies have all found strong and reliable relationships between the difficulty of the words in a text and text comprehension (Anderson & Freebody, 1981). Vocabulary knowledge and reading comprehension correlate so highly (in the 0.85 to 0.95 range) so that some authors have argued that they are psychometrically identical (e.g., Carver, 2003; R. Thorndike, 1974). Others have found that prose literacy has modest but significant correlations with occupational status and participation in society (Guthrie & Hutchinson, 1991). It may overstate the case to say that vocabulary knowledge is central to children's and adults' success in school and in life, but not by much.

The English language, with its penchant for borrowing and its worldwide use, probably has a stock of words larger than that of any other language. It is not surprising, then, that among speakers of English, a large vocabulary is one of the most important parts of verbal proficiency. In fact, the statistical

relationship between vocabulary size and intelligence is so strong that a vocabulary test alone is often used in place of a full-scale test of verbal IQ
(Anderson & Freebody, 1981).

Vocabulary is closely associated not just with intelligence, but also with
knowledge. Although "a rose by any other name would smell as sweet," a
person knowing not only *rose* but *nasturtium, bluebonnet, black-eyed
Susans,* and so on understands more about flowers than does a person who
knows only *flower* and perhaps a few common flower names.

A person who knows more words can speak, and even think, more precisely about the world. A person who knows the terms *scarlet* and *crimson*
and *azure* and *indigo* can think about colors in a different way than a person who is limited to *red* and *blue.* A person who knows about *balks, bunts*
and the *double switch* can think about baseball in a different way than a person who doesn't. A person who can label someone as *pusillanimous* or a
recreant can better describe a person's cowardly behavior. Words divide
the world; the more words we have, the more complex ways we can think
about the world.

For teachers, vocabulary is important most of all because of the huge differences that exist among their students. Differences in word knowledge occur early in life, and there are dramatic differences in the exposure to new
words among families of different social classes. One study (Hart & Risley,
1995) found that children in the households of professional parents were exposed to 50% more words than were children in working-class families, and
twice as many words as children in homes receiving Aid to Families with Dependent Children. Hart and Risley noted that the poorest children had con-
comitantly fewer words spoken to them, with more words spoken in
imperative sentences and fewer in descriptive or elaborative sentences. As an
outcome of these differences in exposure, the children from the most advantaged homes had receptive vocabularies five times larger than did the children from homes with the lowest incomes. The picture that Hart and Risley
presented was that of a dramatic gap in word knowledge between well off
and poor, one that begins early in life and threatens to grow with time.

This does not mean that children from poor homes are condemned to
linguistic poverty. On the contrary, it is not hard to find successful people
from humble beginnings. Education can make a difference. Some studies
have found that good school experiences can overcome the effects of inadequate home experiences (Snow, Barnes, Chandler, Goodman, & Hemphill,
1992). Going to school does not guarantee vocabulary growth; other studies have found no impact of school attendance on young children's vocabularies (Cantalini, 1987; Morrison, Williams, & Massetti, 1998). However,

teachers are clearly in a position to have a powerful impact on children's language development (Dickinson & Smith, 1994).

Vocabulary is also one of the primary challenges facing students who come from non-English-speaking homes. Students from low-income or non-English-speaking homes come to schools with rich funds of knowledge and experience (Moll, Amanti, Neff, & Gonzalez, 1992) that teachers need to recognize and build on. However, ultimately success in school requires linking personal knowledge and experience to the vocabulary of the school. A child may achieve fluency in conversational English in a year or so; but even under optimal circumstances, it may take an English language learner 5 or more years to catch up in terms of the vocabulary of academic English (Collier, 1989; Cummins, 1994).

Past electronic revolutions—telephone, radio, and television—increased the role of oral language in communication. However, despite the increasing use of multimedia, the current wave of information technology shows no signs of making written language an endangered species. Although the word *literacy* is continually being redefined to take into account changes in the contexts in which people encounter written language and the purposes for which they use it, the level of literacy one needs in order to participate fully in society continues to rise.

Perhaps one of the most important reasons why teachers need to pay attention to vocabulary is that vocabulary knowledge is cumulative. The more words you know, the easier it is to learn yet more words. For example, Shefelbine (1990) looked at children's ability to infer the meanings of new words they encountered from context. He found that one of the biggest obstacles facing the less successful children was that they didn't know the meanings of the other words in the context—the words that were supposed to provide the clues for the meanings of the new words. This is a classic case of a "Matthew effect" described by Stanovich (1986). The notion of a Matthew effect comes from the passage from the gospel in which it is foretold that the rich will get richer and the poor will get poorer. Children with weak vocabularies in the early grades will not be able to take advantage of richer texts due to their lack of word knowledge. Because they cannot understand more difficult texts, they will learn fewer words and hence fall further and further behind. Thus, individual differences in vocabulary size, and vocabulary differences related to socioeconomic status or home language, tend to widen over time. Students with smaller vocabularies will fall progressively further behind—unless something is done.

Although the importance of vocabulary seems obvious enough to us, this perception is not universally held. Every year, *Reading Today* (the bimonthly newspaper of the International Reading Association) includes an article on "What's Hot, What's Not." A topic is "hot" if it is judged (by a panel of "literacy leaders") to be receiving increasing and positive attention. In the December 2003/January 2004 poll, for the fourth time in 4 years, vocabulary/word meanings was considered by the majority of the leaders to be "not hot." That is, in their estimation, people in reading-related professions were not especially interested in or concerned about this topic (Cassidy & Cassidy, 2003/2004).

The opinion that vocabulary is "not hot" is backed up by research. A number of studies have shown that, in general, very little classroom time is given to vocabulary instruction (e.g., Durkin, 1978/1979; Scott, Jamieson-Noel, & Asselin, 2003).

Why is vocabulary instruction relatively unpopular? We think that there are two main reasons for this. One is the tendency to treat word-level reading processes and higher-level processes as "either/or" rather than as "both/and." That is, some teachers think they should be focusing on issues of interpretation and critical thinking *instead* of vocabulary. Another reason for the neglect of vocabulary is the tendency to think of vocabulary instruction in terms of traditional methods that have been shown to be ineffective—for example, "memorize the definition, and write a sentence using the word."

It should be noted, however, that rating vocabulary as "not hot" did not reflect what these literacy leaders thought should be the case. On the contrary, vocabulary/word meanings was also listed as a topic that "should be hot" (Cassidy & Cassidy, 2002/2003, 2003/2004). This judgment that vocabulary should be a hot topic is consistent with the National Reading Panel's decision to consider vocabulary as one of five key areas to be addressed in reading instruction.

What needs to be done? That's what the rest of the book is about.

We need to be honest with you, though: Helping students gain large reading vocabularies is neither simple nor easy. An effective approach to promoting vocabulary growth has to be multifaceted and sustained. To make the effort that is needed, you have to know not only the importance of vocabulary knowledge to educational success, but also the complexity and difficulty of the vocabulary problems that many students face. In other words, we think that it's best to tell you the bad news before we tell you the good news. The next two chapters, then, are devoted to complexity and difficulty. Chapter 2 is about the relationship between vocabulary knowledge and reading comprehension. The common-sense understanding of this relationship—that knowing more words makes you a better reader—is true,

2

Vocabulary Knowledge, Reading Comprehension, and Readability

The difference between the *almost*-right word & the *right* word is really a large matter—it's the difference between the lightning bug and the lightning.

(Mark Twain, 1888 letter to George Bainton, published in Bainton, 1890, *The Art of Authorship*, pp. 87–88)

One of the main reasons teachers are interested in improving students' vocabularies is to help make them better readers. In fact, it has been known for a long time that the size of a person's vocabulary is one of the strongest predictors of how well that person can understand what he or she reads (Anderson & Freebody, 1981; Davis, 1944). This relationship between vocabulary and comprehension, which is hardly surprising, seems to have an obvious interpretation: Having a big vocabulary makes you a better reader. The instructional implication also seems obvious: If you teach students more words, they will understand text better.

This implication isn't completely off track. In fact, one of our main goals in promoting students' vocabulary growth is to make them better able to understand what they read. However, the relationship between vocabulary knowledge and reading comprehension is more complicated than just knowing more words makes you a better reader. If we want to increase students' vocabularies as a way of improving reading comprehension, it's important to have at least some understanding of this complexity. In particular, considering the nature of the connections between vocabulary and reading comprehension can tell us some important things about how we should approach the task of trying to increase students' vocabularies.

Hypotheses

Richard C. Anderson and Peter Freebody (1981) were the first to lay out some of the different possible explanations of why a larger vocabulary is associated with better reading ability. The first possibility they labeled the *instrumental hypothesis*—the idea that it is simply knowing more words that makes you a better reader. This idea seems so obvious that you might wonder why they bothered to give it a special name. The reason for this label becomes clearer when you realize that there are some other possible explanations of the relationship between vocabulary knowledge and reading comprehension that are almost equally plausible.

A second possible explanation is the *knowledge hypothesis*. According to this hypothesis, it is not the knowledge of the words per se that makes one a better reader, but instead the knowledge of the concepts that the words represent. An example may be helpful in distinguishing the knowledge hypothesis from the instrumentalist hypothesis: Imagine that you give students a simple vocabulary test containing one word, *photosynthesis*, and only half of the students pass. Next you give them a text to read, on the subject of "how plants make their own food." Imagine further that this text is written in relatively simple language, and does not contain the word *photosynthesis*. Finally, you give the students a comprehension test covering the contents of the passage they read.

It's probably going to be the case that students who knew the word *photosynthesis* did better on the comprehension test. But why? It isn't vocabulary knowledge per se that made the difference, because the text didn't contain the word *photosynthesis* and we are assuming that all the words actually used in the text were familiar to the students. The difference is that the students were not all equally familiar with the *concepts* discussed in the text. Those students who knew the word *photosynthesis* were the ones who knew more about plants, and how plants produce food.

Although this example may seem a little contrived, it illustrates a general principle that has been strongly documented: A readers' knowledge of the topic of a text determines how well he or she will understand that text. It is not that knowledge of the individual words plays no role, but instead that the knowledge of individual words is simply the tip of the iceberg—it is the rich, interconnected knowledge of concepts that really drives comprehension.

Another way to make the same point is to emphasize the connections that exist among word meanings. In dictionaries, each word has a separate definition, and you might be tempted to think that words are stored in your memory in the same way—each word in its own separate little file drawer. However, that's not how human memory works. A somewhat more accurate picture is to think of word meanings as stored in semantic networks. Each word is connected to other words, and to other concepts, facts, and specific memories. When a word is recognized, the connections to other words in the network are also evoked. Hence, when a person reads the word *whale*, for example, any knowledge the person has about whales could be activated. Whether or not a particular text contains the word *orca*, the reader who knows that word probably has a more elaborated network of information about whales than does a person who doesn't know this word. Thus, even if the word *orca* is not in a particular text about whales, a person who knows that word will understand the text more thoroughly than a person who doesn't. The richer the knowledge a person has about the topic of a text, the more that person can learn from that text. Thus, even in the case of children reading simplified texts, children with more knowledge may recall more (Stahl & Jacobson, 1986).

A third hypothesis about the relationship of vocabulary knowledge to reading comprehension is the *aptitude hypothesis*. According to this hypothesis, vocabulary knowledge and reading comprehension are correlated, not because one causes the other, but because both reflect a more general underlying verbal aptitude. Students with high verbal ability will be better word learners, and end up with larger vocabularies. Students with high verbal ability are also better at understanding what they read. Thus, such students will get high scores on both vocabulary tests and comprehension tests, but a direct link between reading ability and vocabulary is not, according to this hypothesis, logically necessary.

The aptitude hypothesis can be further refined or subdivided, according to which aspects of verbal ability one thinks are most important to the connection between vocabulary knowledge and reading ability. Sternberg and Powell (1983), for example, suggested that the relationship between vocabulary knowledge and reading comprehension may lie in the ability to make inferences. This ability is crucial to comprehension, and it is vital to figuring out the meanings of unfamiliar words.

Sternberg and Powell's (1983) interpretation of the aptitude hypothesis focused on inferencing ability as a way of explaining the relationship between vocabulary knowledge and reading comprehension. However, there are other aptitudes or abilities that might also explain some of the connection between vocabulary knowledge and reading comprehension. We believe that metalinguistic awareness is one such ability. Hence, another account of the relationship between vocabulary knowledge and reading comprehension could be labeled the *metalinguistic hypothesis*.

Actually, metalinguistic awareness encompasses a range of abilities that may be involved in the link between vocabulary and reading comprehension. One type of metalinguistic ability that is known to play an important role in early reading is phonemic awareness (Ehri et al., 2001). There is some evidence that vocabulary knowledge contributes to phonemic awareness (Fowler, 1991; Metsala, 1999; Metsala & Walley, 1998). Therefore, one of the reasons for a correlation between vocabulary knowledge and reading comprehension is that young children with large vocabularies tend to have higher levels of phonemic awareness. Higher levels of phonemic awareness result in more success in early literacy, which in turn contributes to greater comprehension.

Another aspect of metalinguistic awareness that may relate vocabulary to reading comprehension is morphological awareness—the awareness of the structure of words in terms of morphemes (i.e., prefixes, roots, and suffixes). Students with bigger vocabularies are likely to have more morphological awareness, and vice versa. However, morphological awareness also contributes to reading comprehension (Nagy, Berninger, Abbott, Vaughan, & Vermeulen, 2003), in part by helping children decode long words more accurately and fluently.

There are other types of metalinguistic awareness that may also be related to both vocabulary knowledge and reading comprehension. The concept of word in text (i.e., the ability to finger point, or match written and spoken words in text) is one that may be important in early stages of learning to read (Morris, Bloodgood, Lomax, & Perney, 2003). Later on, other types of awareness of language—for example, the ability to understand figurative language—may be important.

Another type of metalinguistic awareness is sensitivity to polysemy, or multiple meanings. As we have already noted, most common words have multiple meanings. The meaning of a word shifts at least to some extent every time it is used in a new context. The variability of word meanings is far greater than one typically realizes. If you look at the dictionary entry for a common word, you find more meanings than you might have expected. On reflection, one has to admit, for example, that the meaning of *strict* is different in *a strict interpretation* than it is in *a strict parent*, even though the two are clearly similar. This proliferation of shades of meaning is an ongoing process; Green (1984) estimated that 15% of the words in newspapers, for example, are used with senses not listed in any dictionary.

What does this have to do with the relationship between vocabulary knowledge and reading comprehension? It gets back to another twist on the aptitude hypothesis, similar to the two that have already been mentioned. A person with a larger vocabulary not only knows more words, but also knows more meanings for many words (Qian, 1999; Vermeer, 2001). The process of understanding text requires a certain flexibility in dealing with words that enables one to adjust the meaning of the word to fit new contexts; this same ability is obviously crucial in learning these new meanings.

Karen Mezynski (1983) added another hypothesis to the three suggested by Anderson and Freebody—the *access hypothesis*. This hypothesis highlights the importance of automaticity of word knowledge in comprehension. People who know more words also have deeper, and more fluent, knowledge of the words they have in common with people possessing smaller vocabularies. This is especially important to get the correct shade of meaning used in a particular context. A person with a larger vocabulary therefore has an advantage in terms of being able to access the meanings of even common words more quickly. Because automaticity, as well as accuracy, of word knowledge is important for comprehension (LaBerge & Samuels, 1974; Samuels, 2002), being able to access word meanings more quickly results in better comprehension of text.

Finally, Stanovich (1986) and others have suggested what could be called the *reciprocal hypothesis*—that the relationship between vocabulary knowledge and reading comprehension goes both ways. On the one hand, it seems plausible (as asserted by the instrumental hypothesis) that knowing more words would make one a better reader. On the other hand, being a better reader generally means that one reads more; and if much of a person's vocabulary is gained through reading, one would expect better readers to develop larger vocabularies.

One can think of this relationship in terms of a circle: Having a bigger vocabulary makes you a better reader, being a better reader makes is possible for you to read more, and reading more gives you a bigger vocabulary. This circular relationship tends to increase differences over time. On the positive side, better readers tend to read more, acquire bigger vocabularies, and become even better readers. On the negative side, poorer readers tend to read less, fail to develop large vocabularies, and find reading to be increasingly difficult as the vocabulary demands of the texts they have to read become greater.

It's important to note that it is not just vocabulary knowledge that is involved in this kind of reciprocal relationship, but also any kind of knowledge that can be gained from reading and can contribute to reading. For example, people who know more about the world are better readers because of this fact; therefore, they read more, and in reading more they gain still more background knowledge. The same goes for decoding fluency and knowledge of text structures.

Because this reciprocal relationship involves more than just vocabulary knowledge, the student with a smaller vocabulary has more than just a vocabulary problem. Stanovich and his colleagues have done extensive research on the variety of cognitive benefits that accrue to readers (e.g., Cunningham & Stanovich, 1998). Using a variety of measures of recognition of titles and authors of common books, they found that both children and adults who read more (or who have read more) have significantly greater vocabularies than do those people who have read fewer books. Those people who read more also know more—about history, current events, and practical everyday topics (Stanovich & Cunningham, 1993).

We have now presented quite a few different possible accounts of the relationship between vocabulary knowledge and reading comprehension. Which of these accounts is correct?

The answer is: Probably all of them! As Anderson and Freebody (1981) pointed out when they introduced the first three hypotheses, these different hypotheses are not mutually exclusive. The fact that one may be correct does not make the others wrong. In fact, none of them are likely to be completely false. Rather, the relationship between vocabulary knowledge and reading comprehension is complex.

What conclusions can we draw about vocabulary instruction from this complicated picture? First of all, the very complexity of the picture suggests that any single approach to vocabulary instruction is likely to be inadequate. In fact, we think that each of the hypotheses has implications for vocabulary instruction; each one supports one or more of the multiple components (wide reading, teaching individual words, teaching strategies for learning words independently, and fostering word consciousness) that Graves (2000) claimed are necessary parts of the vocabulary curriculum.

Let's review the different hypotheses with a specific example in mind, a classroom with which you're familiar. (We'll talk about a fifth-grade classroom, but the points would work for almost any grade above the primary level, so keep the classroom you thought of in mind.) Some of the children in the class have large vocabularies, and, not surprisingly, understand their textbooks better. Some have relatively small vocabularies, and even if they can decode reasonably well, they stumble over the meanings of many words. You're about to have the students read a segment of text that contains some words you know will be difficult for some of your students. What do you do to address this vocabulary problem?

The instrumentalist hypothesis suggests an obvious response—teach the meanings of the hard words in the text to students who don't already know them. In fact, teaching the meanings of unfamiliar words can help a student understand a text. In a meta-analysis of vocabulary instructional studies, Stahl and Fairbanks (1986) found that teaching individual words could have significant effects on reading comprehension. This finding was confirmed by the National Reading Panel (2000).

Stahl and Fairbanks (1986), however, did not discern that all approaches to teaching word meanings significantly improved comprehension. For example, approaches that only had children memorize definitions or only presented a word in a single context were not effective in improving children's comprehension. Hence, if the teacher in our hypothetical fifth grade classroom tries to teach students the meanings of the hard words in a text they are about to read by having them copy and then memorize the definitions, there is little reason to believe that the students' comprehension of the text containing those words will be improved at all.

The instrumentalist hypothesis suggests that teaching word meanings may help, but by itself does not tell us *how* we should teach words. However, the access hypothesis—that people with larger vocabularies understand text better because they not only know more words, but they also know most words more thoroughly—makes a specific claim about what is necessary for effective vocabulary instruction. In particular, it suggests that vocabulary instruction should aim not just for accuracy of word knowledge, but also for fluency of word knowledge. A minimum requirement for fluency of word knowledge is that there be sufficient practice with an instructed word so that its meaning can be accessed relatively quickly. This means that children need to see words repeatedly, in different contexts (e.g., Beck, McKeown, & Kucan, 2002), so that the words' meanings will be easily accessible. Furthermore, it is important that words be learned in an environment that encourages them to make connections to other words. This would involve presenting words in meaningful contexts, connected to domain knowledge, rather than presenting words only in lists.

The knowledge hypothesis—that it is not just knowing words but knowing the network of concepts and facts that go with them that improves comprehension—also tells us something about what may make vocabulary instruction more effective. The implication is that instruction about word meanings should be embedded in instruction about content.

This is obvious in the case of content area vocabulary. In the case of general vocabulary, on the other hand, it may not be as easy to do this. However, the implication is that even for words that are not tied to specific domains of knowledge, instruction should emphasize the connection of the instructed words with other words and concepts. Teaching words in clusters is easy to do (and makes a good "sponge" activity, or an activity that can be used to fill in time between activities in the school day). Having children, for example, come up with words that mean "ways of moving" (*walk, stroll, gallop, run, lumber, waddle*) might be a nice activity that can be done while lining up or on the way of a special activity.

The aptitude hypothesis—that smart people are both better readers and better word learners—may not at first seem to offer any suggestions for instruction. However, Sternberg and Powell's (1983) analysis of this hypothesis in fact leads to a very specific instructional conclusion. Sternberg and Powell argued that comprehension and word learning are related because both involve the ability to infer, and furthermore that the ability to infer the meanings of unfamiliar words can be learned. Hence, their version of the aptitude hypothesis suggests that students be taught strategies for figuring out the meanings of unfamiliar words. In the case of the fifth-grade class about to read a text containing some difficult words, knowledge of these strategies may help them make more effective use of the clues to the words' meanings that are already present in the text. In fact, a number of approaches to comprehension strategy instruction include strategies for dealing with unfamiliar words (see, e.g., Klinger & Vaughan, 1999). Teaching students word-learning strategies does not always have an immediate measurable effect on comprehension (Baumann, Edwards, Boland, Olejnik, & Kame'enui, 2003). However, there is at least some hope that such strategies may increase the rate at which students acquire vocabulary from context, which could have a long-term positive impact on their vocabulary growth.

The metalinguistic hypothesis—that people with larger vocabularies understand text better because they are more adept at reflecting on different aspects of language—directs our attention toward the role of "word consciousness" in vocabulary growth. (See chap. 10 for more detail on the role of word consciousness in vocabulary instruction.) In the case of a particular fifth-grade class about to read a text containing some difficult words, the metalinguistic hypothesis does not make any strong claims about what instruction would be most effective in the short run, for improving comprehension of that particular passage. However, this hypothesis does suggest that, in the long run, vocabulary instruction will be most effective if it increases students' awareness of and interest in words.

Finally, the reciprocal relationship between vocabulary knowledge and reading comprehension underlines the importance of volume of reading in increasing students' vocabularies. In the case of the fifth-grade classroom about to read a text containing some difficult words, this hypothesis offers an explanation of why teaching low-vocabulary students the meanings of the hard words in the text is unlikely to bring them up to the level of the students with larger vocabularies. The students with larger vocabularies gained much of their superior vocabulary knowledge in the process of doing extensive reading. In doing this reading, they also accumulated all sorts of other knowledge that would give them an advantage: a variety of topical knowledge, knowledge of text structures and genres, and fluency in word recognition, to name a few. The reciprocal hypothesis thus supports wide reading as one component of an approach to promoting vocabulary growth, even if it doesn't tell us anything about how to teach specific words more effectively.

Our point in this chapter, as in the following chapter, has been to help you understand the need for a comprehensive, multifaceted approach to increasing students' vocabularies. Such an approach obviously will require time and effort, so you need to have solid reasons for making that kind of investment.

So far, we have talked about the severity and complexity of the problem—why it is difficult (although absolutely necessary) to work for large-scale, long-term gains in students' vocabularies. From this point on in the book, we discuss how to take on this challenging task in the most effective ways possible.

Before we discuss instruction, however, we are going to take a slight detour, exploring the relationship between vocabulary and readability—a relationship that is parallel in many ways to the relationship between students' vocabulary knowledge and their ability to comprehend text.

Vocabulary and Readability

So far in this chapter, we have looked at the relationship between readers' vocabulary knowledge and their ability to understand text. Although vocabulary knowledge does contribute directly to comprehension (the instrumentalist hypothesis), the relationship between vocabulary knowledge and reading comprehension turns out to be complex. These complexities tell us that the instrumentalist hypothesis is not the whole picture, and provide some support for the idea of a comprehensive, multicomponent approach to promoting students' vocabulary growth. Readability gives us another window on the vocabulary–comprehension relationship—in this case, from the perspective of the vocabulary load of the text, and how this load impacts on comprehension.

Readability refers to the factors that relate to the relative difficulty of different texts. This is a research tradition that goes back to the beginnings of the 20th century. Prominent researchers such as E. L. Thorndike and Edgar Dale devised approaches to determine for whom a particular text was appropriate (see Chall, 1958). The factors involved in matching texts to readers were an early approach to developing theories of reading comprehension (e.g., Thorndike, 1917).

Readability research attempted to identify factors that would predict text difficulty. Almost invariably, a vocabulary factor of some kind was found to be the single strongest predictor of text difficulty. Hence, readability research would seem, at least at first glance, to support the instrumentalist hypothesis. However, just as the relationship between vocabulary knowledge and reading comprehension turned out to be more complex, so does the relationship between vocabulary load and text difficulty or readability. The vocabulary load of a text can certainly be one of the causes of a text being more difficult, but the vocabulary of a text can also be a symptom of other text features that relate to comprehension.

Word Difficulty

Readability research generally produces formulas that purport to be able to estimate the relative difficulty of a passage by a combination of factors. Usually, these factors are a word factor and a sentence length factor (Chall, 1958; Harrison, 1980). The word factor, which could be measured by the number of syllables in the average word or the number of difficult words, usually accounts for more of the variance in difficulty than the sentence factor (Chall, 1958; Harrison, 1980). However, despite general agreement that word difficulty is the primary factor predicting readability, how word difficulty is measured is often problematic.

Counting Syllables. Different readability formulas use different ways of determining the number of "difficult" words. The easiest to calculate is simply counting the number of syllables per 100 words, as in the Fry (1977) formula, among others. Because more difficult words are likely to be polysyllabic, the higher the percentage of polysyllabic words, the more likely the text will contain difficult words. This is not altogether accurate, because three-syllable words like *together* are easier than are some one-syllable words like *din* or *phlegm*. Counting syllables is a compromise that allows a person to calculate vocabulary difficulty easily, without checking each word against a word frequency list or some other list of word difficulty.

Word Frequency. Another approach to finding difficult words is to divide words into "easy" or "not easy" categories and calculate the percentage of "not easy" words per 100-word sample. In these formulas, "easy" words are considered to be words on a list, such as the Dale-Chall (Chall, 1995) or Harris-Jacobson (Harrison, 1980) lists. These lists are generally comprised of high-frequency words, often as many as 3,000 or 4,000 words. Whether a word is or is not on a list is a rough measure of whether it is frequent or not. If a word is not on one of these high-frequency lists, it is considered "not easy."

There are several problems with the word frequency approach. One is that frequency distinctions among words within the list are ignored. Words like *the* and *when* are more frequent than are words like *easy* or *step*. The first or second most common words in a 4,000-word list are more likely easier to understand than is the 3999th word. For beginning readers, these distinctions may be important.

Another problem with frequency lists is that the frequency of a word in the language in general does not always correspond closely with the probability that individual students will be familiar with those words. Especially in the primary grades, reading programs vary considerably by the number of words introduced. Furthermore, there is also surprisingly little overlap in the actual words introduced (Foorman et al., 2004).

Still another problem is that simply counting word frequency ignores words with multiple meanings. The word *line*, for example, has two distinct word meanings and over a hundred variations of these meanings. A dotted "line" may be easier to understand than to "line" one's pockets. (These two meanings have separate derivations.) A related problem may come from some highly frequent words. The word *that* may be easy when it points out "that" thing (you know, the one over there), but more difficult when it signals a relative clause. A general problem with word frequency approaches is that the more common the word is, the more likely it is to have multiple meanings. Common meanings of words might not cause problems, but uncommon meanings might.

Idioms are a related source of difficulty. This is especially true for English language learners, but idioms can cause problems for all learners. Phrases like "Don't bug me" or "That shirt is cool" may present especial difficulty or may be easier than a readability formula would calculate.

Word frequency approaches also have a problem with proper nouns, which are generally uncommon but may not cause serious difficulties to a reader. Once the reader knows that the character is named "John" or "Jennifer" or "Julio" or "Jamil," the name does not cause further difficulty. (For readers of English encountering Russian novels, names are often ignored or the characters are referred to as "that 'R' guy.") In the earlier Dale-Chall formula, for example, all proper nouns, including place names as well as person names, were designated as familiar. In the current version, however, they are designated as unfamiliar the first time they are encountered. Presumably, a passage with many names is going to be more difficult to read than is a passage with fewer characters. This notion is addressed in the new Dale-Chall formula.

It should be clear that although these two approaches—syllable counting and word frequency—dominated readability measurement for most of the 20th century, they are compromises, providing only a rough guide to a passage's difficulty in exchange for the possibility of hand calculation. A more precise approach to vocabulary difficulty would have each word examined as to word frequency, the number of children who knew its meaning (see Biemiller & Slonim, 2001), or some other metric of word difficulty. This precision is impossible to achieve if readability has to be hand calculated. Furthermore, hand calculation is only possible on samples of text. It would be ideal to calculate readability based on the whole book. Computers can calculate a total word frequency index on entire books with ease. Commercial publishers have employed computer-calculated readability formulas, using precise lists of word frequency, for years. The DRP (Carver, 1992; Freeman, 1987; Wood, Nemeth, & Brooks, 1985) and Lexile (Glick & Olson, 1998; Smith, 2000) approaches have been used to calculate readability; lists of graded books based on each of these approaches are available from Touchstone Associates (DRP) or Meta-Metrics (Lexile). These are proprietary approaches.

Mechanical counts of word frequency also ignore the effects of derivational prefixes and suffixes. Children who know the meanings of the prefix *pre* and the root *meeting* would have no difficulty with the made-up word *premeeting*, although any formula would count it as difficult. English generates new words continuously through the application of prefixes and suffixes to roots. This has been done historically with words whose meanings are established, but can also be done "on the fly." Thus, if one understood the verb *smoke*, one could understand *smoke* as a noun, *smoked* as both a verb and an adjective, *unsmoked, smokeless, smoke-free, unsmokable,* and so on. Anglin (1993) found that over half of children's word knowledge could be accounted for by growth in derived words. White, Sowell, and Yanagihara (1989) noted that a small list of affixes, if taught in third grade, would make a significant impact on children's word learning. Growth in affixes would seem to relate to what is taught in school. If children receive instruction in prefixes and suffixes, derived words should present no difficulty.

For children who know affixes, derived words are no problem and may be overcounted in readability formulas. (By the way, the spell-checker we are using does not recognize *overcounted* as a word, although we hope that you as a reader had no difficulty with this word.) For children who do not know an affix, on the other hand, even a common word may present uncommon difficulty. Thus, metalinguistic awareness—in this case, students' ability to use their knowledge of prefixes and suffixes to interpret new words—plays a role in the relationship between the vocabulary load of a text and its readability.

Knowledge and Readability

Whether a text is difficult, easy, or just right depends on a number of factors, not just the vocabulary difficulty and sentence length. One such factor is knowledge. If you have a high knowledge of the topic, you should be able to read a text that would be relatively difficult. If you have a low knowledge of the topic, you might not be able to understand a relatively easy text. As noted earlier, vocabulary difficulty is likely a measure of the commonness of the ideas in a text. A text written about *home, mother, family, sister,* and *brother* is likely to contain more common words, and thus would rate as easier on a readability formula than would a text that discusses *convertible bonds, options,* and *golden parachutes,* or a text that discusses *jibs, mainsails, gunwales,* and *tacking.* Each specialized knowledge area has its own terminology. The less common the knowledge area, the rarer the words that are part of the specialty will be. Thus, the words associated with football (*punt, block, tackle, quarterback*) may be more common than might the words associated with a less common sport, such as lacrosse. For most children, a text containing these football-related words might make sense, but it would not for a recent émigré, for example, who might not know much about American football, but might know a lot about soccer (*football* in the rest of the world). For that reader, a passage about soccer would be easier than one about American football.

Readability formulas tend to be developed based on an "average" child. Such a child may not exist. Children have highly specific interests. Many high school students, for example, have a great deal of knowledge about cars. High school remedial teachers often report that such students read magazines about racing or auto repair that are well "above" their level. Actually, these magazines are not above these students' level, because their vocabulary, although counted as difficult, really is not given these students' knowledge base.

The knowledge hypothesis discussed earlier suggests that the comprehensibility of a text is determined not just by the words that are used but also by the concepts they represent. If a text is about a complex or difficult topic, substituting easy words for the hard ones will not necessarily make it more readable. In fact, such substitutions may make the text harder to understand, because the easier words are likely to be less precise.

Readability and Younger Children

Most of the issues involving vocabulary and readability imply older children, say those in third grade and up. Although there are formulas developed for and used with younger children (see Harrison, 1980), most of the strict formulas were validated on texts for older children.

More recently, readability of texts for younger children has received more serious attention (Hiebert, 1999; Peterson, 2001). These formulas not only look at word frequency and sentence length, but also at the predictability of sentence patterns, the relationship of the words and the pictures, the placement of text on the page, and other factors that are relevant only for the youngest readers. The vocabulary factor is less important in these formulations of readability, especially those related to Reading Recovery (Peterson, 2001), because the reader has other sources of information to compensate for word difficulty. For example, if there is a *helicopter* in a picture, this word may not present especial difficulties for a child. Similarly, if a word is part of a repeated pattern, such as "'Fire, fire,' said Mrs. McGuire," it may also not present the same degree of difficulty that it would in a less predictable context. This is important to point out because, in early readers, words that would seem to be difficult by traditional readability notions, such as *helicopter* or other longer words, may not in fact be difficult at all. Teachers should not necessarily teach these "difficult" words, because they do not present real problems for comprehension, but instead should devote their effort to less predictable words, often high-frequency words. These high-frequency words, which are less predictable by the context and pictures, may create problems for children learning to read.

In some ways, for young children the vocabulary and readability issues flip-flop, with the more conceptual words creating fewer problems than do the more frequent words. Caution should be taken to avoid spending too much time on teaching these concrete nouns.

In part because of the issues we have outlined, readability measures are at best only rough guides to text difficulty. The Flesch Reading Formula is based on the number of characters per word and the number of words per sentence. Up to now, this chapter has 16.5 words per sentence and 5.1 characters per word, resulting in a Flesch Reading Ease of 42.6 or a 11.1 grade level. Whether high school students can read and understand this book is not certain. Hopefully, our intended audience of professionals can understand it and the high school rating of the prose represents an easy-to-understand style.

Another problem with formula is that readability formulas are fairly vague, with most having large standard errors of measurement of a full grade level or more (Chall & Dale, 1995; Zakaluk & Samuels, 1988). That is, the 11.1 grade level of this book could be as much as plus or minus one whole year. A passage might be understandable to a child a year below what the formula says or might not be understandable to a child on the grade level intended. Over many different passages these errors would average out, but for a particular child and a particular text, a readability formula might be very inaccurate and should be taken with a proverbial grain of salt.

Readability and the Vocabulary-Comprehension Connection

A person's knowledge of word meanings is strongly related to his or her ability to comprehend text. This much we know from studies comparing children's performance on vocabulary measures to their performance on comprehension measures. We also know this from readability formulas, which have found that the most important factor in determining the difficulty of a text is the difficulty of the words in the text.

Earlier in this chapter, we proposed five hypotheses about the relationships between knowledge of word meanings and reading comprehension. These same hypotheses come into play when discussing readability. Traditional readability formulas capture a limited feature of vocabulary—either a word's length or its frequency. This is useful, up to a point. It is easy to count word length by hand or, using computers, to count word frequency. However, capturing these aspects of words does not capture what makes text difficult. Differences in a child's knowledge about the domain a word is in, such as "dinosaurs," "weather," or "Revolutionary War history" will make a difference in how that child comprehends a text, a difference that might be glossed over by merely simplifying the vocabulary. Even if the words are known, if they are not known well or if they cannot be easily accessed they may cause difficulty. In other words, the difficulties that words can present for children's reading comprehension are the same for readability. Substituting easier words do not eliminate those difficulties.

The reason why rewriting texts does not always make them easier is because of the relation between vocabulary and knowledge. Vocabulary knowledge in readability formulas represents children's knowledge of the world. As children learn more words, they learn to think about the world in more sophisticated ways. It is this sophistication, rather than a particular bunch of words, that leads to understanding.

To be fair, readability formulas were always intended to be diagnostic, not prescriptive (Chall, 1958). That is, they were developed to match texts to children, not the other way around. That they have been used both ways is not a fault of the formulas, but rather of the users.

If the instrumentalist hypothesis were the whole picture—if it were only the presence of hard words in a text per se that made the text difficult—then readability formulas might serve as a guideline for editing text to make it more comprehensible. On this point, there is a consensus in the research: Readability formulas were not designed to be, and should not be used as, a basis for simplifying text (Davison & Green, 1988; Davison & Kantor, 1982).

Summary

In this chapter, we considered the relationship of vocabulary to comprehension: first, how individuals' vocabulary knowledge contributes to their ability to understand text, and second, how the vocabulary load of a text impacts its difficulty or readability. In both cases, vocabulary is found to be the single most important factor. However, a simple, instrumentalist interpretation of these relationships is not the whole picture. Knowing the words in a text is not the only factor that makes a person comprehend material well, and the fact that a text contains hard words is not the only thing that makes that text difficult.

We presented five hypotheses about the relationship between knowledge of word meanings and text comprehension. These hypotheses were not presented as competitors, but instead as complementary parts of a complex picture. The reason we have spent so much time exploring this complexity is its implications for instruction: Because the relationship between vocabulary knowledge and reading comprehension is complicated, an effective approach to vocabulary growth must be comprehensive, multifaceted, and long term. In the remainder of this book, we fill in what this comprehensive, multifaceted, long-term instruction looks like.

3

Problems and Complexities

Before we begin our banquet, I would like to say a few words. And here they are: Nitwit! Oddment! Tweak!

(Rowling, 1998, *Harry Potter and the Sorcerer's Stone*, p. 123)

The main purpose of this book is to support teachers in doing something to increase their students' vocabularies. However, before we can talk about what needs to be done, we have to clearly understand the nature and severity of the problem we are facing. We do not pretend to offer any easy solutions. Producing substantial, long-term gains in students' vocabularies requires a serious investment of planning, time, and energy. It would be foolish to take the kind of comprehensive approach to promoting vocabulary growth that we present if there were some simple, inexpensive alternative that would do the job. Thus, we would like to set the stage by portraying the seriousness of the situation as vividly as possible. Please bear with us as we try to paint a realistic, even bleak, picture of the difficulties associated with vocabulary learning.

Undoubtedly, it would not take much persuasion to get many teachers to agree that increasing students' vocabularies is a demanding undertaking. In fact, some teachers might consider the task hopeless. That is not the impression we are trying to convey; it *is* possible for schools to have a positive impact on students' vocabularies. For example, Dickinson and Smith (1994) found that the way that teachers talked with preschool children about texts had a powerful impact on the children's vocabulary development. However, in general, the available evidence suggests that schools are not having

26

as strong an impact on children's vocabularies as they could, especially in the primary grades (Biemiller, 1999; Cantalini, 1987; Morrison, Williams, & Massetti, 1998).

We want to present the difficulties of the task of promoting vocabulary growth as clearly as possible, not just to motivate teachers to make heroic efforts, but also to help them make effective and efficient efforts. For any attempt at promoting vocabulary growth to be effective and efficient, it has to address causes and not just symptoms. A careful consideration of the obstacles to vocabulary growth can tell us a lot about what an effective response to these obstacles should look like. Failure to address these obstacles is likely to mean wasted effort.

There are three fundamental obstacles to developing a large, productive vocabulary:

- The number of words that children need to learn is exceedingly large.
- The vocabulary of literate English is a foreign language for many children, even for many of those who come from English-speaking homes.
- Word knowledge involves much more than knowing a definition, and simply memorizing a definition does not guarantee the ability to use a word in reading or writing.

We discuss each obstacle in turn, and then explain how teachers can address these problems.

So Many Words

One reason why it's hard to make sure that your students develop adequate reading vocabularies is the sheer number of words involved. Average students may add 2,000–3,000 words a year to their reading vocabularies (Anderson & Nagy, 1992; Anglin, 1993; Beck & McKeown, 1991b; Nagy & Herman, 1987; White, Graves, & Slater, 1990). This is a large number, from six to eight new words each day. Individual differences in vocabulary size also involve large numbers. Some children in the same fifth- grade classroom may know thousands, perhaps even 10,000, more words than may others among their classmates.

Say you had a third-grade student (whom we will call "Sam") with a relatively small vocabulary—say in the 20th percentile—and wanted to help this student reach an average (50th percentile) vocabulary by sixth grade (i.e., in 3 years). This is perhaps an optimistic goal, but not an utterly unreasonable one. But how many words a year would this student have to learn to catch up? If the student is 3,000 words below the average third-grade student—not an impossibility if the average third-grade student knows around 5,000 words or more (cf. Anglin, 1993)—that's at least 700 words a year that this student must learn, above and beyond the 2,000–3,000 words a year that the average students are learning. This would be an additional 35% of the average growth in word knowledge, a difficult task at best. In other words, for every three words an average child learns, Sam must learn four. Fig. 3.1 compares Sam's hypothetical growth with that of an average child.

Although there is still debate over how large students' vocabularies actually are, and what words are essential for them to learn, there is no question that good readers learn words by the thousands, and that without intervention the vocabulary gap between more successful and less successful readers in your classroom will continue to widen. One important implication is that vocabulary instruction per se can only account for a limited proportion of students' vocabulary growth, and that a successful approach to increasing students' vocabularies will require increasing their independent word learning as well.

Is the number of words that students must learn really that large? Our argument depends on the estimate of 2,000–3,000 words learned per year being reasonably accurate. Where do these numbers come from, and how sure are we about them? The reasons for our embrace of the higher estimate are explained in the accompanying box. Our numbers come largely from Nagy's research (Nagy, Anderson, & Herman, 1987; Nagy, Herman, &

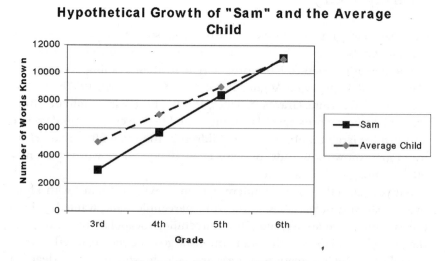

FIG. 3.1. Catching up on vocabulary growth.

Anderson, 1985). Other researchers suggest smaller yearly growth (e.g., D'Anna, Zechmeister, & Hall, 1991; Goulden, Nation, & Read, 1990). Trusting readers can accept our larger figures as they are and skip the material in the box. More skeptical readers can read the information in the box for a more in-depth treatment of the growth of word meanings.

How Many Words Do Children Know?

The history of research on the absolute size of children's vocabularies has produced a wide range of estimates. For example, estimates of the average vocabulary of high school seniors has ranged from about 8,000 words (Dupuy, 1974) to about 50,000 words (Smith, 1941). From these calculations, one could infer estimates of annual vocabulary growth rates from about 650 words to 2,700 words.

We have concluded that an average child learns between 2,000 and 3,000 new words per year. This is a lot, and this is the high estimate of how many words children learn. There are other scholars who have lower estimates, as low as 1,000 words per year. These lower estimates have different implications for instruction.

We have come down on the side of the higher estimates, as did Beck and McKeown (1991b) in their review of vocabulary research. To explain why we took the position that we did, we'll need to give you a little more detail about the history of this issue.

It is impossible to count all the words a person knows, so estimates of a person's absolute vocabulary size are necessarily based on a sample intended to reflect the total vocabulary of English. One of the reasons why published estimates of students' absolute vocabulary size differ so much is that they are based on very different estimates of the total vocabulary of English. Nagy and Herman (1987) attempted to reconcile previous published estimates of absolute vocabulary size by using Nagy and Anderson's (1984) estimate of the number of words in "printed school English" (i.e., the vocabulary found in printed materials used in schools, Grades 3–9). Nagy and Anderson concluded that, given a reasonably conservative definition of what counts as different words, there were around 88,000 different words in printed school English. Adjusting previous estimates of absolute vocabulary size on the basis of this measure, Nagy and Herman concluded that the average student adds somewhere around 3,000 words per year to his or her reading vocabulary. They made this adjustment because they felt that most earlier researchers had underestimated the number of words in the language.

Much of the disagreement about the size of English vocabulary stems from different assumptions about which words should be counted. For example, are proper names to be counted as part of vocabulary? How about idioms and phrasal verbs? How about derivatives? Should *anticipation* be counted as a word distinct from *anticipate*, or should the person who knows both of them be given credit for only one word, because the meaning of the second is predictable from its parts?

A few researchers have argued that students learn only about 1,000 words a year (D'Anna et al., 1991; Goulden, Nation, & Reed, 1990; Zechmeister, Chronis, Cull, D'Anna, & Healy, 1995). Their estimates are based on tests that we believe embody very conservative assumptions about how vocabulary size should be determined. For example, these estimates exclude proper names. In some ways, it might seem odd to include words like *John, Mary, Susan,* and *Annette* as part of one's vocabulary. One reason is that, as some philosophers have argued, such words do not have meaning; they refer by convention to particular individuals. However, we believe there are several reasons to question excluding proper names from estimates of vocabulary size.

In the studies resulting in the small estimates, "proper names" includes anything listed as capitalized in the dictionary being used (*Webster's Third New International*). First of all, *Webster's Third* does not include proper names among the entries, unless they have taken on some additional meaning. The capitalized words include categories of words that have potentially high utility: geographical terms (*America, Europe, Africa, Paris*), names of days and months (*Tuesday, January*), trade names (*Xerox, Kleenex, Google*), and so on. In other words, *Webster's Third* has already, at least in principle, excluded proper names that would be excluded by philosophers. To further exclude words that are listed in *Webster's Third* as capitalized or sometimes capitalized would be to exclude vocabulary that can sometimes be crucial to the understanding of a text.*

Another area in which we tend to disagree with the smaller estimates is the treatment of derived words. It makes sense not to count *slow* and *slowly* as two separate words: Someone who knows the first does not have to learn the second as a separate item of vocabulary. On the other hand, many prefixed and suffixed words have meanings that are only partly (if at all) predictable from the meanings of their parts: *somewhat, understand, pigment, homely, indifferent, highway, withstand,* and so on. Many words fall into a somewhat gray area: Should *trackless* (as in "a trackless wilderness") be considered a separate word because it is based on a rarer meaning of *track*? Should *shadowy* and *shady* be counted as distinct from *shadow* and *shade*, because they take on nuances of meaning not predictable from their roots?

We would argue that conservative estimates of vocabulary size have overestimated students' ability to make connections between such derived words and their roots. Of course, some skilled readers might be able to figure out the meanings and connotations of derivatives like *trackless* or *shadowy* with some help from context. However, students who are in greatest need of help with vocabulary are also the least likely to be able to take advantage of the clues provided by word parts. Using word parts to figure out the meaning of morphologically complex words is a great tool—but this works best for the people who already have larger vocabularies. Someone who doesn't know the meaning of *explicit* is not helped a whole lot by taking the suffix off of *explicitly* to find the root. Likewise, word parts are more useful to those who know multiple meanings for words—which will likewise be those who have larger vocabularies (Vermeer, 2001). It may not help to take the *ment* off of *contentment* if you don't know the relevant meaning of *content* (or even the pronunciation, which follows the meaning). Another set of problems occur when the common meaning of the root is tangentially related to the derived words. Would taking the *ance* off of *importance* really help a person know the meaning of that word?

For someone with a smaller vocabulary, then, or with less ability to analyze words into their parts, the number of "different words" in the language is greater than it is for someone with a larger vocabulary and more morphological awareness. The conservative estimates of vocabulary size and growth that we are arguing against make assumptions that don't match the learners who need the most help.

Another way in which most published estimates of vocabulary size are conservative is that they do not take into account the multiple meanings that many words (especially common words) have. Just because *bear* the animal and *bear* "to carry" are spelled and pronounced the same, does it make sense to say that a person who knows both meanings of *bear* has learned only one word? Perhaps there is some advantage in not having to learn a completely new spelling and pronunciation—but perhaps there is also some disadvantage in having to keep the two meanings distinct.

Jeremy Anglin's (1993) study of vocabulary growth helps explain the sources of differences among estimates of vocabulary size. He measured first, third, and fifth graders' knowledge of entries randomly selected from a dictionary, and divided the entries into categories on the basis of their relationship with other entries: root words, inflected words, derived (prefixed or suffixed) words, literal compounds (multiple word entries whose meanings were predictable from the words of which they were composed, e.g., *beehive*), and idioms (e.g., *lady's slipper*, a type of orchid). Children's knowledge of root words was found to increase by about 1,000 words a year, consistent with the estimates of Goulden et al. (1990) and D'Anna et al. (1991). However, Anglin also attempted to estimate vocabulary growth in terms of "psychologically basic words"; that is, not just root words, but also idioms, and derivatives that children recognized as units rather than inferring their meanings from their parts. Anglin suggested that children learned psychologically basic words at a rate of around 3,500 words per year. Anglin admitted that this figure is far from exact, but his figure gives us some confidence that our estimate of 2,000–3,000 words per year is not excessively high.

---

*It should also be noted that Nagy and Anderson's (1984) estimate that the vocabulary of printed school English contained about 88,000 words excluded proper names. Hence, Nagy, and Herman's (1987) upward adjustment of previous estimates of vocabulary size could in this regard be considered an underestimate.

If we accept that children learn 2,000–3,000 words per year, as trusting readers had accepted before reading the box and (hopefully) skeptical readers have been convinced by the box to accept, we must put this figure next to an estimate of how many words can usefully be taught. Our experience and our discussions with other teachers over the year suggest that teaching 10–12 new word meanings per week seems to be the norm in English/language arts. Given 40 weeks in a school year, it seems reasonable to assume that a teacher can teach 400–500 words over the course of the year. Of these, an average of 75% might be learned (a guess based on our experience, that of others, and a few studies), meaning that children might learn

300–375 words through direct teaching in English/language arts. Even if we double that number to include words taught in science and social studies, we are nowhere near the number that children are going to learn ordinarily. (We discuss later where these words might come from, but it is important to stress at this time that teachers cannot possibly teach all the words that children need to learn.)

Our estimate is intended to represent how many words average children add to their reading vocabularies per year. It does not necessarily follow, however, that a child actually *needs* to learn all these words. Perhaps some proportion of these words are relatively low in frequency (words like *quotidian, calliope, azure*), or otherwise not part of the core vocabulary every student needs to master. After all, a 4-year-old may know names for dinosaurs that many adults would not be able to identify.

So even if children *do* learn 2,000–3,000 words per year, perhaps many of these are not really necessary. Hence, our pessimistic conclusion that vocabulary instruction cannot possibly cover all the words that children need to learn may be misguided. The only words we *need* to make sure that children learn are a relatively small core of high frequency, high-utility words, and this core is small enough that it could be covered by instruction.

Thus, some scholars interested in vocabulary instruction have suggested that children need to be taught the meanings of a core of high-frequency words (e.g., Coady, Magoto, Hubbard, Craney, & Mokhtari, 1993). Certainly it might well be useful to identify a core of high-frequency, high-utility words, and to teach some of them to children. (We present a set of high-utility words in chap. 7.) However (especially because this is the section in which we want to emphasize the dire nature of the situation), it is far too simplistic to assume that instruction on such a set of words could solve our children's vocabulary problems.

Perhaps the biggest problem with the proposal to teach a small set of high-frequency words is the multiplicity of meanings involved. The higher the frequency with which a word appears in text, the more meanings it is likely to have. A relatively infrequent word like *pusillanimous* has one meaning (we are not going to tell you what it is, as a way of calling into question the practice of *always* sending students who ask about a word meaning to dictionaries to look up the word for themselves). A more common word like *line*, on the other hand, may have 120 or more dictionary entries, including two distinct families of meanings: *line* as in "straight line" and *line* as in "line one's pockets" (derived from *linen*). Most of the common words have multiple meanings, sometimes three or four, sometimes, as in the case of *line*, many more. The 3,000 most frequent words in the language may represent

10,000 or more distinct meanings. Each of these meanings may represent a different learning experience, or a possible source of confusion.

Certainly, it could be worthwhile to identify a core of high-utility words to teach to children, although frequency would certainly not be the only criterion one would want to use to define such a set. However, it has to be understood that knowledge of such a core of words, although it might be necessary, could not be sufficient. A comprehensive approach to vocabulary must have some way of addressing all the other words that children will encounter in their reading.

It seems quite plausible to suggest teaching students a set of carefully chosen, especially important words. We are not denying that this might be useful, but we want to make it clear as possible why this is not a sufficient approach to vocabulary learning.

What's wrong with the assumption that the student who possesses only "core vocabulary" knowledge is at no disadvantage? One problem has to do with the interconnectedness of word meanings (see Nagy & Scott, 2000). The idea that the noncore words are not essential rests on the assumption that words are completely separate items in memory, like piles of index cards. However, it is more accurate to think of human knowledge as being richly interconnected. It may help to think of each word as part of a network of other words. That is, each word is connected to other words that a child knows. The more words to which a word is connected, the richer the network is and the better known the word will be. (These networks are not the only knowledge that children have; in addition, words are connected to experiences, contexts in which the words were experienced, etc.)

Consider the two semantic networks depicted in Figs. 3.2 and 3.3.

In both cases, the word *whale* is known and each child knows something about it. However, the second child knows a minimum about the word, mainly that it is an "animal" and that it swims. That child is not sure whether a whale is a fish or not. The first child, on the other hand, knows somewhat more about whales and can distinguish between mammals and fish. If each child encounters the word *whale* in a text, the first child brings a great deal more to the text and probably will understand the text better.

As we mentioned in chapter 2 in the discussion of the knowledge hypothesis, it is not just knowledge of words per se that contributes to reading comprehension. Knowing words contributes to reading comprehension, to a large extent, because these words represent conceptual knowledge that goes well beyond the knowledge of the meanings of individual words. To understand a text about photosynthesis, it isn't enough simply to know the definitions of *carbon dioxide* and *photosynthesis*—one needs to know

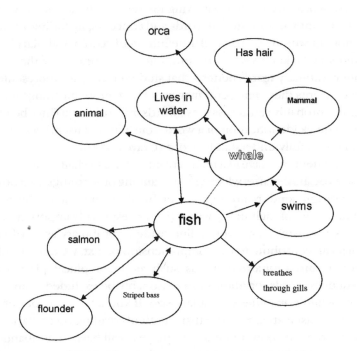

FIG. 3.2. More developed semantic network for *whale*.

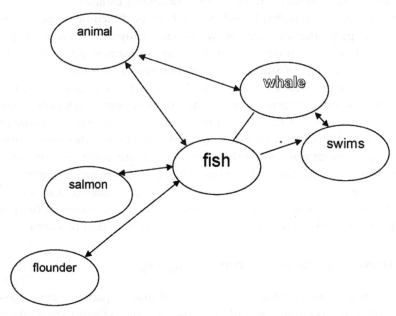

FIG. 3.3. Less developed semantic network for *whale*.

how these words are related. Knowing the relationships among words often involves knowing additional words and concepts, including words that might not fall within any particular definition of "core vocabulary."

A student who knows words beyond some core vocabulary, then, knows the core vocabulary words better—that student has richer representations for the concepts they represent, may well know more meanings for these words, and probably can access these words more quickly. Thus, being able to make a quick identification of a word from a list is a useful first step, but not enough to fully understand a word (Graves, 1986).

The arguments we have just made are intended as a challenge to small estimates of vocabulary size, which assume, among other things, that noncore words of various kinds really don't count. In other words, it may be possible to identify a core of high-utility words that are especially important for students to know. However, if you define reading vocabulary as word knowledge that can contribute to the comprehension of text, we don't think that technical terms, capitalized words such as geographical place names, low-frequency words, or idioms can reasonably be excluded from an estimate of a child's absolute vocabulary size. If you accept any of our arguments, the conservative estimate that children's reading vocabularies grow (on the average) by only 1,000 words are year will have to be abandoned. The claim of 2,000–3,000 words as a rough estimate of the average child's vocabulary growth seems to be a more reasonable estimate.

So far, then, we have explained the first of three difficulties to be covered in this chapter—the sheer size of the task facing anyone who wants to promote students' vocabulary growth. There are so many words to learn that you cannot teach your students all that they need to absorb.

What conclusion do we want you to draw from this dilemma? As we have already said, our goal is not to make the situation look hopeless (although we do hope that you acknowledge the situation to be serious). The main implication at this point is that teaching individual words, although it is often necessary, cannot possibly be the whole picture. An effective approach to improving students' vocabularies has to include ways of increasing their independent word learning, including their word awareness, and this will necessarily involve increasing their exposure to rich but comprehensible language. We talk more about how to do this in part III of this book.

Written English as a Foreign Language

The second major problem is that this vocabulary is part of a language— we'll refer to it as literate or academic English—that is likely to be a foreign language to the student whether or not the student comes from a home in which English is spoken.

For those of us who are comfortable with both conversational and academic English, it is easy to underestimate the differences between the two. However, the differences are substantial. First of all, it needs to be made clear that the difference is not simply a matter of spoken versus written. This is an important difference, but even more important are the differences in style, syntax, and vocabulary that follow from the different communicative demands typical of these two modalities.

Some researchers interested in language development and literacy consider the most important distinction to be between contextualized and decontextualized uses of language. In *contextualized language,* the meaning is supported by the context. The shared physical context allows the speaker to point, or use words such as *this* and *that.* In conversations between friends and acquaintances, shared knowledge makes precise communication possible without precision in wording. Intonation, facial expressions, and gesture provide additional channels of information. Typically, precision of word choice is not an important factor in contextualized language—accuracy of communication is achieved by reliance on feedback and negotiation. Spoken language is usually contextualized; normal conversation is a good example of this type of language.

The following is an example of very contextualized language; in this case, a conversation between a 4-year-old child and an adult:

Child:	This is me and that's you.
Adult:	Okay.
Child:	No. This is me and that's you and that's me.
Adult:	No. No, that's me. Wait. That's me?
Child:	Yeah.
Adult:	Okay. So that's you?
Child:	Yeah.
Adult:	All right.

This conversation, although it may have been significant to the participants, makes little sense to an outsider. The meaning in the conversation is tied to the context. (In this case, the context was some sort of pretend play involving Legos. Pretend play often provides opportunities for rich language use, but in this case, that apparently wasn't happening.)

One might wonder whether the 4-year-old in this example was suffering from some deficiency in language development. The vocabulary and syntax used by the child in this conversation (and by the adult, for that matter) seem impoverished. However, a few minutes later, when asked about a topic that was not quite as here-and-now as Legos, the same child displayed a much richer command of the language:

Adult: Where did you find out about *Star Wars*?
Child: I dreamed that I was in *Star Wars* and I saw this strange pack of ooie and I saw mud.
Adult: You saw a strange pack of ooie?
Child: I saw a big pack of stinky, ooie garbage. He lives in there, in a stinking pack of garbage.
Adult: Who does?
Child: Jabba!
Adult: But where did you first find out about *Star Wars*?
Child: I saw it first, and, but then how Jabba, I just taught myself and then I found it.
Adult: Oh. What happens in that movie *Star Wars*?
Child: Jabba catches Han. But he has a gun and he goes like this, pow pow. And guess what happens?
Adult: What?
Child: Luke and Han disguise themselves as storm troopers and they jump into a stink pack garbage. That's where Jabba lives.

This latter example represents language that is more decontextualized; that is, the meaning is not so strongly supported by the context. There are a number of factors that can contribute to language being decontextualized: The topic is nonpresent (i.e., not something to which you can point). Less knowledge is assumed to be shared. (In this case, the adult's question "What happens in that movie *Star Wars*?" suggests to the child that the adult has not seen, or does not remember, the movie, so more detail must be given.) Language tends to be more decontextualized when the individuals communicating are separated in space or time. You can't depend on gestures when talking on the phone, and when writing a book you can assume very little about the person who might read it so you have to be more explicit.

Spoken language is typically contextualized, and written language is more decontextualized, but the preceding examples make it clear that the contextualized/decontextualized distinction is not the same as the oral/written distinction. Some oral language (e.g., storytelling, lectures, and speeches) can be relatively decontextualized, and some written language (e.g., notes or e-mail among friends) can be rather contextualized.

Gordon Wells (1986) described this distinction in terms of the relationship between words and the world. In contextualized language, the words fit the context; whereas with decontextualized language, one in effect creates a context by using words. One of our favorite examples of how language can create its own independent context comes from a short story, "The Cleveland Wrecking Yard," by Richard Brautigan (1967). In this story, he described his visit to a salvage yard:

… There was also a big sign that said.

USED TROUT STREAM FOR SALE.

MUST BE SEEN TO BE APPRECIATED.

I went inside and looked at some ship's lanterns that were for sale next to the door. Then a salesman came up to me and said in a pleasant voice, "Can I help you?"

"Yes," I said. "I'm curious about the trout stream you have for sale. Can you tell me something about it? How are you selling it?"

"We're selling it by the foot length. You can buy as little as you want or you can buy all we have left. A man came in this morning and bought 563 feet. He's going to give it to his niece for a birthday present," the salesman said.

"We're selling the waterfalls separately, of course, and the trees and birds, flowers, grass and ferns we're also selling extra. The insects we're giving away free with a minimum purchase of ten feet of stream."

"How much are you selling the stream for?" I asked.

"Six dollars and fifty-cents a foot," he said. "That's for the first hundred feet. After that it's five dollars a foot." (Brautigan, 1967, p. 104)

After a bit more discussion with the salesman, the author finds the stream in the back of the salvage yard. He views a number of waterfalls stacked up and priced for sale:

I went into another room where there were piles of sweet-smelling lumber, glowing a soft yellow from a different color skylight above the lumber. In the shadows at the edge of the room under the sloping roof of the building were many sinks and urinals covered with dust, and there was also another waterfall about seventeen feet long, lying there in two lengths and already beginning to gather dust.

I had seen all I wanted of the waterfall, and now I was very curious about the trout stream, so I followed the salesman's directions and ended up outside the building.

O I had never in my life seen anything like that trout stream. It was stacked in piles of various lengths: ten, fifteen, twenty feet, etc. There was one pile of hundred-foot lengths. There was also a book of scraps. The scraps were in odd sizes ranging from six inches to a couple of feet.

There was a loudspeaker on the side of the building and soft music was coming out. It was a cloudy day and seagulls were circling high overhead.

Behind the stream were big bundles of trees and bushes. They were covered with sheets of patched canvas. You could see the tops and roots sticking out the ends of the bundles.

I went up close and looked at the lengths of stream. I could see some trout in them. I saw one good fish. I saw some crawdads crawling around the rocks at the bottom.

It looked like a fine stream. I put my hand in the water. It was cold and felt good. (Brautigan, 1967, pp. 106–107)

This story illustrates the power of language alone to create a world. In this case, it is a world that can't even exist—a salvage yard containing a trout stream, broken up into lengths, in which the trout are still running.

There are a number of differences between contextualized and decontextualized language, one of the most obvious being richness of vocabulary. It should not be surprising that written language, which is normally decontextualized and relies heavily on word choice for communicative effect, has a much richer vocabulary than does typical conversation. The size of the difference is striking, however. It turns out that conversation among college-educated adults has a richness of vocabulary comparable to preschool books. Children's books have a vocabulary almost twice as rich as adult conversation. As discussed later, comic books, adult books, and popular magazines have a vocabulary three times as rich (Cunningham & Stanovich, 1998; Hayes & Ahrens, 1988). The language of television shows, on the other hand, is about the same as that of adult conversations.

Cummins discussed this type of distinction and its impact on English Language Learners. A student who comes to school with no knowledge of English may achieve proficiency in conversational English in a year or two. However, it may take 5 to 7 years for those children to be academically proficient in English (Collier, 1989; Cummins, 1994).

Failure to recognize the distinction between different types of language can lead to a serious misunderstanding of an English language learner's abilities. For example, a fifth-grade English language learner may have been in school for 2 years, and be quite competent at using English with peers on the playground, and yet still have serious trouble understanding the textbook.

These differences in the use of English in different settings may be partially because of the differences in the richness of knowledge, as discussed earlier, but also because written English uses different words than does casual conversation. In school, various content areas have their own vocabulary. In mathematics, words such as *hypotenuse, octagon, divisor,* and *denominator* are used. In social studies, words such as *representative, act, revolution,* and *population* are common. Science, literature, music, and art all have their own specialized vocabularies. Outside of the content areas, certain words are used in school writing that rarely appear in conversation. These might include words such as *hypothesis, practically, absolutely,* and *dependent.* Even for younger children, many of the words in children's texts occur rarely in natural settings. Words such as *erected, renovate, restore, delve,* and *elude,* which might appear in a story from a fifth-grade reader, are rarely encountered in everyday speech. If school personnel are not aware of the difference in the time it takes to achieve conversation fluency and proficiency with the language of textbooks, they might wrongly diagnose the fifth-grade student mentioned in the last paragraph as having a learning disability or a reading disability.

Although richness of vocabulary is one of the major differences between contextualized and decontextualized language, the differences go beyond just vocabulary. Children who are not experienced with decontextualized language may not understand the communicative demands that lead to the use of rich vocabulary in written language. They may not understand how much of the meaning they want to express is dependent on tone of voice, gesture, or shared knowledge.

The second main obstacle to vocabulary growth, then, is that written (i.e., decontextualized) language is a foreign language to many students, even those who live in homes where English is spoken. The language of conversation, and of television, simply is not adequate preparation for the language that students will encounter in their texts.

In one sense, this is a vocabulary problem—these students have not been exposed to the rich vocabulary that they need in order to comprehend what they need. However, what these students are lacking goes beyond simply not knowing specific words. They are also likely to lack a feel for the ways in which written language differs from conversation. They write like they talk. This may be adequate for beginning writers, and even a gift when writing dialogue, but it is not an adequate foundation for most of the kinds of writing that school requires. Students need to develop an understanding of how written language works—and, in particular, how well-chosen words are one of the most powerful tools available for making your meaning clear to someone who doesn't already know what you are going to say.

Understanding this obstacle—many students' unfamiliarity with both the words and the ways of written language—helps us see more clearly what an effective approach to vocabulary development must look like. As we discuss later in this book, it is important not just to help students gain a richer vocabulary, but also to understand the role and power of word choice in effective written communication.

The Complexity of Word Knowledge

The third major obstacle to increasing students' vocabularies is the complexity of word knowledge. What do we mean by the "complexity of word knowledge"? We can begin to answer this by posing a second question: What does it mean to know a word? A simple answer might be to equate "knowing a word" with "knowing its definition," so that if one learns a definition, one has learned the word. Knowing a definition can be important, but it turns out that this conception of what it means to know a word is far too simplistic, in a number of ways.

First of all, there are plenty of words that you know for which you could not easily provide a definition. The word *the* may seem like an unfair example, but for many perfectly ordinary words, you might be hard pressed to come up with a definition on the spot. (Try it: Give a definition immediately for the following words: *embarrass, know, find, cute, world, comfortable, beauty.* Okay, time's up! How did you do? And how often did you have to resort to using words that were less familiar or frequent than the word you were trying to define?)

Simple introspection tells us that when we hear or see a word, we are aware of its meaning within a fraction of a second—far more quickly than we could remember or produce a definition, even if there were such a definition stored in our memories. And even if we are able to think of definitions for some words, there are a number of reasons to believe that however word meanings may be stored in our memories, this information is not in the form of definitions (Anderson & Nagy, 1991).

As we mentioned earlier, it isn't just definitional information about a word that one needs in order to understand a text containing that word. For example, a text containing the word *snake* might assume knowledge of various types of folklore about snakes—the fact that many people are afraid of them, they are commonly believed to be dangerous, the role of the serpent in the Garden of Eden—all kinds of information that would not be likely to make it into a definition of the word. Our knowledge of the meanings of words is also closely tied to other aspects of our knowledge about words:

their part of speech, how they function in sentences, what other words they are likely to combine with, how frequently they tend to be used, and in what types of situations and styles of language they are employed.

There is a second aspect of complexity that has to be taken into account—not all words are alike. In fact, words differ from each other in a number of ways, posing problems for any simplistic approach to vocabulary instruction.

Sometimes words are simple, easily described by a one- or two-word synonym. Other times, words are complex concepts, requiring not only long explanations but also extensive content knowledge. These differences in complexity create difficulties for word learners.

Michael Graves (1986) suggested that words may differ from each other in ways that have implications for instruction—differences in the type of learning that the words require. In particular, Graves distinguished among:

- Words already in the student's oral vocabulary, which he or she needs to learn to recognize in print. These are words that a child must learn to decode or recognize by sight.
- Words not in the student's oral vocabulary, but which are labels for concepts already familiar to the student. For example, the student may need to learn that *apologize* means to say one is sorry, or that *elaborate* means pretty much the same thing as *complicated*. These words may represent different shades of meaning from their synonym, but knowledge of the more frequent synonym will usually get a reader through a text containing that word. The different shades will be learned through continued exposure. For these words, less intensive vocabulary instruction methods may suffice.
- Words not in the student's oral vocabulary that refer to concepts new to the student. For example, the student may not know the words *osmosis, feudalism,* or *exponential.* In such a case, it is not simply a matter of not knowing the word; the student is likely to be totally unfamiliar with the concept. In this situation, a definition or other brief explanation is unlikely to help. Rather, a teacher would need to spend a great deal of time examining such concepts. Spiro and his colleagues described the process of learning complex concepts as "criss-crossing the landscape." They suggested that people need to learn complex concepts through repeated encounters in a number of different contexts, with a great many connections made to examples of these concepts, like a naturalist learns a terrain (Spiro, Coulson, Feltovich, & Anderson, 1994). We discuss techniques for building concepts—such

as semantic mapping, semantic feature analysis, concept of definition maps, and so on—later in this book.

What are the implications of recognizing the complexity of word knowledge? One is the insufficiency of definitions as a source of word knowledge. Definitions are important; at times, they are essential; but they are often not enough. To really know a word, the student needs types of information that are not included, or at best only poorly conveyed, in definitions. Hence, whatever an effective approach to promoting vocabulary growth looks like, it cannot rely simply on definitions.

Another implication of the complexity of word knowledge is that word learning is necessarily incremental—it takes place in many small increments or steps (Nagy & Scott, 2000; Schwanenflugel, McFalls, & Stahl, 1997). It requires quite a number of different experiences with a word to get to the point of ownership. Therefore, teachers should not expect too much from any given instructional activity or episode. If you want students to get to the point of using words effectively in their writing, or even understanding text containing the instructed words, you will have to invest some time and effort. Powerful forms of vocabulary instruction that take students from no knowledge of a word to being able to use the word in understanding text are labor intensive (Beck et al., 1982).

There may be times when it is appropriate simply to move a student one notch higher on the scale of word knowledge—for example, by giving a brief explanation of the word during a read-aloud, or in response to a question. However, don't expect this explanation to lead to full knowledge of that word. For example, in the sentence "Papa bought a frame wagon that farmers had used to haul crops," knowing that *haul* means the same as *carry* would be enough to understand the sentence. Other words, such as *frame wagon,* may not have to be taught at all, because the concept of the type of wagon is not needed to understand the general idea of the story.

Sometimes authors use rare words as ornamentation. For example, in *Stuart Little*, when the title character is manning (or should we say *mousing?*) a toy boat, he uses a variety of nautical terminology. None of it is really essential for getting the gist of the story; it is there pretty much for flavoring. In *Charlotte's Web*, some of the elaborate descriptions of the barn—for example, "It smelled of grain and of harness dressing and of axle grease and of rubber boots and of new rope" (White, 1952, p. 13)—seem to play a similar role. For us, the sentence calls to mind a faint but specific memory of what fresh rope smells like, which enriches the experience of the book, but the fact that we don't know what harness dressing smells like doesn't undermine the effectiveness of the writing. In fact, we assume that one could get the gist of the story perfectly well even if one had no idea what harness dressing was.

In other texts, however, the rare words are much more central to the content. In a science text, for example, one has generally *not* gotten the gist of the text if one doesn't understand the meaning of some of the key terminology. In a text on the development of penicillin, the words *bacteria, antibiotic, disease,* and so on would seem essential to understanding the discovery and its importance.

How complex a word meaning is may determine how complex the instruction needs to be. Words that are conceptually complex and integral to the story may need elaborate explanation. Other words that are less complex may not need such intense instruction. Still other words may not need any instruction at all, either because their meaning is conveyed well through context or because they are not needed to understand the story. One of the lessons of this chapter—that children learn far too many words for a teacher to be able to teach—can be carried over to making instructional decisions. If one cannot teach all the words that children need, then one must make good decisions about what should be taught.

The fact that there are different types of words that place different types of demands on the learner means that there cannot be a single, one-size-fits-all approach to vocabulary instruction. What constitutes effective vocabulary instruction depends on the type of word, the type of learning this word demands from the learner, and the role of the word in the text.

Summary

In this chapter, we have discussed three factors that make word learning difficult. The first problem is that there are so many words that children have to learn. Accepting our estimates, the average child learns between 2,000 and 3,000 words per year. Assuming (for the sake of math) that children do not learn any words on Saturday, that means that the average child learns about 10 new words a day. This is, on one hand, too many to teach one by one. (As discussed later in this text, one of the contradictions to this view is that vocabulary instruction does seem to significantly improve children's word knowledge and comprehension.) However, the size of the task should give us pause and cause us to make sure that we are providing other word learning opportunities.

The second problem is that the vocabulary of written English is like a foreign language to many children. Ordinarily, our speech is contextualized so that we are relying on shared experiences for communication. Because the author of a written text is not usually present (and may, in fact, be dead), written language needs to be more explicit and less dependent on shared knowledge. In addition, the words used in written English are somewhat different. There is a formal register of "academic" words that are rarely used in oral language. These could include content words, such as *photosynthesis* or *oligarchy,* or general academic words, such as *absolutely* or *hypothetically,* that do not pepper the speech of casual conversations. For many children, these words represent another learning task.

The last problem discussed in this chapter is the complexity of word knowledge. First of all, to "know" a word means knowing not only a definition, but also something about how the word is used in context. The different senses of a word are further discussed in the next chapter. However, to know a word also means knowing its pronunciation, knowing how it is used in different social settings, knowing what part of speech it is, and so on.

Furthermore, some words are simple; that is, they are synonyms or near-synonyms for other words that one knows. An example might be the relation between *amble* and *walk*. Other words represent brand-new concepts, such as *nucleus* or *parasite*. Complex concepts require a different type of instruction than do simple concepts. As we address in chapter 6, complex concepts require examples, nonexamples, categorization, and descriptions so that the learner can create a rich and full understanding of the word's meaning. Simple concepts can require considerably less.

We have tried in this chapter to inspire a little awe in the face of the difficulties confronting anyone who hopes to increase the vocabularies of their students. Even though it is a difficult task, children do learn words, and do so readily and fluently. In fact, if you are a reader of this book and are not totally flummoxed by our purple prose, then you must have a reasonably good vocabulary.

4

A Comprehensive Approach
to Vocabulary Learning

All hope abandon, ye who enter here!

(Dante, *The Inferno*, Canto iii, Line 9. Alighieri, 1314/1960)

OK, the situation for those teaching vocabulary is not as bad as it is for those entering Dante's *Inferno*. We have tried to be realistic about vocabulary, but we did not want to make the task of teaching word meanings to seem impossible. We hope it is clear by now that increasing students' reading vocabularies is a complex and difficult matter. We have gone over the difficulties and complexities in some detail. The point was not simply to make the situation look bleak—although a realistic appraisal of the difficulty is a good starting place. Showing the seriousness of the problem may serve as a motivation to work harder at increasing students' vocabularies. However, more important than working harder is working smarter. In describing each of the difficulties, we intended to foreshadow the solutions,

As we turn now to the task of laying out the solutions, the first point we want to make is that there is no simple solution. We have spelled out many reasons why growing students' vocabularies can be difficult, and each of these reasons must be addressed in some way.

Although solving students' vocabulary problems is not simple, neither is it impossibly complex. Rather, we think that the various parts of the solution can be put into a coherent whole. Our goal in this chapter, then, is to give you the "big picture," so you can see how the pieces fit together. In following chapters we explore each of the pieces in more detail.

We are going to try two different ways to make the big picture as clear as possible. First, we describe the components of a comprehensive approach to vocabulary instruction. Then, we'll present a graphic, the "vocabulary pyramid," as one way of talking about how these parts fit together.

Components of a Comprehensive Approach to Vocabulary Instruction

There are three main components to a comprehensive approach to promoting vocabulary growth:

- Teaching specific words.
- Immersion in rich language.
- Developing generative vocabulary knowledge.

This list is a slight modification of that suggested by Michael Graves (2000). Each of these components is essential for promoting vocabulary growth. However, each by itself also has limitations that must be kept in mind. It is the combination of the three that is essential. We now go over each of these in a little more detail.

Teaching Individual Words

One of the ways we help children learn new words is to teach them the words' meanings. We hope it is clear from our discussion of the amount of words children must learn that teaching words one at a time is not sufficient to produce large-scale, long-term vocabulary growth. However, just because teaching individual words can't be the whole process doesn't mean it isn't *part* of the process.

It should also be clear from our discussion of the complexity of word knowledge that some traditional methods of vocabulary instruction, which rely largely on definitions to convey information about new words, are not effective. However, there are many ways to teach words that address these problems. We discuss methods of teaching individual words in part II of this book, chapters 5 though 8.

Immersion in Rich Language

This is the second component of a comprehensive approach to vocabulary, which we discuss in more depth in chapter 9. You can't learn a language well without being immersed in it. For children to develop large vocabularies, they have to delve deeply into the world of words. Part of this can be accomplished through wide reading. But although wide reading is essential, it is also essential that teachers make the most effective use possible of oral language as well.

Encouraging Wide Reading.   We believe that wide reading is the single most powerful factor in vocabulary growth. Even a moderate amount of daily reading with appropriate text could lead to most of the vocabulary growth a student needs. However, many of the students who need the most vocabulary growth are not capable of sustained independent reading of reasonably challenging text. In addition, it is especially important for young children and struggling readers to be read to by teachers, parents, or others. For children who have difficultly in reading, read-alouds assume greater importance for vocabulary development (Stahl, Richek, & Vandevier, 1991).

Exposing Children to Rich Oral Language.   Even for students who are learning to read at the expected pace, we cannot wait until they are able to read independently to begin addressing their vocabulary needs. Vocabulary growth requires massive exposure to rich language, so at least until children are able to fluently read challenging material on their own, oral language is a crucial channel of vocabulary growth. (Of course, there is no reason to cease using oral language as a tool for promoting vocabulary growth even when children have become proficient readers.) We want to highlight this point because we are thinking about a broad range of grades and ages, including kindergarten and even prekindergarten, in which oral language is especially important for vocabulary growth.

There are a number of ways that oral language can be used to promote vocabulary growth. Reading aloud is one way to help children who cannot read well enough on their own to experience rich language. However, teachers can also learn one of the skills of good children's authors—to talk slightly above children's heads, but in a way that engages them rather than losing them. We talk more about using oral language in chapter 9.

Developing Generative Word Knowledge

This is the third essential component to a comprehensive approach to vocabulary development. By *generative word knowledge* we mean knowledge about words that goes beyond the knowledge of individual words, and that makes a person a better word learner. It's the vocabulary analog of "teaching a person to fish" rather than "giving a person a fish." There are two related aspects to generative word knowledge: word consciousness and word-learning strategies.

Word Consciousness. Exposure to rich language, whether written or oral, is a necessary condition for vocabulary growth. However, it may not be a sufficient condition for all children. Earlier in this text, we mentioned one of the possible reasons, when we discussed the fact that literate English is a foreign language to many children, whether or not their home language is English. Conversational English, even among educated adults, does not generally use a very rich vocabulary. As a consequence, children who are not familiar with the written language (whether through reading it themselves, or having heard it read aloud) may not appreciate the power of word choice as a communicative tool. They are therefore less likely to attend to unfamiliar words or to the shades of meaning that the words are used to convey.

Word consciousness can be the difference between the number of words taught per year and the number of words learned. Children who are strongly conscious about learning new words can be presumed to pick up more words from their reading than do children who are less focused on words. A classroom environment that emphasizes the important of learning words, from a variety of sources, will be better at promoting vocabulary growth.

Word-Learning Strategies. As Nation (1990, 2001) pointed out, the English language has a huge number of low-frequency words. According to one estimate (Carroll, Davies, & Richman, 1971), half of the words in English occur less than once in 10 billion words of text. Any particular word from this pool of low-frequency words is unlikely to show up more than once every few years, even for very avid readers, so it would be hard to make a case for trying to teach students their meanings. On the other hand, low-frequency words do show up in texts, even texts written for children. Students must therefore have strategies for dealing independently with words they encounter in reading. Chapters 11 through 13 tell more about how to teach such strategies.

The Vocabulary Growth Pyramid

The components we have just described are all essential to promoting students' vocabulary growth. However, simply listing these components doesn't go very far in telling us how to fit them together. As one more step in trying to give you a clearer overall picture of how to deal with vocabulary in the classroom, we offer the vocabulary growth pyramid, depicted in Fig. 4.1.

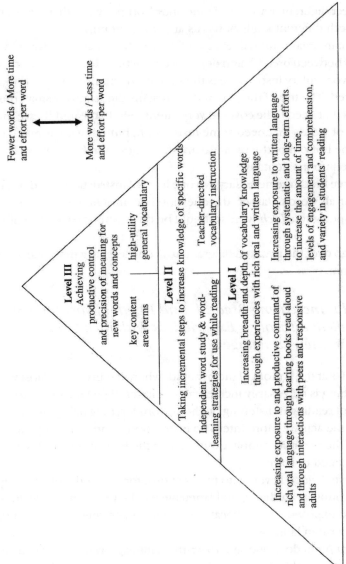

Fewer words / More time and effort per word

More words / Less time and effort per word

Level III
Achieving productive control and precision of meaning for new words and concepts

high-utility general vocabulary

key content area terms

Level II
Taking incremental steps to increase knowledge of specific words

Teacher-directed vocabulary instruction

Independent word study & word-learning strategies for use while reading

Level I
Increasing breadth and depth of vocabulary knowledge through experiences with rich oral and written language

Increasing exposure to written language through systematic and long-term efforts to increase the amount of time, levels of engagement and comprehension, and variety in students' reading

Increasing exposure to and productive command of rich oral language through hearing books read aloud and through interactions with peers and responsive adults

FIG. 4.1.   The vocabulary growth pyramid.

This diagram is based on an analogy with the food pyramid. The food pyramid was designed to convey two basic points: variety and proportion. (It may require some effort for younger readers to imagine a pre-Atkins world in which carbohydrates were still widely recognized as the mainstay of a healthy diet.) The vocabulary growth pyramid likewise represents the need for both variety and proportion in vocabulary instruction. The three levels of the pyramid reflect different amounts of time and effort per word that are appropriate for both different kinds of words and different purposes.

The main organizational scheme of the vocabulary growth pyramid is the trade-off between breadth and depth of instruction. That is, the more intensive the vocabulary instruction is the smaller the number of words that can be covered. The top of the pyramid represents the relatively small number of words that need to be covered very intensively. In the middle are a larger number of words that need some instruction, but not with as much intensity. At the bottom of the pyramid are the largest number of words, which are picked up incidentally.

All three levels are necessary. No one level of instruction could be appropriate for all words. Rather, the question becomes how many words, and more important, *which* words, should be dealt with at each level of intensiveness.

Let's go over the pyramid diagram now, one level at a time, starting from the bottom.

Level I: Increasing Breadth and Depth of Vocabulary Knowledge Through Experiences With Rich Oral and Written Language

Level I is at the bottom of the pyramid, where it is broadest. Most vocabulary learning is necessarily incidental—a matter of picking up words in the process of reading or listening, without word learning being an intentional focus of the activity. More intensive instruction, represented by the higher levels of the pyramid, simply cannot cover the huge number of words that children need to learn.

We have divided Level I into two sections, for oral and written language. For the youngest students, oral language will be the primary way in which they'll be exposed to rich vocabulary; with older children, the emphasis shifts to written language.

At what point does one shift to written language as the primary means of vocabulary growth? Up to a certain age, the maximum level of text difficulty that children can understand when text is read aloud to them is higher than the level of difficulty they would be able to understand if reading on their own. That is, their listening comprehension exceeds their reading comprehension. As long as this is true, listening is likely to be a more effective way of picking up new words than reading. For most adults, on the other hand, the situation is reversed: They can successfully read text on their own that they would not be able to understand if it were read aloud to them. Somewhere in between, one's reading catches up with one's listening comprehension, and reading can become the major contributor to vocabulary growth. (This doesn't mean, of course, that exposure to rich oral language ceases to play a role.)

Where is this middle point? One study that addressed this question found it to be at about seventh or eighth grade (Biemiller, 1999; Sticht & James, 1984). In other words, up to seventh grade, students are able to comprehend text read aloud to them that is more complex than what they would be able to comprehend when reading on their own. Furthermore, this is for average students; there may be many students at higher grade levels who are still better able to understand text read aloud than text that they read to themselves.

This is one argument for maintaining the practice of reading aloud to students, for the sake of exposing them to rich, challenging language and concepts that they might not be able to understand if they were reading independently. Biemiller (1999) made a strong case for the necessity of using oral language to promote vocabulary growth during the years that children are still developing the mechanics of reading.

There are, of course, other reasons for reading aloud to students; in poetry, for example, the sound is an important part of experiencing the text. Hence, we are not arguing that reading aloud to students should stop after the eighth grade. Instead, our point is simply that oral language plays an essential role in vocabulary growth, and that the importance of oral language to vocabulary growth continues past the early elementary years.

Promoting Word Consciousness.   We included promoting word consciousness in Level I with some trepidation. We put it here because word consciousness, by itself, will not result in the kind of deep knowledge and ownership of words that is the target of Level III instruction, or even the level of definitional knowledge that may result from Level II instruction. However, word consciousness should permeate the vocabulary program. If one is teaching specific words, as in Level III, one should teach in a way that makes children curious about other words, so that when you teach one word the students may end up learning other words as well. If one is talking about words in a more casual manner, as in Level II, the talk should encourage children to look for other words. In short, we do not want to create students with piles of words, but instead develop students who are curious about words and language in every form, so that they will extend their reading to be more productive in learning words.

Of course, getting students to read as much and as widely as possible is essential for their continued vocabulary growth. Level I of the vocabulary pyramid—the level that covers the most territory—means doing everything you can to increase students' exposure to rich oral and written language, while at the same time creating in students an interest in words and delight in language that makes them receptive to the new words they encounter.

Level II: Taking Incremental Steps to Increase Knowledge of Specific Words

Incidental learning of words from continued massive exposure to rich oral and written language is essential for vocabulary growth, but it is not everything. Exposure to rich language will help children learn lots of words, but it will not necessarily help them learn those particular words that may be needed for some particular purpose.

A key concept underlying the vocabulary growth pyramid is the incremental nature of word learning. Words are learned in many small steps, not all at once. It takes repeated encounters with a word to bring it to the point where you really own it—where you can use it in your own writing, or understand why someone used that word rather than a different one in a text.

As we describe in more detail in chapter 5, vocabulary instruction that brings new words into children's active vocabularies is relatively time intensive. This is the kind of instruction at Level III of the pyramid, which we address in a moment. However, sometimes it's enough to take the child just a few steps further along the journey at a given time. For example, while reading a story aloud, a teacher might offer an explanation of a new word. Sometimes students only need to learn a word well enough to understand what a sentence means, and then move on.

There are a variety of instructional activities that can take a student one step further in the process of learning a word. Explanations by a teacher are one example. In fact, such explanations can have a significant impact on students' word learning (Elley, 1989; Penno, Wilkinson, & Moore, 2002). Although definitions have limitations, there are times when simply looking up a word is appropriate. Word and concept sorts (e.g., Bear, Invernizzi, Templeton, & Johnston, 2004) are another example of tasks that can incrementally increase students' familiarity with word meanings. Chapter 8 gives more detail on Level II vocabulary instruction.

The important thing is to recognize both the value and limitations of activities that take students a few steps further on the journey of learning a word. Any progress in word knowledge is, of course, valuable. The limitation is that one should not expect ownership—the ability to use a word in writing, or to fluently read text containing the word—from instruction that achieves only a partial level of word knowledge. In other words, there are times when it's okay to simply tell a student what a word means, or ask him or her to look it up, but don't expect the student to be able to use it correctly in a sentence at that point.

Level II also includes teaching students independent word learning strategies (see chaps. 11–13). As we have already pointed out, it is essential for students to have strategies for dealing with unfamiliar words that they encounter while reading. As valuable as such strategies are, however, one must recognize that they are likely to result in only a partial level of word knowledge—hopefully, enough to enable the student to go on reading and get the gist of the text, but not necessarily enough to have the word become part of the student's active vocabulary.

Level III: Achieving Productive Control and Precision of Meaning for Completely New Words and Concepts

Level III is the most intensive level of dealing with vocabulary. This is the level of instruction that aims at bringing students to full ownership of words—being able to use the words in writing, and understanding their meanings quickly and automatically when reading text.

Such instruction is not quick or easy, which is why we put it at the top where the pyramid is narrowest. Only a relatively small number of words can be covered with this type of instruction. A text of, say, 3,000 words may have 100 words that might be problematic to some children in a typical class. If one can profitably teach 10–12 new words per week in a literature class (a best guess based on the experience of teachers with whom we have worked), this means that the majority of problematic words cannot get direct and sustained attention without spending so much time on vocabulary teaching that there would be no time left for reading of literature.

How do we choose these words? We believe that two major factors should go into the choice of which words to teach: importance and utility. We discuss these in turn.

Importance.   The first principle of choosing words to teach should be that the words chosen should be important to the literature or the content area passage that the children are about to read. If you are teaching literature, the words you choose to teach should be central to the story. If you are teaching from a social studies, science, or other content area text, the words should be key concepts in the chapter. In both cases, you need to ask yourself, "Will the child understand this [story or passage] without knowing this word?" If the answer is no, then you need to teach that word. If the answer is yes, then you might decide to talk about the word during reading, or hope that the child might learn the word incidentally.

It is important not to be diverted by "seductive details" (Garner, Gillingham, & White, 1989). These are interesting, but irrelevant, tidbits embedded in a text. The purpose of these factoids are to keep the students' interest in the text, but they can distract from the overall meaning. Consider the following passage, from *To Kill a Mockingbird* (Lee, 1960), a book commonly taught in middle school:

> For reasons unfathomable to the most experienced prophets in Maycomb County, autumn turned to winter that year. We had two weeks of the coldest weather since 1885, Atticus said. Mr. Avery said it was written on the Rosetta Stone that when children disobeyed their parents, smoked cigarettes, and made war on each other, the seasons would change: Jem and I were burdened with the guilt of contributing to the aberrations of nature, thereby causing unhappiness to our neighbors and discomfort to ourselves. (Lee, 1960, p. 63)

This was the first paragraph of a much longer chapter, with many more challenging words. A teacher might choose to teach perhaps one or two of the words in the paragraph, or not, because other words may be more important. Of the words in the paragraph, we would probably not teach *Rosetta Stone*, because although it is an interesting literary conceit, it does not relate to the rest of the story. We would probably ignore *prophets*, because it too seems rather unrelated. *Aberrations* would be questionable. On one hand, it is central to one of the main ideas of the paragraph, that the weather was unnaturally cold. On the other hand, it is relatively obscure and probably not too useful for middle schoolers. Furthermore, its meaning is somewhat predictable from the context, and hence it is redundant. All in all, then, although this paragraph offers some intriguing opportunities for vocabulary learning, it is not obvious that any of the words is essential. This is, in fact, often the case with narratives. Difficult vocabulary is often present, but it is less likely to be essential to grasping the gist of the text.

For content area texts, on the other hand, difficult vocabulary is likely to be central to the meaning of the text, and is likely to be highlighted in some way in the text. Each chapter or book section has key terms that should be covered. Some of these represent new concepts; others represent synonyms for concepts the child likely already has mastered. These two types of words present two different teaching problems, as discussed in chapters 5 and 6. In teaching content area texts, it is more likely that words will fit together in a coherent domain. For example, words like *crater, satellite, phases, waxing, waning, sea,* and so on might be taught together, using a semantic map (see chap. 6) or another knowledge-based technique that would allow the students to see the relations among the words.

Utility.   In addition to importance, the teacher should also take into account the word's utility. Utility has several dimensions. First, a word should be useful for children to learn—that is, it should be a word that they are likely to encounter in a variety of contexts. The words in the Academic Word List (chap. 7) are examples of high-utility words. These are words that can be used across a number of different subject areas.

Second, the word should be useful for the student at the time it is taught—that is, the word needs to be one that is not already known, as well as one that is not too difficult for the child to learn. As teachers report, many words chosen by basal reading programs are already known by most if not all children in the class. If a word is known, then, obviously, you do not have to teach it. We recommend using a quick checklist such as that shown in chapter 7, or even a show of hands, to get a quick idea of who knows a particular word. Other words are too difficult. Biemiller and Slonim (2001) found that children's word knowledge develops in a fairly similar manner. They suggested that words build on each other—that learning more difficult words depends on understanding more simple words. Although Biemiller and Slonim used a vocabulary survey to determine how difficult words were, a good teacher's intuition can suffice. It is because of our intuition that we thought that *aberrations* might have been too difficult for our middle schoolers.

Remember that the time available for teaching in this Level III instruction is too valuable to waste. Treat each minute of teacher time as if it is gold; spend it wisely. The words you choose to teach should be words that propel the child's comprehension of the text as well as help the child read future texts.

Summary

In this chapter, we have laid out our blueprint for vocabulary instruction, as exemplified by our vocabulary growth pyramid. This model asserts that effective vocabulary instruction involves different levels of intensity for different types of word learning. The pyramid suggests that the majority of time in a classroom should be spent on increasing the breadth and depth of children's word knowledge through experiences with language. This includes both wide reading and rich oral language experiences. A somewhat smaller amount of attention should be devoted to talking about words in an informal way, through teacher explanations of words during reading, providing simple definitions for words that do not need long explanations, as well as some independent word learning strategies. Finally, Level III of the pyramid involves direct instruction of word meanings. In this chapter, we discussed briefly how to choose words for instruction; in the remaining chapters of this book, we go into more depth about components of vocabulary instruction.

What is important to understand is the importance of *all* levels of this pyramid, including word consciousness that should permeate the entirety of a word learning program. Vocabulary learning is not just talking about words in class, nor is it just memorizing definitions, nor it is just learning word parts—it is all of this and more.

II

Teaching Specific Words

In the first part of this book, we tried to give a clear picture of the problem—reasons why it is absolutely essential for students to develop large reading vocabularies, and the nature of the obstacles that make it difficult for many to attain this goal. In part II of this book, we present part of the solution: teaching students the meanings of specific words.

Let us stress again that this is only *part* of the solution. Students must not only be taught words, they must be taught to become better independent word learners, and they must be immersed in the rich language, oral and written, from which they will gain much of their vocabulary knowledge. With apologies to St. Francis, we might offer as a motto, "Always promote vocabulary growth—and when necessary, teach words." We emphasize this point because there is always a danger of thinking that teaching the meanings of specific words is all there is to vocabulary instruction.

There are a variety of reasons to teach students the meanings of words, and a variety of words that can be taught. The four chapters in part II of this book address different categories of words, and different types of instruction.

Chapter 5 is called "Teaching Words for Ownership." In this chapter, we explain what kind of instruction is necessary if you want students to "own" words—that is, to be able to easily understand text that contains these words, and to be able to use the words in their own writing. This kind of instruction is useful for general vocabulary, or what some have called "Tier Two" words—words that are unlikely to be familiar to students from their spoken language experience, but that are used frequently across a variety of genres of written language.

Chapter 6 is about teaching new concepts. General vocabulary words, dealt with in chapter 5, often provide new ways of talking about ideas and experiences that are already familiar to students. For example, students may not yet know the word *animosity*, but they are likely to have had sufficient experiences to grasp what this word is all about. When learning content area vocabulary, on the other hand, students usually face a different situation—words referring to new and difficult concepts that cannot be reduced in simple ways to their existing base of knowledge and experiences. The task of learning a new concept is more challenging than simply adding a new word to one's vocabulary, and the instruction that supports this kind of learning is necessarily more intensive.

Chapter 7 is about teaching high-frequency words. The bulk of the text that students read in school is made up of a relatively small set of common words that are essential for students to know. Of course, many of these words may already be familiar to your average and above-average students, but you cannot assume that your students know all of them, especially those students whose home language is not English.

Chapter 8, "Talking About Words," deals with vocabulary instruction when learning of words per se is not center stage. The school day should not *feel* like one long vocabulary lesson. And yet, throughout the day, students should be encountering new words and ideas, and teachers should be helping students learn and remember them. Talk about words should be a natural, and pervasive, part of the classroom.

5

Teaching Words for Ownership[1]

A word in a dictionary is very much like a car in a mammoth motorshow—full of potential but temporarily inactive.

(Anthony Burgess, 1992, *A Mouthful of Air*, p. 48)

A comprehensive approach to promoting vocabulary growth has three main parts: teaching specific words, increasing students' exposure to rich oral and written language, and increasing students' generative word knowledge (i.e., their awareness and interest in words, and their ability to make effective use of context, word parts, and definitions). In this part of the book, we look at methods for teaching specific words. In this particular chapter, we discuss what has been called *intensive* or *rich vocabulary instruction*—that is, at Level III, the top level of the vocabulary pyramid.

This chapter is about teaching words for ownership—bringing students to the point where they can quickly and easily understand text containing these words, and can use these words in their own writing. Not all words deserve such treatment; some of the words that students encounter in their reading are not likely to show up again for another year or so. However, there are many words that, although they may be uncommon in everyday conversation, are part of the core of the written language that students encounter in their texts.

Which words fall into this category depends on the grade level of the student, but it's easy to think of words that students are unlikely to know but you would expect to be part of a literate person's vocabulary: *abolish, ban-*

---

[1]Some material in this chapter taken from Stahl (1999). Reprinted with permission.

ish, chamber, deliberate, exceed, frequent, genuine, hospitable, and *initiative*, to take examples from the first nine letters of the alphabet. Such words are essential tools for both reading and writing; to be used as tools, they must be learned thoroughly.

Three Principles of Teaching Words

To lead to ownership of words, vocabulary instruction must meet three criteria:

- Include both definitional information and contextual information about each word's meaning.
- Involve children more actively in word learning.
- Provide multiple exposures to meaningful information about the word.

Include Both Definitional and Contextual Information

When you think back to vocabulary instruction in school, you immediately remember learning lists of definitions (with a test on Friday). Such instruction is not only boring, it is also ineffective in improving comprehension. We found that approaches providing only definitional information did not significantly affect children's reading comprehension (Stahl, 1986). In contrast, methods that provided both definitional and contextual information did significantly improve comprehension.

Consider teaching the word *debris*. Jenkins, Pany, and Schreck (1978) found that learning that *debris* meant "trash" did not transfer to being able to better understand passages containing the word *debris*. There were two problems with this study. First, the number of unknown words was a relatively small percentage of the number of words in a passage. Readers can compensate for a small percentage of unknown words while reading. Studies of informal reading inventories disagree on the percentage of words that readers can tolerate not knowing without impairing comprehension, but estimates range from 5% to 10% of the text (Freebody & Anderson, 1983; Hsueh-chao & Nation, 2000; Laufer, 1989). This is a relatively large number, and suggests that readers are flexible in using their ongoing comprehension of the text to compensate.

Second, knowing that *debris* means "trash" may be insufficient for comprehension. *Debris* does not precisely mean "trash." Instead, it is a particular kind of trash that results from a cataclysm such as a car or plane accident or a storm. The implication of cataclysm may be lost if a person only knew that *debris* meant some sort of trash. This may or may not be important in any given passage, depending on how important the term *debris* is to the overall theme of the passage.

Children may not need to know the full meaning of each word in order to understand any given passage. For some words in some contexts, knowing a definition may be good enough to understand the word. This depends on the importance of the word in the passage and the depth of meaning that the word contributes to the passage (Graves, 1986). Consider these two examples:

1. He stepped over the debris on his way to the car. He heard someone quietly moaning inside.
2. He stepped over the debris on his way to the car. He put his key into the ignition and took off.

In the first example, the meaning of *debris* might be essential to understanding what is going on. The reader can make an inference, based on knowledge that *debris* is often associated with accidents or catastrophes, that the car in question may have been involved in an accident serious enough to do substantial damage to the car, and hence also serious enough to cause injury to the driver or passengers. In the second example, *debris* may be incidental to the plot. The basic gist of the story can be understood without knowing the word at all.

It is not the individual words that make texts easy or difficult, it is instead the cumulative amount of difficult words. Thus, a reader can tolerate one unknown word, especially if it is relatively unimportant to the text, but may not be able to tolerate a critical number of unknown words. It is important to look at the entire text.

Finally, knowing the meaning of *debris* means learning a further differentiation of the category of "trash." As one learns more about these categories, one learns more about the world. Contrast the memorization of the debris–trash association with a more elaborate explanation, such as:

What does *debris* mean? Debris is kind of like trash, in that debris is something left over, but it is not just any trash. Think about a car crash, for instance. You might see broken headlights or pieces of a bumper left over after the crash. That would be debris. Debris is something left over after an event. So you might have debris after a car crash, or after a plane crash, or after a hurricane or tornado. You might have debris left after a party, if it was a good one.

This explanation relates the term to a larger context, and to the learner's knowledge and experience of car crashes. Extending the meaning of *debris* to hurricanes, airplane crashes, or even high school football games should be fairly easy once the overall meaning is learned. The discussion can go on to distinguishing between *debris* and *trash* and *garbage*. By looking at the word from multiple directions, the teacher is "criss-crossing the landscape" (Spiro, Coolson, Feltovich, & Anderson, 2004, p. 652) and creating a rich mental representation for the word. That mental representation will be available for the children when they encounter *debris* again.

Learning the word *debris* also means that the child has gained in knowledge overall. Being able to break the domain of trash into *trash, debris,* and *garbage,* as well as *recyclables* and so on, means that the child can talk about that domain in more precise terms. Although the category is an unimportant one, the same is true for more important venues. This is an example of the knowledge hypothesis discussed earlier in this text. The more knowledge a person has of a domain, even a mundane domain like trash, the more the person will be able to read texts that use any of these words.

Just having children memorize definitions leaves them to the mercy of the "phone number" syndrome. When you look up a phone number, ordinarily you remember it just long enough to dial it and then forget it almost immediately. This is the way children handle those memorized definitions. They remember the definitions long enough to pass the test, or do whatever they need to do with them, and then forget them. The definitions can be arbitrary pieces of information. For the definitions to be remembered, they need to be tied into already existing information in the child's head. So tying *debris* to images that children may have of accident sites would make the word *debris* more memorable. The more connections the child can make, the better he or she remembers the word.

Some things that a teacher might do to provide definitional information include:

- *Teaching synonyms.* This should not be overdone, but synonyms can be useful. Often, a synonym is all a person needs to understand a word in context.
- *Teaching antonyms.* Not all words have antonyms, but thinking about antonyms requires a child to identify the crucial aspects of a word. For example, a word like *pandemonium* implies lawlessness, or clutter, but its antonym, *order*, focuses the meaning on the "chaos" part of the word's meaning. (However, it should be noted that teaching a word and its antonym at the same time when both are unfamiliar can be confusing, especially to English language learners; (see Higa, 1963; Tinkham, 1993; Waring, 1997).
- *Rewriting definitions.* Having students state a definition in their own words is more powerful than having them remember the exact word-

ing of the definition. Definitions can be confusing to children (Scott & Nagy, 1997). Having children restate definitions may be the only way a teacher can find out whether the children actually understand them.

- *Providing examples.* This is another way for a teacher to ascertain whether students understand definitions. These examples may be drawn from personal experiences ("My room is pandemonium") or from school content ("After the Civil War, there was pandemonium all over the South").

- *Providing nonexamples.* This requires the student to think about the critical attributes of a word, similar to the task of providing antonyms. A nonexample is a word that is similar to the target word, but different in a very important sense. For example, for the word *habitat* a non-example might be *box* or *bedroom.* A person could live in a box but a box would not comprise a total environment for living. The same would be true for *bedroom.* For *debris,* a nonexample might be something orderly, such as index cards in a box, or something not broken. Discussion of nonexamples can key the student onto the important attributes of a concept.

- *Discussing the difference between the new word and related words.* For example, a discussion of the word *debris*, defined as "trash" or "waste," might include a discussion of the differences between *debris* and *trash* (trash could include anything; debris results after some sort of accident or disaster), *garbage* (which generally refers to organic material, e.g., food leftovers), or *waste* (which implies something left over, rather than something resulting from a disaster). Such a rich discussion focuses the meaning of the word. (This can be similar to semantic mapping, discussed in chap. 6.)

Similarly, a teacher could provide contextual information by:

- *Having students create sentences containing the target word.* Sentences should show the meaning clearly, and cannot be vague. One suggestion might be to give different credit for sentences, which show better use of the word. One might give no points for a sentence frame, such as "I like pandemonium," one point for a sentence that includes the definition, such as "Pandemonium is when everything is chaotic," or two points for a sentence such as "It was complete pandemonium—people were running in all directions, often bumping into each other and knocking each other over."

  When having children write sentences, it is important to share them with a class or a small group. When children only write their own sentences, it is just a single repetition and tends to be another memorized fact. Having students compare sentences forces them to think about the word's meaning in different contexts. It should be kept in mind, of course, that simply providing students with a definition for a word generally does not give them an adequate basis for writing sentences that use that word, especially if the word is not a concrete noun. Asking students to write sentences for a word is most helpful if some activities for supplying definitional or contextual information described here have already taken place.

- *Sometimes it is useful to ask students to use more than one word in each sentence.* Using more than one word in a sentence forces students to look for relations among words. In one classroom we worked in, the children spontaneously competed among themselves to produce sentences that contained as many of the six words being taught as they could jam into one sentence. The sentences got fairly absurd, but the children remembered the words. It is important to keep in mind that the definition must be maintained and that the sentences should be somewhat plausible.

- *Discussing the meaning of the same word in different sentences.* It is important that a teacher use multiple sentences, so that a student is not locked into a particular context. If possible, the contexts should be as varied as possible. For the word *pandemonium,* sentences might include topics such as chaos in the classroom, chaos in terms of clutter and mess, chaos in relations among people, and so on.

- *Creating a scenario.* This involves not just a sentence, but making up a complete story. An alternative for younger children might be drawing a picture story for a new word.

- *Silly questions.* This involves pairing the words being taught and creating a question out of each pair (Beck et al., 1982). For the words *actuary, hermit, philanthropist,* and *villain,* a set of questions might include "Can an actuary be a hermit?" "Can an actuary be a philanthropist?" "Can a philanthropist be a hermit?" "Can a philanthropist be a villain?" These can be made out of any words. Often, it works well just picking words from a list, culminating with playfully bizarre results.

It is often difficult to generate realistic contexts. It is especially tough to make up contexts on the fly. We recommend that you devote some time to plan effective contexts. In principle, the Internet should be a useful source of authentic contexts to illustrate the use of words, but we have yet to find resources that would be ideal for most teachers. There are an increasing number of sites making a variety of texts available for free (e.g., Project Gutenburg http://www.promo.net/pg/ and others like http://digital.library.upenn.edu/books/ and http://etext.lib.virginia.edu/ebooks/ebooklist.html). To find examples of specific words, a concordance is most helpful, but the concordances available on the Web are mostly for specific texts or corpora—the Bible, the works of Shakespeare (http://www.it.usyd.edu.au/~matty/Shakespeare/test.html), a corpus of sentences used in the Voice of America's Special English programs (http://www.manythings.org/voa/sentences.htm), and even a large corpus of British English (http://sara.natcorp.ox.ac.uk/lookup.html). Some of these may be helpful, but we hope that more easily searchable and comprehensive corpora come to be available so that teachers can easily locate authentic examples of how instructed words are used.

One could also use the Internet as one way of helping students find uses of the word outside of the classroom. Even a simple Internet search, using Google or some other search engine, could be motivating just because the students become aware of the fact that what seem like "rare" words are actually used tens of thousands of times on the Internet.)

Involve Children in Actively Processing New Word Meanings

A second principle of effective vocabulary instruction relates to how active students are at constructing links between new information and previously known information. Children remember more information when they are performing cognitive operations on that information. Such operations might include relating it to known information, transforming it into their own words; and generating examples, nonexamples, antonyms, and synonyms.

Lessons in one study of exemplary vocabulary instruction (Beck, Perfetti, & McKeown, 1982) were conducted in a 5-day cycle. On the first day, words were defined. Then students discussed how each word is used in context. This discussion could take a number of different forms, including discussion of examples and nonexamples, pantomimes, or having students say "Thumbs up" if the word was used correctly in a sentence or "Thumbs down" if it was not. On the second day, after a review of the definitions, students might have worked on log sheets, completing sentences for each word. On the third day, students completed another worksheet with the vocabulary words and then worked on a "ready, set, go" activity. (This is a timed activity in which pairs of students attempt to match the words with their definitions in the shortest amount of time.) This activity was repeated on the fourth day. After completion of the second "ready, set, go" activity, students were asked silly questions. On the fifth day, students took a posttest.

These are only examples of activities, which varied somewhat with different units. Students also completed a "word wizard" activity each day (see chap. 10). They were given credit toward becoming a "word wizard" by finding examples of each word used outside of class.

This program, or variations of it, was found to significantly improve students' comprehension of texts containing words that were taught (Beck et al., 1982; McKeown et al., 1985). They also found that their approach, which involved active processing of each word's meaning, had significantly greater effects than did the definition-only approach on measures of comprehension.

Provide Multiple Exposures to Meaningful Information About the Word

The third principle of effective vocabulary instruction is that it takes repeated meaningful encounters with a word to learn it to the point of ownership. In the studies by Beck, McKeown, and their colleagues just described, they discovered that it took 12 encounters with the word to reliably improve comprehension. Four encounters with the word, even if they were rich, meaningful, instructional experiences, did not suffice to increase the students' understanding of text containing the instructed words. Thus, this research suggests that vocabulary instruction can improve comprehension, but only if the instruction is rich and extensive, and includes a great many encounters with to-be-learned words.

Teachers might object that such intensive instruction is not feasible. How can a teacher carry out vocabulary instruction in such depth and still have any time left for anything else in the curriculum?

Our answer to this objection is that you should not attempt to teach very many words this way. As we said in chapter 4 in the discussion of the vocabulary pyramid, only a small proportion of the words that students are to learn can be covered at this level of intensity—words of especially high utility that students will encounter frequently in the reading, and need to be able to use in their own writing. Many other words will have to be taught less intensively, or left up to students to learn on their own.

If research has shown that it takes 12 instructional encounters to thoroughly learn a word, what is the use of less intensive instruction? Here we think it helpful to remember that learning a word is a matter of many small steps. Often, there is only enough time available to help a student take one step forward, by providing a definition or explanation for an unfamiliar word. This step is not wasted, if the student is also immersed in rich oral and written language that in the course of time will provide additional meaningful encounters with that word.

Another possible objection to intensive vocabulary instruction, involving a dozen encounters with each instructed word, is that devoting such an amount of time to vocabulary instruction would be insufferably boring. However, this objection stems from an overly narrow conception of what can constitute an instructional encounter with a word. Students found the intensive vocabulary program of Beck, McKeown, and their colleagues described earlier to be very engaging. Some of the activities already discussed in this chapter (e.g., the "silly questions") can provide a number of encounters with words in a relatively short amount of time, and in a way that actively involves students. In the next section, we consider discussion, another important way to provide students with multiple experiences with instructed words.

Use Discussion to Actively Teach Word Meanings

Discussion adds an important dimension to vocabulary instruction. First of all, children benefit from the contributions of other children. It is our experience that children who enter a vocabulary lesson without any knowledge of a target word seem to learn a great deal from their peers, who may have partial or even fairly good knowledge of the word. We have found that, in open discussions, children are often able to construct a good idea of a word's meaning from the partial knowledge of the entire class. (When the class as a whole does not know much about a word, however, the teacher may have to interject some information about the word, such as a quick definition.)

Discussion can clarify misunderstandings of words by making them public. For words that a child partially knows, or knows in one particular context, the give and take of discussion can clarify meanings. When misunderstandings are public, the teacher can shape them into the conventional meaning.

In addition, discussion seems to involve children in other ways. While waiting to be called on, students practice or prepare a response to themselves. Even though only one child is called on, many children anticipate having to come up with an answer. Because many children are practicing a response covertly, discussion seems to lead to increased vocabulary learning (Stahl & Clark, 1987). Because of the importance of each child expecting to be called on, teachers should allow all children in the class some think time before calling on one individual. Also, a teacher should be sensitive to his or her patterns of calling on children, and avoid calling on only the "smart" kids. If a child does not think that he or she will be called on, the child will not practice a response. Without practicing a response, discussion is not as valuable a learning experience.

Drama and Charades. Another approach to getting children engaged in learning word meanings that makes them think about the words in a way that helps them remember a word's meaning is drama and charades. Charades, of course, are a game in which a person on one team gives a clue that is acted out, and the other team must guess the word. This can be done with small groups of children, preferably at the end of the day because it involves a great deal of high energy. Foil and Albers (2002) suggested breaking the class into four teams and giving each team a list of vocabulary words. Each team member would take turns acting out one of the words on the list. The first team to identify the word would get a point. The winning team would be the one with the most points at the end of the game.

Another alternative would be to give credit for making the words easy to guess by having as accurate a pantomime as possible. In this activity, you would use pairs of teams. Each team would consist of four to six students. Consider the following words from a fifth grade story: *beloved, desire, permit, heaved, marveled,* and *bid.* One could add another group of similar words to this, such as *sweetheart, need, sanction, tossed, amaze,* and *hail,* so that there would be a contrast. Children from one team would have to pantomime the words and children from the other team would have to make guesses. Points would be given for making the words easiest to guess.

As in the adult version of charades, team members could use hand signals to indicate the number of syllables in the word. (Putting one finger on the opposite arm would indicate one syllable, two fingers would indicate two syllables, etc.) Also, team members could indicate that the word sounds like another word by touching their ears. However, the meaning of the word would have to be conveyed through pantomime alone, without any verbal interactions. An easier version of charades, one that might be used for younger children, is simply having children volunteer to pantomime words, without a game format.

Short skits could be developed from lists of words. Again, using the same set of words *(beloved, desire, permit, heaved, marveled,* and *bid)*, groups of children could develop short skits using each word. As the word appears in the skit, one member of the group could hold up a word card, to reinforce the words.

Charades can force children to think about how to convey a meaning. This thinking is generative and forces children to think about the contexts, especially physical, in which a word can be used. We recommend charades as a reteaching approach, rather than as an initial teaching approach, because if a word is totally unknown it would be difficult to guess. However, charades might be a way of getting children to go back over words from previous lessons.

Word Guesses is very similar to charades, except that in Word Guesses the students use verbal descriptions instead of pantomimes. The steps are as follows:

1. The teacher places vocabulary words on small slips of paper.
2. The class is divided into two different teams. (Again, four to six seems like a good number of students for each team.)
3. A member of each team draws a slip of paper out of a bag.
4. That team member will try to describe the word's meaning without using the word itself.
5. That student's team will try to guess the word.
6. If the team can guess the word, they get a point. If not, the other team can try to guess the word and get the point.
7. The team with the most points wins.

For the word *ghost,* the student might say, "This is a spirit, possibly someone who died, you can't see it."

Again, Word Guesses requires children to convey the meaning of the word, in this case using both definitional information and contextual information. The active guessing makes children think about the information provided; not only the word given, but also other words with similar meanings.

Drama could be used to teach even simple words, such as *before, during, first, last,* and *next,* that often cause difficulty among young readers and ESL children. Children could be asked to act out, by moving to the *first* place in the line, to the *next* place, to the *last* place, *before* one child, *after* another, and so on.

Some of these can be filler or sponge activities that can be used between activities.

Story Impressions. This is a reading/writing activity, used both pre- and postreading. McGinley and Denner (1987) created Story Impressions to be used to develop an anticipatory set for comprehension. Richek (in press) suggested that, with the addition of talk about word meanings, it could be used for vocabulary instruction as well.

To use Story Impressions, prior to reading a story the teacher prepares an ordered set of words or short phrases. These words should represent the key concepts in a story and could be used to retell many of the major points in the story. It is important not to include too many details, but to cover the main points. To modify Story Impressions for vocabulary preteaching, the teacher should make sure that some of the words will be likely to cause problems for children's reading. This list is put on an overhead slide or a piece of chart paper, or copied and distributed to the class.

Prior to reading, the class writes a story or stories using the words on the list, *in exactly the order that they are on the list*. Words or phrases can be combined within a single sentence or in multiple sentences. If desired, sentences can be included that do not contain any of the list words. As the list is brought out, the teacher should go through it, discussing the meanings of the words on the list. For the Story Impressions depicted in Fig. 5.1, based on the book *The Wreck of the Zephyr* (Van Allsburg, 1983), words such as *wreck, gust, boom, bow,* and *till* might be discussed. For *boom, bow* and *till,* the teacher might want to point out other parts of a sailboat as well, so that the children have a clear idea of how these parts connect to each other.

Children can write stories in small groups, as a whole class, or individually. After they write their stories, these stories should be shared with the rest of the class. After sharing the stories, children should read the story for the first time. After reading, they can compare their stories with the actual story. In addition, they can talk about how the targeted words were used in the story, and what other words it would have been useful to know.

We have used Story Impressions successfully with children from Grades 2–8. McGinley and Denner (1987) actually developed this approach for high school students. We find that it makes children more active readers. Children report that they are compare the story they are reading with the one that they wrote before reading. These comparisons can be made explicit after reading. By adding vocabulary discussion, children can focus on the new words during reading, making them more likely to internalize the words' meanings.

The activity also includes both reading and writing, and, if small groups are used, discussion as well. This allows it to serve many different functions. The writing makes it a generative vocabulary activity, because it forces children to integrate the new word meanings into an ongoing story, and then addresses the relation of those words to other words when the children's stories are discussed both pre- and postreading.

wreck
|
sailboat
|
old man
|
Zephyr
|
boy
|
sail better than anyone
|
gust
|
caught the sail
|
boom
|
hit the boy's head
|
on a beach
|
two boats
|
sailing above the water
|
sailor
|
learn to sail
|
new sails
|
took the till
|
fly
|
evening wind
|
bow
|
began to lift
|
over the village
|
fell to the ground

FIG. 5.1. Story Impressions for *The Wreck of the Zephyr* (Van Allsburg, 1983).

A Bingo game can be played with new vocabulary words. (Chap. 7 gives an example of playing such a game with high-frequency words.) In this game, the caller would given a sentence with the word omitted or a definition, and each child would have to recognize the word and put a marker by it. As with regular Bingo, the first person with five in a row would win.

Other games, such as Memory using a word on one card and its definition on the other, could be adapted for vocabulary practice. These should be a minor part of a vocabulary program, but they can add some spice to practicing word meanings.

Limitations. Although vocabulary instruction does seem to significantly improve comprehension (at least when the words being taught are in the text), there are some limitations. Teaching vocabulary can, under certain circumstances, distract a reader from the main ideas in the text. One study found that teaching words that were associated with low-level information encouraged students to focus on that information. Because students were focusing on unimportant details, they were not as good at recalling important information as were students who did not get vocabulary instruction recall (Wixson, 1986). Thus, it is important that a teacher choose words that are important to the ideas in a text, rather than words that are interesting but not related to the main ideas of a story or passage.

If one wants to teach some words that are tangential to the story, because they are useful or interesting, it would be best to do that teaching after reading the story. This would allow students to focus on the story during reading, but still receive vocabulary enrichment.

A Sample Lesson

To put these concepts together, Stahl (1999) suggested a sample lesson for the following words, taken from the story *The Talking Eggs* by Robert San Souci (1989): *backwoods, contrary, dawdled, groping, rubies,* and *silver:*

> For *backwoods*, one might read this sentence from the story: "Then the old woman took her by the hand and led her deep into the backwoods" (p. 7). I would ask students to predict what *backwoods* meant. This word is a compound and should be fairly clear from the word parts, combined with some context. Students could be asked to describe the backwoods briefly.
>
> Similarly, I would teach *contrary* beginning, again, with this sentence from the book: "You do as I say and don't be so contrary" (p. 19), and asking students to predict its meaning. I would then discuss a definition, such as "disagreeable, raising objections" and how it fits into that sen-

tence. Next, students might provide some sentences that use *contrary*. I might also discuss the other related meaning for *contrary*, that of "from another point of view," as in the expression "to the contrary."

For *rubies* and *silver*, we might discuss what precious things are, and possibly provide pictures of rubies and of silver. Together, the class and I could make a list of precious things, including rubies and silver, as well as gold, diamonds, and so on.

Groping and *dawdled* are verbs. I might begin again with sentences from the story, and also do a pantomime, rather than provide merely a verbal definition. Then, students would add their own sentences. I would suggest some nonexamples for *dawdled*, because it seems to be a word that has some clear antonyms, such as *hustled, ran, went quickly*, and so on.

The words in this sample lesson are highly dissimilar, grouped together only because they happen to come out of the same story. This is often the case in literature-based classrooms. The techniques used to teach the words are somewhat similar. When I actually taught this sample lesson, for four of the six words I started with the text sentence in which they were used. I chose those sentences to make a link to the text. Then I asked for additional sentences to extend the meaning of the words beyond the text. Finally, I also included a definition, either a verbal or a gestural one, for all of the words. Otherwise, I tried to adopt my instruction to the words, using the general principles discussed previously. (p. 35)

This is relatively minimal instruction, designed to support the reading of the text. More elaborate instruction would shift the focus from the story to the vocabulary, and might be useful in a classroom with many ESL learners or in other situations in which a greater emphasis on vocabulary is appropriate. More elaborate instruction might include additional sentence contexts for each word, a "yea or nay" activity ("Would you dawdle in the backwoods?"), having students write a scenario containing these words, and the like.

Vocabulary instruction needs to be both planned and opportunistic. Much of the time, teachers will be explaining words, or pointing out opportunities for applying word learning strategies, "on the fly." However, there is also a place for the more formal, planned vocabulary instruction discussed in this chapter. Of course, even in preplanned vocabulary lessons, much of the instruction will involve reacting to what children say, scaffolding their correct responses, and pushing them toward cognitively challenging thought about words.

Different levels of vocabulary instruction are appropriate for different purposes. For students to know words well enough to make a difference in understanding text—that is, text in which the instructed words play an important role—relatively intensive instruction is required. Such instruction must include both definitional and contextual information about the words, involve children actively in word learning, and provide multiple exposures (at very least, more than four) to meaningful information about the word. In this chapter, we've given examples of a variety of activities that can help students attain this level of word knowledge. In the following chapter, we talk about instruction that is intensive in a slightly different way—instruction for teaching students new and unfamiliar concepts.

This chapter has described how to teach words for ownership—that is, how to help students move from little or no knowledge of a word to the point where they can understand text containing that word, and use that word in their own writing. There are three characteristics of vocabulary instruction that can do this: It must include both definitional and contextual information about a word, must actively involve students in word learning, and must provide multiple instructional encounters with the word.

Such instruction is relatively labor-intensive, both in terms of classroom time and preparation time, so teachers need to be selective about which words to give this amount of attention to. In short, such instruction is appropriate for words of high utility—words that students will encounter frequently in their reading, that they should be able to use in their own writing, and ideally, words that are related in some way to major themes or concepts in the curriculum.

Teaching words for ownership can be intensive, but it need not be onerous. In fact, to actively involve students in word learning requires activities that are engaging. For vocabulary instruction to be truly effective, it must not only ensure that children learn specific words, but also help engender in them a delight in words and appreciation for language.

6

Teaching Concepts

It is impossible to dissociate language from science or science from language, because every natural science always involves three things: the sequence of phenomena on which the science is based; the abstract concepts which call these phenomena to mind, and the words in which the concepts are expressed. To call forth a concept a word is needed; to portray a phenomenon, a concept is needed. All three mirror one and the same reality.

(Antoine Laurent Lavoisier, 1789, Traité Élémentaire de Chemie, *Bartlett's Familiar Quotations*, 17th ed., 2002, p. 359)

The principles discussed in the last chapter are sufficient for teaching words that are labels for concepts that children already know, or at least that can be explained in terms of experiences that are already familiar—that is, words that have easier synonyms or can be easily defined. However, often a teacher needs to teach complex concepts, such as *DNA, independence, quadratic equation,* and so on. What makes something a complex concept depends not only on the word, but on the background knowledge and experiences of the students, and on how thoroughly they need to learn it. In general, what makes something a complex and difficult concept is not just that the idea itself is new to the child, but also that it is part of a new set or system of ideas. Learning the meaning of the word *ventricle*, for example, depends not just on mastering one concept, but also on understanding how the different chambers of the heart are related to each other.

Complex concepts require multidimensional teaching techniques. Generally, if one is going to teach a concept, one must (a) identify the critical attributes of the word, (b) give the category to which it belongs, (c) discuss examples of the word, and (d) discuss nonexamples of the word. For example, for the word *prehistoric,* it is important to note that *prehistoric* means "before history" or before things were written down, and then to explain that this word is used to describe things in terms of when they existed. One might discuss prehistoric times, what people looked like in those times, and so on. Students could be asked to tell whether dinosaurs and lions were prehistoric, and explain why. The object is to give students as full as notion of *prehistoric* as possible.

Consider a complex concept that all children encounter in their social studies—*liberty*. My *Encarta* dictionary defines it as follows:

lib•er•ty (*n*)

1. the freedom to think or act without being constrained by necessity or force

2. freedom from captivity or slavery

3. any of the political, social, and economic rights that belong to the citizens of a state or to all people (often used in the plural)

See also civil liberties

None of these definitions truly captures the subtleties in the word's meaning. The first definition is close to it, but *liberty* involves more (and less) than "freedom to think or act." One cannot, for example, act in a way that results in the death of another: *Murder* is not *liberty*. Nor can one have complete freedom of action in noncriminal matters. As Oliver Wendell Holmes famously put it, freedom of speech does not extend to yelling 'fire' in a crowded theatre. Liberty is constrained by the obligations of living in a society, and a child's definition of *liberty* should reflect both the positive aspects of liberty as well as the limitations. A fully developed concept would contain both.

So how would we teach the concept of *liberty*? First, we might begin by talking about the context in which we are discussing liberty, saying something like, "The Constitution guarantees 'life, liberty, and the pursuit of happiness.' What do we mean by *liberty*?" We would get responses from children, some of which would be wrong or misleading. We would, however, accept those responses without comment. By soliciting responses, we are both investing children in finding out whether their answer is right or wrong and getting them to activate their prior knowledge about the concept. Then, we might define *liberty,* perhaps conversationally as "the freedom to think or act." We might write this on the blackboard. We would then discuss an example of *liberty*, preferably one that is personal to the children. We might talk about the things that one is allowed to do on a weekend, for example. This would be an extended example.

Next we would write on the blackboard "Liberty" and "Not Liberty." We would again solicit student responses, asking for examples of *liberty*. If a child comes up with examples of "the freedom to think or act" that go beyond the concept of *liberty*, we would discuss them, and put them under the "Not Liberty" column. If students do not produce enough examples of "Not Liberty," we would specifically ask for them.

When there are five or six responses under each category, we would add the category "Slavery," explaining that *slavery* is the opposite of *liberty*. (More precisely, *slavery* is the opposite of one sense of *liberty*—but how we would deal with this refinement would depend on the age of the students, and on the role of the concept of *liberty* in the overall lesson.) We would then discuss what slaves could and could not do, again putting examples under the category. Nonexamples, both limitations and opposites, sharply focus the concept. We might follow this up with a writing activity, such as having children write about the importance of *liberty* in their own life.

We would have devoted a fair amount of classroom time to the development of this concept, but it is an important concept. We would not recommend spending the same amount of time on all words. At the rate of 10 or 15 minutes per word, one would not be able to cover many words. However, key concepts such as *liberty* (which is also fairly abstract), *democracy, protest, republic,* and so on are important concepts that need to be established as an underpinning to the content in American history. Without these concepts, a student could not understand much of what would follow.

Developing Concepts

What we have done with *liberty* is follow some general principles of concept development (Klausmeier, Ghatala, & Frayer, 1974; Wixson, 1986). First, we defined the concept. Because a concept such as *liberty* is too complex to be defined in a simple phrase, we really would not expect the student to learn very much from that definition alone. The first extended example is an example of "inflexible knowledge" (Willingham, 2003). Inflexible knowledge is knowledge of a single example, one that is fairly context bound. Associating *liberty* with what one can do on the weekend is only partially correct, but it gives a base for the flexible knowledge we desire. The other examples, from different realms and contexts, will broaden the concept. However, nonexamples and opposites are needed to fully map the concept, because each concept has limits. The use of opposites further requires children to think more deeply about what the concept means. We find that, even in less extensive vocabulary instruction, having children come up with antonyms (even for words without obvious antonyms) is useful in getting children to think about the meanings of words.

Two simple approaches to concept teaching are to use word maps or the "four square" vocabulary activity. Word maps could be used to teach children elements commonly found in definitions. These word maps can help children learn new word meanings from context, in addition to being used to directly teach new words. They are also called "concept of definition" maps (Schwartz & Raphael, 1985) because they were originally based on that Aristotelian notion of definitions discussed earlier in this text. To generate a word map, one might use a blank diagram and have children discuss the category to which a new concept belongs, some examples, and some nonexamples (see Fig. 6.1). A filled-in map is provided in Fig. 6.2.

We see the use of word maps as being more appropriate for abstract words, such as *friendship, liberty, evolution, abstract painting,* and so on. These concepts are difficult to learn, and truly need a "criss-crossing" of the conceptual landscape to be understood (Spiro, Coulson, Feltovich, and Anderson, 1988). By providing examples, nonexamples, categories ("What is it?"), and descriptions ("What is it like?")—all through active class discussion—the teacher and class can build up the meaning of the concept, break down misconceptions, and cement the word into the child's memory. For prereaders, this can be done orally, but we feel that the diagram adds measurably to children's learning.

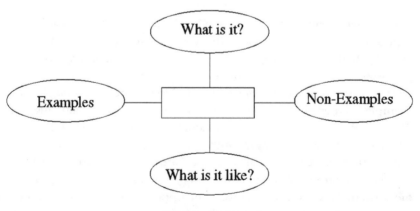

FIG. 6.1. Word map.

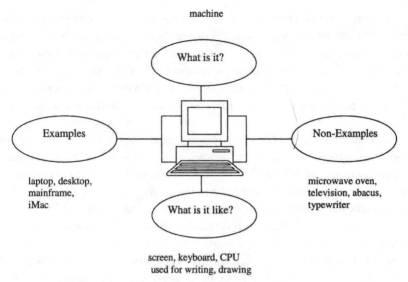

FIG. 6.2.   Word map 2 for the word *computer*.

Four Square Vocabulary Learning

The "four square" activity is based on an activity developed by Eeds and Cockrum (1985). This is a simpler variation of word maps. In this activity, each student takes a sheet of paper and folds it so there are four sections, as shown in Fig. 6.3. The students then write the target word (such as *soothing*) in the upper left section.

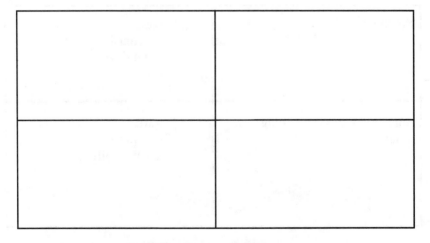

FIG. 6.3.   Sheet of paper folded for "four square" map.

The teacher then gives a definition for the word, possibly from a dictionary. This definition is not written down, because it is intended only to start a conversation. The teacher next solicits examples of the concept from the students, commenting on how good a fit the students' words are with the concept. Examples of the concept are written in the upper right section (e.g., for *soothing*, examples might include *baths, soft music,* and *chocolate*).

The teacher then asks for some things that are *not* [target word]—in this case, *soothing*—and puts those nonexamples in the lower right section (e.g., *loud music, traffic,* and *crying babies*). Finally, the students are asked to compose a definition for the term in their own words and write that definition in the lower left section. Fig. 6.4 depicts a completed concept map.

The "four square" approach is what we call a "hip pocket" approach, because it can be used for any word with which the students are having difficulty and it does not need much preparation. It can be used with nouns, verbs, and adjectives, as can be seen from the examples of *fad, dote,* and *soothing*. Activities such as the "concept of definition" maps require that maps be photocopied in advance and readily on hand, but all this requires is a piece of paper. Fig. 6.5 gives two more examples of completed four square concept maps. Fig. 6.6 gives the generic format for these maps.

Four Squares can be done with the whole class or in cooperative groups. We do not recommend it as an individual activity, because we feel that students gain a great deal from the interactions with others.

Soothing	bath soft music lying down chocolate
Something that is soothing relaxes you	traffic rap music teacher yelling

FIG. 6.4. Completed four square concept map.

fad	rap music low riding pants certain types of sneakers hula hoops (in the 1950s)
something that is popular for a while, but disappears quickly.	classical music jeans

dote	son granddaughter daughter grandson plants books pet
to care for someone or something very much, even overlooking their flaws	villain neighbor's child who plays in your yard someone you don't like

FIG. 6.5.   More examples of completed four square concept maps.

word	examples of the concept • example • example • example (3-6 examples)
definition of the word (in students' own words)	non-examples • non-example • non-example • non-example (3 – 6 non-examples)

FIG. 6.6.   The generic form for a four square concept map.

Semantic Mapping

Semantic mapping is another "hip pocket" activity, because it can be done on the spur of the moment, as well as in a planned-for manner. Semantic mapping is usually used to prepare students to read a content area selection or to introduce a content area unit, such as *water, weather,* or *astronomy*. In our work, we have used semantic mapping primarily in science lessons, but we have seen examples of semantic mapping used in such diverse content areas as music and mathematics, and we even have seen it used by a librarian to teach the Dewey decimal system! (See Heimlich &

Pittelman, 1986, for more examples.) It is a very flexible approach to teaching word meanings in relation to other words and to develop concepts.

A semantic mapping lesson has four parts:

- *Brainstorming.* The teacher and the class brainstorm ideas that relate to a topic. For example, for *weather,* a class might come up with *rain, snow, wind, hot, thermometer, hurricane, blizzard,* and so on. The teacher might stop and explain some of terms that the students come up with, in a discussion forum. The teacher might also add some terms, again explaining what they mean. These terms can be written on the board, or pictured for young children.
- *Mapping.* These terms can be drawn into a map. To draw the map, children (with the aid of the teacher) would come up with three or four categories that describe the terms on the board. These are arranged into a map. Fig. 6.7 gives an example of a possible map for the concept of *weather.* A map made of pictures, for prereaders, is given in Fig. 6.8. Such a map might be used to introduce terms such as *insects, mammals,* or particular types of each.
- *Reading.* After the map is complete, the students and teacher read a book or selection about that topic. For younger children, the teacher

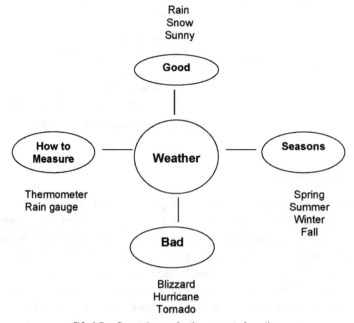

FIG. 6.7.   Semantic map for the concept of *weather.*

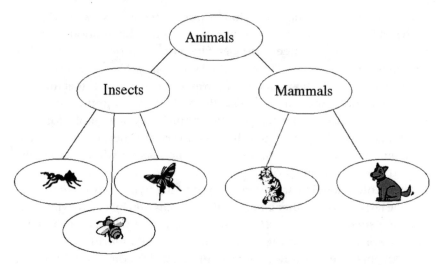

FIG. 6.8.   A semantic map using pictures.

can read the text aloud; for children who can read, they might read in partners or by themselves. An alternative might be an observation. For a lesson on *weather,* this might involve going outside to see the current weather. For a lesson on *plants,* this might involve growing a plant.

• *Completing the map.* After the reading, teachers and children as a group discuss what they have learned from the book. At this time, they might change categories or add another category to reflect what they have learned.

It is important that semantic maps not be just the end in themselves. Instead, they should be connected to a book, an observation, or some ongoing part of the curriculum.

An Example

Prior to reading a story that takes place in the Middle Ages, a fourth-grade teacher wants to activate students' prior knowledge about that time period. Although the major theme of the story is "wisdom and age," she still wants to cover the terms related to the Middle Ages, because these terms and the concepts that she would cover also connect to her social studies curriculum this includes this era. Included in the story are the words, *scroll, banner,* and *conquered.* These are words that she will highlight in the discussion.

The teacher begins the discussion by putting the words *Middle Ages* up on the whiteboard. She then asks the class what they know about that time period. One child volunteers *knights*. She writes this on the board. Then she asks where knights live. Another child says *castles*. She writes this on the board. Because of the few responses, she makes a mental note that this class does not seem to know much about the Middle Ages and that she might have to stress these concepts, possibly by picking a few books for read-alouds that cover this period. She then asks a series of questions designed to elicit children's knowledge of the period. She asks for whom the knights worked, and, after some prodding, elicits the word *king*. Then she explains that kings often fought each other, with one king trying to *conquer* or take over the territory of another king. She then solicits other words having to do with war, such as *invade, attack,* and *occupy*. She talks about how the knights wore *armor* to protect themselves and used *lances* to *joust* with other knights. She asks how people identified which army was which. One child volunteers that the knights carried a flag. The teacher then says that another name for the flag they carried was a *banner* and that a banner was a long piece of cloth, either attached to a pole or strung between two poles. She draws a quick picture of the banner on the whiteboard. She asks who else worked for the king. When no one responds, she talks about the *peasants* who farmed the land, and the *scribes* who wrote things down because few people could read or write during that time period. Rather than writing in books, she offers, scribes wrote in *scrolls*. A child mentions that the Bible used to be written on scrolls and the teacher compliments her.

The teacher has been writing all of these terms on one half of the white board, which looks like Fig. 6.9. At this point, she asks children to read each word aloud, and tell briefly what each word means. Next she writes the words *Middle Ages* in a circle in the middle of other half of the white board. She asks the children in what categories these words belong. One child suggests *peo-*

knights	**lance**
castles	**joust**
king	**banner**
conquer	**peasants**
invade	**scribes**
attack	**scrolls**
occupy	
armor	

FIG. 6.9.   Words relating to the Middle Ages.

ple. The teacher asks which words fit into the category "people." Students reply *king, knight, scribe, peasant*. She draws a circle containing the word *people* and writes those words above the circle, crossing each one out after it is written. Another child suggests words meaning "fight" and the words *conquer, invade, attack,* and *occupy*. The teacher draws a circle, writes the word *fight* inside the circle, and adds these words below, again crossing each word out as she writes. She then asks about the word *joust* and the students agree that it too belongs under *fight*. This leaves *castles, lance, banner,* and *scrolls* on the list. One student suggests a "weapons" category for *lance*. The teacher makes a circle with *weapons* in the middle, placing *lance* underneath. The teacher then solicits other medieval weapons. One student suggests *gun*, but the teacher says that people did not have guns yet in the Middle Ages. Another student suggests *mace*. The teacher asks him how he heard of a mace and the student says that he saw one used on a video game. The teacher and class look up the word *mace* and read aloud the definition: "a medieval weapon in the form of a heavy club with a round spiked metal head." This definitely belongs. The class finally decides that *scroll* and *banner* belongs under a "writing" category and that *castle* belongs under a "home" category, along with *house, hut,* and *dungeon*. Finally, one circle is drawn and left blank, to be used after reading the story, for other categories of information that may come up during the reading.

The result is the map shown in Fig. 6.10. This kind of map should by kept up on the white board for a few days, as the class works through the story and any additional read-alouds of stories that take place in the Middle Ages. Included in the "people" section after the additional reading can be words like *vassal* and *serf,* with *parchment* and *quill* added in the writing section. In a relatively short lesson, a great deal of content can be covered. This includes not only the vocabulary in the story, but also connections to social studies content.

For a lengthier unit, the words can be transferred from the white board or chart paper to a content area word wall. In this way, the map can be used by the students throughout the unit, for reading and writing activities. Displaying the words over time with the expectation that they will be used repeatedly increases the likelihood of student ownership.

Discussion seems to be a crucial element in the effectiveness of semantic mapping (Stahl & Clark, 1987; Stahl & Vancil, 1986). An individualized mapping procedure, in which students studied maps on their own, did not work as well as a group procedure. Discussion in semantic mapping instruction seems to engage children by making them rehearse possible answers. One study found that children who knew they were not going to be

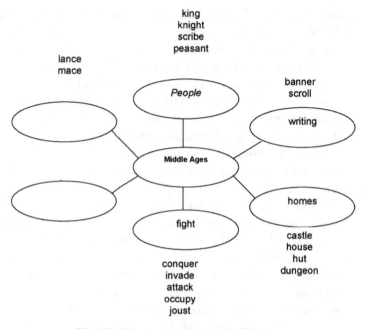

FIG. 6.10.   Map of words relating to the Middle Ages.

called on in class did not recall as many word meanings as did children who thought they might be called on (Stahl & Clark, 1987). This was true, even though all children could listen to the same discussion.

Discussion may be especially important for the children who begin with lower vocabularies. For high-vocabulary children, most of these related words are known, and thus reinforce the target words. For low-vocabulary children, more of the related words may be unknown, and thus may be learned as well. For children with reading problems, this class discussion provides a chance for the kind of learning that they might not glean through a plain reading task.

Discussion also forces children to attend to the concepts and process them deeply. As noted earlier, processing information deeply makes it more memorable, and thus improves the chances that children will retain the information.

Fig. 6.11 gives a semantic map for the concept of *meteorology*.

Comparing and Contrasting

Often, it is important to compare and contrast two different concepts. One simple approach to doing this is the Venn diagram, adapted from math-

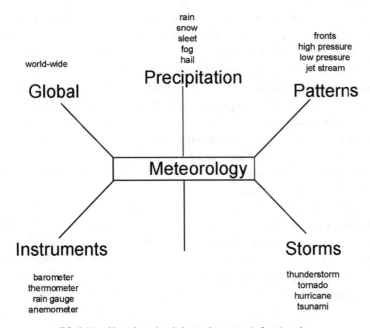

FIG. 6.11. Map of words relating to the concept of *meteorology*.

ematics to show how two sets might overlap. Venn diagrams are adapted to a wide range of situations. For example, for a first- or second-grade lesson, words could be sorted into *insects* and *things that fly* (see Fig. 6.12). In this diagram, *ant* and *grasshopper* would be placed under *insects, airplane* and *bird* would be placed under *things that fly*, and *butterfly* and *bumblebee* would be placed in the overlapped section in the middle.

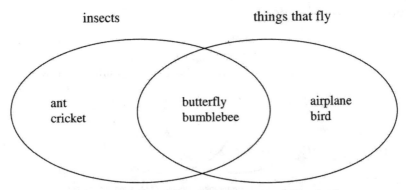

FIG. 6.12. Venn diagram of the categories *insects* and *things that fly*.

For example, when teaching about the American Revolution, it is important to contrast *protest* and *rebellion*. The colonists thought that they were protesting the English taxes by committing acts such as the Boston Tea Party. In contrast, King George III thought that the colonists were rebelling. The difference in perceptions led to increasing tensions and, eventually, revolution. A simple Venn diagram can be a good teaching tool for such contrasts. This diagram can be used to contrast such things as *bacteria* and *viruses*, *monocots* and *dicots*, *symphony* and *concerto*, *republic* and *democracy*, and so forth. One can also make diagrams or charts that distinguish characteristics (respects authority, challenges authority) from examples (*Vietnam War protests, marches*).

Consider a social studies lesson around the beginnings of the American revolution. One of the root causes of the revolution was a difference in viewpoint between King George III and the American colonists. The American colonists saw their actions—the Boston Tea Party, the boycott, and so on—as *protests* against specific British acts that, they felt, unfairly taxed them or took advantage of their status as a colony. King George, on the other hand, felt that these challenges to British rule was a *rebellion*, which had to be put down so that order could be maintained. A thorough understanding of these terms would enable seventh-grade students to understand better the causes of the revolution.

A teacher might begin by putting the Venn diagram on the board and then writing the words *protest* and *rebellion* (see Fig. 6.13). Then the teacher can ask students if they know what *protest* means. Students might contribute by giving examples, but eventually come to the definition that a protest is a "strong disagreement or disapproval with something" that is usually accompanied by an action or a formal complaint. The teacher can do the same with *rebellion*, but stress in the discussion that rebellion is usually against some authority and usually involves refusing to do what an authority tells one to do.

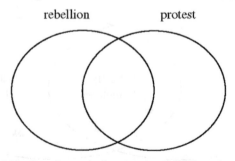

FIG. 6.13. Venn diagram for the categories of *rebellion* and *protest*.

The teacher can then ask for examples of each concept. Under *protest,* students might come up with suggestions like complaining to a parent about curfew, boycotting school lunches in order to get greater variety, and so forth. For *rebellion,* students might suggest *Star Wars*, refusing to go to war, or a revolution. These can be put in the diagram. The teacher can discuss how some of these actions could fit into both categories, depending on one's point of view. This might be a perfect lead-in to a discussion of the actions surrounding the American Revolution.

Through the simple means of a Venn diagram, students can discuss nuances of concepts. Whether an item fits into one set or another is often ambiguous; through discussing the ambiguities, one can learn a great deal about complex concepts. These discussions are perfect examples of "crisscrossing" the landscape of the concepts (Spiro, Coulson, Feltovich, & Anderson, 1988).

Categorization

Basic categorization can be done with children as young as preschool age. In fact, categorization is a basic language process that should be taught from preschool onward. A basic sorting activity can be used with young children. A teacher can take a flannel board divided into two sections and have a group of children sort pictures into two groups. Sample categories might be farm animals and zoo animals, or things found in a kitchen and things found in a living room, and so on. This can be an opportunity to introduce words that refine existing knowledge, such as *sofa* or *couch* or *stool* or *spatula*. Teachers can introduce those terms as they discuss pictures. A basic sorting grid (see Fig. 6.14) can be used, either drawn on a whiteboard or using colored papers. Instead of words, pictures can be used.

The process of thinking in categories, as discussed here, is a basic mental process, underlying a great deal of reasoning. By encouraging this categorization early, teachers can develop children's thinking processes.

Semantic Feature Analysis

Sometimes it is helpful to compare and contrast not just two concepts, but a set of partially overlapping concepts. Semantic feature analysis is a tool that can be used for this purpose.

Similar to semantic mapping, semantic feature analysis draws on students' prior knowledge, using discussion to include information about word meanings into a graphic display. Semantic feature analysis uses a

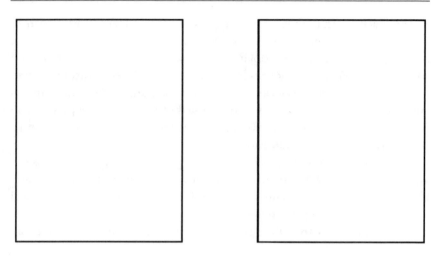

FIG. 6.14.   Basic sorting grid for categorization.

grid such as that in Fig. 6.15 rather than a map, but otherwise they are similar. Down the left side, the teacher writes the names of members of the class. Across the top, he or she writes feature terms. For a unit on transportation, one might place terms such as *car, truck, bicycle, ship, taxi, velocipede, unicycle, dirigible,* and *space shuttle* down the side and *flies, motor, "footpower," wheels, rocket, public, private, land, sea,* and *air* across the top. Students are encouraged to add terms either across the top or down the side during discussion. Groups of students or whole classes can discuss whether each item is an example of each concept, marking + for positive examples, – for negative examples, and ? for items that might be examples under certain circumstances. Fig. 6.15 shows a partially completed semantic feature analysis grid. As with semantic mapping, discussion is an important part of the instruction. Feature analysis grids should not be used as seatwork. In our experience, we've found that even work with groups is suspect, because one member of the group tends to do most of the filling in without a discussion that makes the activity worthwhile. Discussion seems to be key in this activity, because, in our experience, there are many ambiguities. Discussion of the ambiguities seems to clarify the concepts.

Semantic feature analysis would not be appropriate for a set of completely unfamiliar words. Rather, this is a tool for clarifying students' knowledge of words for which they already have at least partial knowledge. One or two brand-new words could, of course, be added to the set, but this activ-

	two wheeled	four wheeled	one wheeled	foot powered	motor powered	on land	in the water	in the air			
bicycle	+	–	–	+	–	+	–	–			
car	–	+	–	–	+	+	–	–			
unicycle	–	–	+	+	–	+	–	–			
airplane											
boat											
hovercraft											
supersonic transport											
velocepede											

FIG. 6.15. Semantic feature analysis for transportation. From Stahl, S. (1999). *Vocabulary Development*. Newton Upper Falls, MA: Brookline Books. Reprinted with permission.

ity presupposes that the students already have sufficient knowledge of most of the words to recognize fairly subtle distinctions in their meanings.

For a prereading activity in a social studies unit on natural resources, a teacher might use the semantic feature analysis grid depicted in Fig. 6.16. The teacher first writes the left column, discussing each term as he or she writes it. (In our example, for space reasons we have chosen to go down in each column rather than across.)

After these terms are discussed, the teacher writes the first word, *natural gas,* and goes down the list, asking students whether it is a natural resource, whether it is renewable, whether it is a fossil fuel, and so on. This is repeated with each of the terms in the first row. We have left space for additional terms, both across and down. For example, the teacher might include *regions of the country,* because this is a section of the chapter. Hence, the terms *West, natural gas, oil, trees,* and *fish* might get a check, but *iron* would not. Or the teacher might include a category for resources that must be processed *(gas, iron, fish)* and those that can be used as is *(trees, oil).* Other items can be added to the top as well.

	natural gas	oil	trees	fish	iron	
natural resource	+	+	+	+	−	
renewable	−	−	+	+	−	
fossil fuel	+	+	−	−	−	
food	−	−	−	+	−	
mineral	−	−	−	−	+	

FIG. 6.16.   Semantic feature analysis grid for natural resources.

For convenience, we have made up a blank semantic feature analysis grid to be photocopied. This grid can be found in Fig. 6.17.

Possible Sentences

Another approach to teaching word meanings is the development of possible sentences. In the possible sentences activity, the teacher first chooses about six to eight words that might cause difficulty for the students. In a content area text, these words are usually key concepts in the text, but they also may be more general words that relate to those key concepts. Then, an additional four to six words are chosen that are more likely to be known by the students. These are used to help generate sentences. We chose *front, barometer, humidity, air mass, air pressure,* and *meteorology* as the target words for a unit on weather, with *high, rain, clouds,* and *predict* as the contrast words (Stahl & Kapinus, 1991). We chose the target words based on our intuition about which words might be difficult for fifth graders, and because these words were central to the concepts taught in the passages. The contrast words were ones we thought would be known to the students and would lend themselves to logical sentences that would relate to the major concepts in the chapter.

These 10 to 12 words are then put on the board. Teachers can provide a short definition of each word if desired or necessary. Most of the time at least one student in the class has knowledge of the word that can be shared. Students are directed to think of sentences containing at least two of these words and that might be in the chapter (or passage) they are about to read. Student contributions are then put on the board. Both accurate and inaccurate guesses are included, and are not discussed at this time. When the students are finished contributing sentences (and all words are included in at least one sentence), the teacher has them read the passage or chapter.

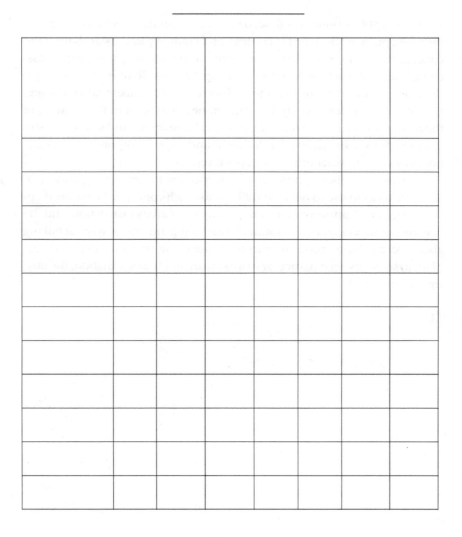

FIG. 6.17.   Blank semantic feature analysis grid.

After reading the selection, the class then returns to the sentences on the board, and the class as a whole discusses whether each sentence could or could not be true based on their readings. If a sentence could be true, it is left alone. If a sentence could not be true, then the class discusses how it could be modified to make it true.

Summary

Most concepts are built over time, bit by bit. The student sees an example of the concept, hears the word in context, and gradually understands what the concept means. In school learning, we often have to compress this process, using intensive teaching to get key concepts across. To develop a concept, the teacher and students need to "criss-cross" the conceptual landscape. For a concept such as *liberty,* the student needs to see it in the contexts of the revolution, one's personal life, historical characters, and so on. The student needs to understand what *liberty* is and, equally important, what it is not, as well as to what other concepts it relates.

We have described a number of approaches to developing concepts. They are tools to use to develop difficult-to-teach concepts. Semantic mapping, semantic feature analysis, four square vocabulary instruction, and the rest are useful as part of a vocabulary teaching program, as ways of talking about words. The graphs and procedures are no more than structures to explain to students what particular words mean. It is the explanation, the talk, that is important.

7

Teaching High-Frequency Words

It depends on what the meaning of the word "is" is. If … "is" means is and never had been, that is not—that is one thing. If it means there is none, that was a completely true statement.

(William Jefferson Clinton, Grand Jury Testimony, August 17, 1998, *Bartlett's Familiar Quotations*, 17th ed., 2002, p. 840)

As we pointed out in Part I of this book, one can't possibly teach all the words that students need to learn. Furthermore, as should be clear enough from the last two chapters, high-quality vocabulary instruction takes time. (There are, of course, times when it is appropriate simply to give an explanation of a word in passing; we'll talk more about that in chap. 8. But if you want students to know words well, you have to be prepared to invest some effort.) Thus, when teachers do take the time to teach words thoroughly, those words should be selected carefully.

What kind of words deserve careful instruction? We believe there are three main categories:

1. *High-utility literate vocabulary*. These are words that occur frequently in most or all genres of written language, but are likely to be unfamiliar to many students because they are relatively rare in conversation. The type of instruction most appropriate for such words was covered in chapter 5.

2. *Key content area vocabulary*. These are words that are specific to a domain but important within that domain, and which probably repre-

sent concepts that are unfamiliar to many students. The type of instruction most appropriate for such words was discussed in chapter 6.

3. *High-frequency words*. These are the core words of the language—the words that make up the bulk of the words in any genre, spoken or written. These are also the words you would probably expect your students to be familiar with already. However, because of the increasing diversity of language and culture among our students, it is no longer appropriate to take anything for granted about what knowledge they might or might not bring with them to the classroom. We certainly don't want you to waste time teaching words that students already know; however, in some cases it may be important to make sure that the foundational vocabulary is in place.

We'll start by looking at what words are in this last category, and then talk about instruction.

Very High-Frequency Words

A relatively small number of words constitute the bulk of the words one encounters while reading. For example, Adams (1990) reported that the 105 most frequent words account for about 50% of the words used in written English. A number of lists of the most frequent words in English have been compiled. Fry, Kress, and Fountoukidis (1993) presented a list, shown in Table 7.1, of the most common 100 words in English. Another common word list was developed by Edward Dolch (Buckingham & Dolch, 1936) of the University of Illinois. This is reproduced in Table 7.2. These words were divided into grade levels, which should be considered as approximate.

It should be noted that such lists of high-frequency words contain two distinct types of words: function words and content words. Function words are words that have a syntactic function—for example, articles, prepositions, pronouns, and conjunctions—that are used to cue a reader or speaker to the structure of the sentence. Consider the previous sentence without the words *are, that, a, to, or, the,* and *of*. It would read, "Function words have syntactic function, used cue reader speaker structure sentence." Although it was not a gem of a sentence before, it becomes unintelligible without function words.

These words are the "glue" that holds sentences together. They contain little of the content that the sentences are intended to convey. Strictly speaking, then, teaching function words is outside of the scope of this book, which is devoted to teaching meaning vocabulary. A few of the highest-fre-

TABLE 7.1
The 100 Most Common Words in English

the	not	people	most
of	have	them	its
and	this	other	made
to	but	more	over
a	by	will	see
in	were	into	first
is	one	your	new
that	all	which	very
it	she	do	my
was	when	then	also
for	an	many	down
you	their	these	make
he	there	no	now
on	her	time	way
as	can	been	each
are	we	who	called
they	what	like	did
with	about	could	just
be	up	has	after
his	said	him	water
at	out	how	through
or	if	than	get
from	some	two	because
had	would	may	back
I	so	only	where

Source: Zeno, Ivens, Millard, & Duvvuri (1995), p. 896.

quency words in our language are content words, however—for example, *number, people, water, word,* and *write.*

For native speakers of English, most of the meanings of the highest-frequency words can be taken for granted, and the goal of instruction for these words would simply be to ensure that they are recognized quickly and effortlessly when encountered in print. One cannot always assume, however, that English language learners will be familiar with these words. Furthermore, the most frequent words in the language tend to have multiple meanings—sometimes very vague meanings—so teachers should not take it for granted that these words will be easy for all their students.

TABLE 7.2
Dolch Word List

Preprimer	Primer	First Grade	Second Grade	Third Grade
a	all	after	always	about
and	am	again	around	better
away	are	an	because	bring
big	at	any	been	carry
blue	ate	as	before	clean
can	be	ask	best	cut
come	black	by	both	done
down	brown	could	buy	draw
find	but	every	call	drink
for	came	fly	cold	eight
funny	did	from	does	fall
go	do	give	don't	far
help	eat	going	fast	full
here	four	had	first	got
I	get	had	five	grow
in	good	her	found	hold
is	have	him	gave	hot
it	he	his	goes	hurt
jump	into	how	green	if
little	like	just	its	keep
look	must	know	made	kind
make	new	let	many	laugh
me	no	live	off	light
my	now	may	or	long
not	on	of	pull	much
one	our	old	real	myself
play	out	once	right	never
red	please	open	sing	only
run	pretty	over	sit	own
said	ran	put	sleep	pick
see	ride	round	tell	seven
the	saw	some	their	shall
three	say	stop	these	show
to	she	take	those	six
two	so	thank	upon	small
up	soon	them	us	start
we	that	then	use	ten
where	there	think	very	today
yellow	they	walk	wash	together
you	this	were	which	try
	too	when	why	warm
	under		wish	
	want		work	
	was		would	
	well		write	
	went		your	
	white			
	who			
	will			
	with			
	yes			

Source: Buckingham & Dolch (1936).

High-Frequency Words

Word frequency is a continuous variable. That is, there is no sharp line between very high-frequency words, high-frequency words, and sort of high-frequency words. Nation (1990) and others treated the most frequent 2,000 or 3,000 words in the language as high-frequency words. One attempt to identify a core vocabulary of high-frequency words was West's (1953) General Service List. This list contained 2,000 headwords, roughly equivalent to main entries in a dictionary. Under some headwords some inflected or derived forms were also listed; for example, under the headword *child* the related words *children, childhood,* and *childish* were also listed. In all, the original General Service List included 1,500 derived words. Several versions of the General Service List are available on the Internet. Web sites that were working when this text was written include the following:

http://jbauman.com/gsl.html

http://www.auburn.edu/~nunnath/engl6240/wlistgen.html

http://www.uefap.co.uk/vocab/select/gsl.htm

http://www.fiu.edu/~dwyere/lists.html

http://www.nottingham.ac.uk/~alzsh3/acvocab/wordlists.htm#gsl

Although the General Service List attempted to cover the most frequent and useful words in English, it is clear that a list of 2,000 headwords is not enough. Laufer (1997), for example, argued that the 3,000 most frequent word families in English constitute an essential core, and that mastery of these is a turning point for English language learners. If one counts inflections and derivatives, 3,000 word families would amount to about 5,000 words. Hence, even according to a very conservative notion of what constitutes an essential core vocabulary, the General Service List is still too small. Thus, it would seem reasonable to try and identify the most important words that lie just beyond a 2,000 word core.

At first glance, it might seem that frequency would be a sufficient basis for determining what the next most important words are. However, especially when one gets away from the small core of very common words, frequency— although important—is not sufficient. The utility of a word depends not only on how often it is used, but also on where it is used—which genres, which stylistic levels, and which contexts. The most frequent words in the language have a pretty broad range of utility. Which words constitute the top 1,000 or so in terms of frequency will not change much whether the corpus on which the frequency is based is spoken or written, formal or informal. Beyond this core, however, differences between oral and written language, and between different registers or styles, become more important.

Several attempts have been made to identify the most important words beyond the General Service List, focusing on those words that are essential for academic success. One of the most recent and most careful attempts to identify such words was Coxhead's (2000) Academic Word List. Some Web sites giving the Academic Word List are:

http://www.vuw.ac.nz/lals/research/awl/

http://www.uni-trier.de/uni/fb2/anglistik/Projekte/stubbs/awl.htm

http://www.nottingham.ac.uk/~alzsh3/acvocab/wordlists.htm#awl

http://www.pu-kumamoto.ac.jp/~jay/class/modeng/handouts/AWL(Coxhead).pdf

http://language.massey.ac.nz/staff/awl/download/awlheadwords.rtf

The top 2,000 words in the language cover about 75% of the running words in text. The Academic Word List covers approximately an additional 10%. The remaining 15% of words in text are likely to be either pretty low in frequency or relatively specialized. Hence, the words in the Academic Word List seem like reasonable candidates for a systematic approach to vocabulary instruction.

This list is probably the most concrete operationalization of what Beck, McKeown, and Kucan (2002) would call "Tier Two" words—words residing somewhere between high-frequency words (e.g., those on the Fry or Dolch lists), and words too low in frequency to be worth teaching. However, Beck and McKeown's concept of Tier Two words is not identical to Coxhead's Academic Word List. The majority of the words Beck and McKeown used as examples of targets for their program of intensive vocabulary instruction are not on the Academic Word List; Beck and McKeown tended to favor words that are somewhat more interesting (e.g., *hermit, virtuoso, philanthropist*) but also somewhat less frequent. One problem with a list like the Academic Word List is that words of high utility are sometimes rather general and boring words—for example, *assess, benefit, consist, define, establish*, and *factor*—rather than the kinds of interesting words that Beck et al. would teach, or the kinds of words that kids would choose to learn on their own.

Please note that we do not recommend merely handing these lists out and having students memorize them and their definitions. As is repeated throughout this book, such instruction is both onerous and ineffective. These lists were developed originally for ESL college students for self-study of academic vocabulary words. We feel that these lists can be used for native English speakers as a guide to words that they need to know. Students can check off words on the list, determine which words they know and which they do not, and use this knowledge to guide their study. A sample checklist is provided in Fig. 7.1. In this checklist, students are asked to indicate which words are totally unknown, which words are partially known, and which words are well known (Curtis, 1987). Checklists such as these can be used for both self-assessment and to help teachers determine what words should be taught.

Teaching High-Frequency Words

It is essential that students be familiar with high-frequency words. In most cases, the meanings of these words will be familiar to students from their oral vocabularies. The primary goal with regard to these words will therefore usually be to make sure that students can read them fluently when they encounter these words in print.

There is some debate whether learning to read high-frequency words is best done in isolation (i.e., in lists), or in context (e.g., Goodman, 1965; Nicholson, 1991). For us, there is no controversy. Both teaching words in isolation and in context have advantages, and both should be used.

Teaching words in isolation allows the child to focus on the features of the printed form of the word. Often, especially when the texts used have predictable sentence patterns (e.g., Bridge, Winograd, & Haley, 1983), children do not analyze the word fully but instead use information available from context to help identify the word. It is important to remember that words live in context, and that they need to be practiced in reading connected text. Nevertheless, a small amount of practicing words in isolation can be useful.

We find, as did Tan and Nicholson (1997), that children do learn words using flashcards. For many years, we have used a simple activity in our clinic

	I've never seen this word before	I've seen this word, it has something to do with ...	I know this word and can use it in a sentence or define it
achieve		X	
acquisition	X		
administration		X	
affect		X	
appropriate			X
aspects		X	
assistance			X

FIG. 7.1.   Example checklist for self-assessment of word knowledge.

with a great deal of success. "Three Strikes and You're Out," it is a basic flashcard activity. Words that children miscall during reading are noted and put on 3" × 5" index cards. These are added to a word bank. Children can practice words from each other's word banks during individual reading time. Words that the child correctly identifies on three different occasions are retired from the word bank. The occasions do not have to be consecutive. As words are retired, they are taken from the word bank and put into a bank of retired words. Retired words can be revisited, but ordinarily are left to grow. As the bank of retired words grows, the child sees concrete evidence of his or her growth in word learning. The activity should take very little time, but seems to be a favorite among children and teachers.

One of the nice things about Three Strikes is that it is a cumulative activity. That is, the number of words will always grow, never diminish. On weekly tests, for example, children's scores will vary, so that even if a child improving week by week, there will be peaks and valleys. For Three Strikes, even if a child learns five words in one session and one word in the next, the pile of retired words will always grow. Three Strikes could be graphed, as in Fig. 7.2, showing continuous progress.

There are other approaches to teaching high-frequency words. The common game "Bingo" can be adapted to teach high-frequency words. In this kind of bingo game, the teacher makes up boards like that shown in Fig. 7.3, using the high-frequency words that his or her students are being taught.

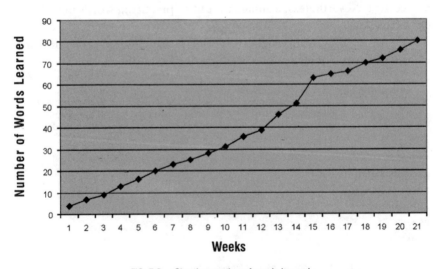

FIG. 7.2. Charting number of words learned.

B	I	N	G	O
are	and	they	was	there
what	is	out	then	to
you	said	from	if	did
his	it	when	on	for
as	have	which	or	by

FIG. 7.3. High-frequency word bingo.

Children are given counters. The teacher calls out words, one at a time. When a child hears a word that is on his or her card, that child puts the counter on the word. The first child who gets five in a row across, down, or diagonally can call "Bingo" and thus win that round. Then the children clear their cards and the teacher begins again.

For more complex words, 8" × 5" cards can be used. Information on these cards might include the word, a dictionary definition, and an example sentence. Children can quiz each other using these cards. One child might give the word to the other, who could provide either a definition or example sentence. The definition should be in the child's own words and not memorized from the card; the example sentence should be a different one from one on the card as well. This can be performed with pairs of students, or with groups, or in teams, as in a game show.

Teaching Words in Context

As noted earlier, words live in context. Teaching new words in context means providing supported reading of connected text. This might involve stopping occasionally during reading to ask the child to explain what a word means in context or what a sentence containing that word means. It is important not to interrupt too frequently, so as not to interfere with the child's comprehension. Some attention to words, however, is important. Reading with a child can be an opportunity to talk about words.

Some techniques for oral reading may be useful in helping children develop knowledge of high-frequency words. These include repeated reading, echo reading, and the use of closed caption television. In repeated readings (Samuels, 2002), students read the same text repeatedly, until a desired level of fluency is attained. There are a number of approaches to having children do repeated reading. We use a specific procedure in our reading clinic, as follows:

1. Choose a passage to read that is slightly above the child's instructional level, but which the child might be interested in reading. This method may be used with grade-level materials for a child reading significantly below grade level.

2. Take a 100-word excerpt from this passage. (You may use different lengths, but the math is more difficult.)

3. Have the child read the passage aloud, and mark all the miscues that the child makes. Time (using a stopwatch or a watch with a sweep second hand) and audio-record the reading. Mark the child's speed and error rate on a chart.

4. Review the child's miscues with him or her. This may be done using the tape or through discussion.

5. Have the child reread the passage. Mark the child's errors and time on the chart.

6. Have the child continue until a speed of 100 words per minute with zero or one miscue per 100 words is achieved. (If this takes more than seven tries, you might want to discontinue and use an easier passage.) This will usually take more than one clinic session. Chart each attempt.

7. Go on to another section at the same level. When the child can read relatively fluently for the first time, move on to a more difficult passage.

The method of repeated reading has been used for a long time. However, we do have some cautions. First, Kuhn and Stahl (2003) found that repeated reading was not as effective as was assisted reading. One reason is that repeated reading does not ordinarily have enough teacher monitoring. We have observed children pretending to read rather than actually reading the text. Repeated reading needs to be monitored. The procedure detailed in the preceding list provides that monitoring when the child's errors are reviewed. This review can help children to recognize high-frequency words.

Another approach to support children in learning high-frequency words in context is echo reading. In echo reading, the teacher reads a section of the text aloud. (This section could be a sentence, paragraph, or longer.) Students "echo" the section back, pointing to each word as they say it. This is a useful introduction to a difficult text. It is a relatively simple approach, but one that does help students read more challenging material.

According to research, children's word identification does improve from watching closed-captioned television (e.g., Koskinen, Wilson, & Jensema, 1985; Newman & Koskinen, 1992). It is relatively easy to suggest that students in need of practice with high-frequency words watch TV at home with the captions function on.

Teaching the Meanings of High-Frequency Words

In most cases, students should already be familiar with the meanings of high-frequency words, or at least with the primary meanings of these words. However, this cannot be taken for granted, especially in the case of English language learners. Hence, it has been recommended that teachers of English as a Second Language devote special instructional attention to the most frequent 2,000 words in English (Nation, 2001).

We agree that it is essential for English language learners to have mastered the core vocabulary of high-frequency words. However, we would want to stress that any instruction aimed at ensuring mastery of a core vocabulary should be done with great care and caution, because there are a number of potential problems. One potential problem concerns efficiency: You don't want to spend time teaching words that students already know. Even a quick, informal assessment of whether or not students already know particular words can be helpful.

The primary problem in teaching high-frequency words is that the more common a word, the more likely it is to have multiple, vague, and slippery meanings. Even in a very compact dictionary, a common verb like *give* might have 20 or more meanings listed. Beyond these meanings, frequent verbs often take part in verb-particle combinations that change their meaning still further; for example, *give up, give out, give in, give off,* and *give way.*

A related problem is the diminished likelihood of cross-language similarities for high-frequency words. For less common, more specific words, there is often enough a reasonably close equivalent in the child's first language. The word *thief* might be translated into Spanish as *ladrón* without too much distortion of the meaning. However, high-frequency words not only have multiple meanings, but the range of meanings of equivalent words in other languages is likely to be quite different.

Another problem with teaching high-frequency words has to do with the limitations of definitions. As we stress elsewhere in this book, definitions by themselves seldom constitute effective vocabulary instruction. In the case of high-frequency words, the weakness of definitions are often far greater. Multiplicity of meanings is only one of the problems associated with high-frequency words; another is the difficulty of defining a common word without using other words that are less common.

We don't want to rule out the use of definitions, even in the case of high-frequency words. However, it needs to be kept in mind that, in the case of high-frequency words, definitions are less likely to be helpful, and students will have even more need of seeing the words in multiple contexts.

Summary

In this chapter, we reviewed teaching high-frequency words. Commonly called "sight words," these are words that children need to be able to read without thinking too much about their meaning. This chapter discussed three types of high-frequency words. One type is very high-frequency words, the top 100 or so most common words in the English language. Most of these are function words, or words that primarily have a syntactic function. The second type is a core vocabulary of about 2,000 words. This core vocabulary is largely common to any variety of English, spoken or written, formal or informal. Although there are more content words than function words in the top 2,000 words of the language, many of these have vague or multiple meanings. A third category of words could be called "academic vocabulary." These are less frequent than the high-frequency words, but important nonetheless because they occur across a variety of academic contexts, and are much less likely to be familiar to students because they are not frequent in everyday conversation.

Words in the first two categories are important for students to know, but in most cases the meanings of these words will be familiar to students from their oral vocabularies. For most students, then, instruction on such words would focus primarily on ensuring that the students could recognize them quickly and automatically in print. However, it is also important to ensure that English language learners have some familiarity with the primary meanings of high-frequency words.

8

Talking About Words

"I'm glad I'm a sedentary spider."
"What does sedentary mean?" asked Wilbur.
"Means I sit still a good part of the time and don't go wandering all over creation. I know a good thing when I see it, and my web is a good thing. I stay put and wait for what comes. Gives me a chance to think."
"Well, I'm sort of sedentary myself, I guess," said the pig. "I have to hang around here whether I want to or not."

(E. B. White, 1952, *Charlotte's Web*, pp. 60–61)

In the second part of this book, we have been talking about various ways of teaching words. Up to now, we have discussed relatively formal procedures for teaching words that need to be known well—high-frequency words, high-utility academic vocabulary, and key content area concepts. These formal procedures are generally rather intensive, and expensive in terms of time, and hence can only cover a relatively small number of words. We now want to expand our scope, moving so to speak one step downward on the vocabulary pyramid. More intensive, formal vocabulary instruction can cover a few words, but there is also the need for less intensive instruction to cover a greater number of words. In this chapter, we discuss the kind of informal talk about words that should permeate a classroom that promotes vocabulary growth.

Talking Versus Teaching About Words

In chapters 5 and 6, we discussed criteria for choosing which words to teach. To warrant intensive (Level III) instruction, words should be either *important* to the story or passage to be read or *useful* for children to learn because they appear in many different contexts. The time available to teach words in a full-blown manner is limited, and teachers need to husband their time so that it is used wisely. But what about the other words? There are many words that are important but not that important, or that are useful but not *that* useful. In other words, what do we do about the words that are not important enough to warrant a significant devotion of time?

Often, these are the words that are defined well enough by their context so that a student reading the story or text will be able to figure the word out independently. However, as we discuss in chapter 12, context is not always informative, and the word may contribute enough to the meaning of the sentence to make it worth knowing, even if it isn't a word you would necessarily want to bring into students' speaking or writing vocabularies. For such words, perhaps a quick definition or a simple explanation will suffice. In this chapter, we address these kinds of words.

Consider the following:

> Factories for *trimming,* boiling, and binding cork in bundles surround the white washed villages…. Local *entrepreneurs* hand out their business cards with their names printed on slivers of cork. Cork, cork, and more cork has brought a measure of *prosperity* to what has otherwise been a dirt-poor region of south-central Portugal. (Tagliabue, 2003, p. B1; emphasis added)

Consider the three italicized words. The first two, *trimming* and *entrepreneurs,* are interesting words, but not essential to the story; nor would a discussion about cork trimming be particularly useful in general. These words do not have to be specially taught. However, a quick mention of the process of making corks (one sentence or two at most) and a quick mention that an entrepreneur is a type of businessperson would be useful. Such a explanation night not be sufficient for the students to know the word, but it might propel them through the article. The next time a student runs into these two words, some foundation will have been established, making it easier for the student to learn. This would allow the teacher to devote time to more important and useful words, such as *prosperity,* which is not only important for the article but also useful in many contexts.

The Story Reading Context

Although talk about words should be found throughout the day, we begin with a discussion of one particular context: teachers reading stories to children. We chose this context because the insights that we can gather from such a setting can be easily generalized to most settings in which teachers and children are interacting around texts. This setting is also the type about which the most research has been done.

Introducing a Book

The purpose of a book introduction is to set the child up to read the book. This may seem straightforward, but it is not. A good book introduction provides children with the background information and vocabulary needed to understand the text. Such an introduction should be focused on the information needed to understand the text, with a minimum of extraneous material. This seems easy to say, but we have observed far too many teachers who use an introduction to do "bird-walking," or talking about information that is tangential at best to the narrative or expository text that they are about to read. Taylor (personnel communication, September, 2002) found that many of the teachers she observed did this kind of "bird-walking," and that these teachers tended to be the less effective teachers in her study.

We first observed "bird-walking" when teaching graduate students. At that time, Stahl used a passage from a social studies text dealing with the Yanamomo, an indigenous people in South America. Although the passage is clearly focused on their warlike nature, there is a mention of the chief having a "second wife." A sizable proportion of my students included polygamy as one of their key concepts, even though it had little to do with the passage. Stahl, Jacobson, Davis, and Davis (1989) compared the recalls of students who were introduced to the passage by talking about polygamy to those who were introduced to the passage by discussing the Yanamomo people's warlike nature. The students who had a more relevant introduction recalled more about the passage than did those who learned about polygamy. In addition, the students who learned about polygamy tended to focus on aspects of the passage dealing with home and family; even though they were of lesser importance overall.

In this study, we found that a poor introduction can impair children's comprehension by focusing their attention on aspects of the narrative relating to the introduction, which may not be related to the thrust of the passage. Book introductions work that way. They tell students what to look for in the passage they are about to read. Good introductions focus children on what is important. Poor introductions send them in another direction.

There are a number of approaches to book introductions. Beck and McKeown (2001; see also McKeown & Beck, 2003), in their work with "Text Talk," favored a minimal approach in which the teacher discusses briefly a key concept in the story and moves toward reading. There is a virtue to brevity. However, we also can see that a somewhat more elaborate introduction, one that is highly focused, can help prepare children for reading as well. Such an introduction might be most useful when the children come to the story with less background knowledge and less knowledge of the vocabulary words.

Picture Walk

K. Stahl (2003) found that a picture walk approach was useful for introducing vocabulary to struggling readers. At present, we see the picture walk as most useful for younger readers. With older readers reading the wonderful picture books available for those ages, we would like those students to focus more on the words than on the pictures.

A picture walk is a guided reading book introduction based on the work of Marie Clay and her descriptions of effective book introductions for novice readers (Clay, 1991, 1993). Fountas and Pinnell (1996) provided more explicit procedures and examples of how to structure an effective new book introduction. These conversations typically occur as the teacher and students preview each page or a few pages of the new book before reading. The pictures are used as a catalyst for discussion of what the book is likely to be about. Unlike the DRTA and the KWL, the picture walk does not have a specific set of procedures. It is used flexibly and in response to the students' needs and the challenges of a particular text to promote fluency and comprehension. Teachers follow a few guidelines to ensure that students have a successful, independent first reading of the text (Clay, 1991; Fountas & Pinnell, 1996):

- The teacher conducts a new book introduction as a conversational, social interaction around the text.
- The conversation prompts student engagement in activating background knowledge and experiences that relate to the text.
- The teacher provides an overview of the plot, theme, or important ideas.
- The teacher directs the children's attention to text structure and language structure.
- For books with predictable patterns or unusual language use, teachers use the book's language structure (e.g., verb tense, predictable patterns) and vocabulary in the conversation about the book.

How extensive the introduction is depends on the expected challenges caused by content or text readability. However, the children are always left with opportunities for problem solving at the levels of both word attack and meaning construction during their first independent reading.

Consider the following transcript, taken from a lesson with struggling second-grade readers who were reading a book about the moon:

K: Let's take a look on pages 8 and 9 now. [Students continue talking.] Let's take a look on pages 8 and 9 now. This is a picture taken with a camera. Can you make any predictions about what this is going to be about on this page? What might they be telling you in this kind of very stark picture? S3?

S3: About them on the moon and footprints all over.

K: Maybe seeing some footprints. What else do you think it's about?

S4: I think they are telling you what the moon is really like.

K: What is the moon really like? What is the land on the moon like because that's all you can see is land and sky. So they might be telling you what the moon is really like. What do you think the moon is really like from the other books you've read? What kind of information ... if you were writing this book and were going to put, if you were going to put the words on this page what would you say?

S3: Oh, I know.

K: S3, what would you say if you were writing the words on this page?

S3: I would say, I think this is when the sun hits the moon and it's really hot.

K: Okay. Because the surface itself looks bright, doesn't it? This may be the part that the sun is hitting. What else if you were describing the moon and the land on the moon and what it's like on the moon, what would you say, S2?

S2: The moon has these little footprints on it. If you look on the second page ... [flipping forward to page 11]

K: But we are writing about this page. Remember your job is, if you were writing the words to go with this page ...

S2: This moon has footprints and sand on it.

K: Okay, so it is sandy and dusty. What would you say, S4, if you were going to write the words describing the moon?

S4: I would tell more like what is on it.

K: Tell me what you would say.

S4: I would say there are rocks, and mountains, and [unintelligible], and craters.

K: Good. What would you say, S1?

S1:   I don't know.

In this transcript, the teacher began by asking children to look at the pictures and anticipate which words would be used on the page. The emphasis was on the concepts in the text, as well as using a written language register. The teacher sometimes subtly changed what the children said to fit the language. An example was when S2 said that the moon has footprints and sand on it, and the teacher changed it to "sandy and dusty," mirroring the language in the text. A more explicit example of word teaching within the context of conversation about the pictures can be found in the following transcript, with the same group of students discussing the same book:

K: Go to page 14. On this page there's an important word that you need to know that will be described for you. (Students can be heard having private discussions in the background.) It describes how the moon travels around ... but you need to be on page 14 with me. There is a word that describes how the moon travels around the Earth on this page. The word is *orbit*. Find the word *orbit* on this page. Good. What are the two little chunks in that word, S1?

S1:   Bit.

K: And what else?

S1:   Or.

K: *Or-bit*. What does *orbit* mean S2?

S2:   Orbit means ... (other children are heard in the background saying, "I know, I know") these corners in the middle of the moon.

K: I am sorry that you weren't listening. S1, can you describe what *orbit* means?

S1:   *Orbit* means like when the light shines, I mean the Earth goes around.

K: Yes, the Earth goes around the sun, but the moon also goes around the what?

Ss: Earth.

S4:   The moon goes around the Earth. Can I tell you something?

K: Sure.

S4:   *Orbit* means like something going around something real big.

K: Exactly.

The students decoded the word, but also discussed the word's meaning. S1 had a misconception about the word—that *orbit* means that light shines on the moon—but quickly corrected it. This kind of interactive conversation is useful for helping children fix misconceptions about word meanings.

A successful picture walk, or any other book introduction, should be interactive in order to allow children to say what they understand and misunderstand about the topic of the story or text. By keeping it at a discussional level, the teacher can respond to children's misunderstandings so that those misunderstandings do not interfere with the children's reading.

Teacher talk should not wholly dominate; children need to be able to contribute. In reality, the teacher is the dominant actor in most classroom interactions, but many teachers overcontrol. It is important to allow for student contributions. This often involves permitting a certain amount of "wait time," or time to permit students to formulate their own responses. It might be useful for teachers to count "one Mississippi" after a question or comment, to allow children to make contributions.

Vocabulary can be introduced informally during these introductions. The talk about words can either reinforce the more formal introductions that we discussed later in chapters 5 and 6, or can be just a mention of a word and/or its definition. The informal discussions can be a valuable place to introduce words that do not need a full-blown explanation, but for which a brief explanation would suffice.

The principles involved in a successful picture walk can be applied other types of introductions. We present these as self-guiding, for teachers to ask themselves as they go through their book introductions:

- Is my introduction focused on the key concepts of the story or text?
- Will the introduction lead the child to focus on unimportant parts of the story or text?
- Is the introduction interactive? Do children participate fully, or is the introduction dominated by teacher talk?
- Did the students bring up misconceptions? Were these misconceptions treated as an opportunity to learn?
- Did you interweave the important concepts or new words into the discussion?

Although pictures can be used effectively to introduce a book, Beck and McKeown (2001, 2003) also offered some important suggestions for avoiding having the pictures become a distraction from, or a replacement for, actually attending to the text. They recommended that, during reading, pictures not be shown to children until after the text corresponding to the picture has been read.

During Reading

Talk Around Words

The type of talk around words is important. The example of "motherese" that follows is a good example of what effective teachers (both teachers and parents) do to expand their children's vocabulary:

> A parent asked a 23-month-old, "What happened to Marlon?" When the child did not answer, the parent gave a hint: "What does he have on his arm?" The child said, "Cast." The parent confirmed, "A cast," and returned to "What happened to his arm?" The child said, "Cast." The parent then supplied the answer she would expect (and the child would be able to give) at 36 months of age: "Yes, the cast is on because he broke his arm. He fell and broke his arm." (Hart & Risley, 1999, p. 103)

In this case, the parent started with what her child knew and expanded it through a series of questions. This type of expansion through questioning seems effective in helping older children learn new words encountered in context. DeTemple and Snow (2003) suggested that nonimmediate and cognitively challenging talk is effective in helping children develop new word meanings.

Nonimmediate talk is talk that goes beyond what is in front of the child that enables the child to make connections to past experiences, to analyze information or draw inferences, or to discuss the meaning of words. Mothers' use of this type of talk was found to relate to their children's later performance on vocabulary measures (De Temple, 1994). De Temple and Snow (2003) used storybook reading for examples of this type of talk, but it can be done when talking about things that one encounters on a walk or on a trip. It can be a "What's that?" kind of discussion, as in the following exchange. In this segment, a mother and her 3-year-old son were reading *The Very Hungry Caterpillar* together:

Mother:	What's that? (pointing to the sun)
Child:	(shrugs)
Mother:	What's that? What make you hot?
Child:	I don't know. Huh?
Mother:	What make you hot?

Child:　　(shrugs)
Mother:　The sun don't make you hot?
Child:　　Mmhm. (nods)
Mother:　It make you real hot? (nodding)
Child:　　Mmhm. (nods). (De Temple & Snow, 2003, pp. 21–22)

In this segment, the mother tries (unsuccessfully) to get her son to use the word *sun*. When he was unable to say it, she gave a defining characteristic (very hot) and then provided the word for him.

In cognitively challenging talk, the adult tries to get the child to extend his or her thinking about the topic. Such talk not only expands vocabulary knowledge, in terms of the numbers of words known, but also expands the depth of that knowledge. The following excerpt involves Domingo, age 5.11 years:

Mother:　That's a tusk see? It's white. Know what Domingo?
Child:　　Hmm?
Mother:　Hunters kill these elephants for that.
Child:　　Why?
Mother:　Because they want it for, um, well, they use it for different things I think um some museums buy them and I don't know about museums but I know that they kill the for this white um.
Child:　　There's no tusk on these elephants though.
Mother:　See? That one's bigger so some of them die because of that. That is sad.
Child:　　I wish there was not such things as hunters and guns.
Mother:　I know it me too. Oh there's a herd. That's a lot of them. See how they walk?
Child:　　Ma here's ones that's dead.
Mother:　I don't think he's dead! Well we'll find out. "They use their tusks to dig." Oh see he's digging a hole! "They use their tusks to dig for salt...."
Child:　　Hmm.
Mother:　Let's look and see if there's another page you might like. It's ivory! The tusks are made of ivory. And they can make things with these tusks and that's why some animals, they die, hunters kill them.
Child:　　No wonder why they have hunters.
Mother:　Yeah that's sad.

Child: I'm never gonna be a hunter when I grow up. (De Temple & Snow, 2003, pp. 23–24)

The talk in this excerpt shows how a mother can take an experience and use it as a springboard to new concepts. In this case, the mother begins by pointing out the tusk, then expands the discussion to the uses of the tusk by the elephant and by the hunters, and finally ends on an emotional reaction to hunting. The richness of the language expands the child's knowledge of the word *tusk*, by connecting it to *hunting, digging,* and so on.

These needs will not be met, however, if the words required for expression are not available. Hart and Risley (1995) found that children in poverty were not exposed to the same quantity of language as were children from higher socioeconomic-status (SES) homes. Regardless of children's cognitive capacity and need to express those cognitive states, their vocabulary will not grow unless the words are available in social and interactive settings. Furthermore, the lower-SES children studied by Hart and Risley were given more imperatives and fewer opportunities for elaboration. In this study, parents in the advantaged homes gave children more "motherese" or repetitions with expansions typical of middle-class households. In this and other examples, parents elaborate on children's knowledge and expand it. This expansion moves from the child's knowledge and increases it.

Cognitively Challenging Talk in the Classroom

We present these examples from parent–child interactions to illustrate the power of cognitively challenging talk. Effective teachers imbue their classrooms with this sort of talk. Taylor et al. (2000), in their study of teachers who "beat the odds" in working with children from low-SES schools, discerned that the most effective teachers used more open-ended questions and higher-level questions than did teachers who were less successful. Open-ended questions and higher-level questions engage children more thoroughly in the reading. This engagement compels children to process the information in the text—both words in the text and the meaning of the text—more thoroughly, leading to both better comprehension and increased word learning. Taylor et al.'s observation checklist of teacher interaction styles included:

- Coaching/scaffolding.
- Modeling/demonstrating.
- Recitation.

- Telling.
- Discussion.

In this study, the most accomplished teachers did more coaching or scaffolding and less telling than did the least accomplished teachers. In coaching, the teacher strives for what used to be called "leading from behind" (Wells, 1986). Person and Graesser (1999), in observing successful tutors, broke down coaching into the following behaviors:

- Hinting.
- Prompting (providing more information to help the student come up with the answer).
- Pumping (asking the student for information that he or she has that is relevant to the word's meaning).
- Splicing (taking two answers and putting them together to make a fuller answer).
- Offering polite, explicit negative feedback to address errors.
- Summarizing (recapping the conversation to summarize the main points).

These conversational moves can be used in teaching larger groups as well. What is important is that the teacher uses conversation, via successive approximations, to help students come up with the answers by themselves.

Coaching needs to be embedded in a discussion about the text. For the purposes of this book, such a discussion might stress words. When the teacher coaches, he or she solicits the child's understanding of the word and pushes that understanding further, through sensitive questions.

Text Talk

McKeown and Beck (2003) used an approach to discussing storybooks with young children in which cognitively challenging talk is employed to support children's learning. Text Talk is an approach to read-alouds that is designed to promote comprehension and language development. It involves the *selection* of texts that exhibit an event structure and enough complexity to prompt discussion and higher-level thinking. The strategic use of open-ended *questioning* encourages children to explain, elaborate, and formulate their own questions surrounding the text.

The purpose of Text-Talk questions is to encourage children to talk about the important ideas in a story as they occur (Beck & McKeown, 2001;

McKeown & Beck, 2003). This takes the form of a dialogue around the important information in the text, rather than an evaluation or, worse, an inquisition. Questions are interspersed with story reading, and are open ended to encourage children to use their language to express and connect story ideas. Open-ended questions were found to be effective in Taylor et al.'s (2002) study, as well as in the observations of effective teachers reported in Allington and Johnston (2002). This is in contrast to the kinds of closed questions that are often observed, which ask children to simply retrieve small bits of text language.

The first set of questions and responses, shown in Table 8.1, was collected from classrooms before implementation of Text Talk (McKeown & Beck, 2003). The second set of questions, shown in Table 8.2, was taken from Text Talk lessons. Note that the questions are not only thought provoking, but are also more engaging. This engagement results in more learning, both of the text content and of the words in the text.

In Text Talk, extensive vocabulary work follows each story. The meaning of three or four words is given with examples of how each word is used. Children are encouraged to generate their own sentences for each word immediately after the reading, and an incentive chart records each child's use of the words over time. The result is that there is a richer discussion about the text.

An example of a dialogue in Text Talk about the word, *absurd,* follows:

absurd from the story *Burnt Toast on Davenport Street* (Egan, 1997).

absurd: In the story, when the fly told Arthur he could have three wishes if he didn't kill him, Arthur said he thought that was absurd. That means Arthur thought it was silly to believe a fly could grant wishes. When something is absurd—it is ridiculous and hard to believe.

TABLE 8.1
Textbook Baseline Questions and Responses

Questions	*Responses*
Is he a new toy or an old toy?	Old
Who is Joe? He's the what?	The baby
Think back in the story. They went to pick up his ...	Big sister
Do you think Nelle is going to be happy or mad?	Mad
Somebody else had already what?	Found him
Was she being nice to her little brother?	Yeah

From McKeown and Beck (2003, p. 164). Reprinted with permission.

TABLE 8.2
Text Talk Questions and Responses After Intervention

Questions	Responses
How did the other kids like Stephanie's ponytail?	First they liked it when she didn't have it to her ear, and then they kept calling her ugly, and now they're gonna be jealous, real jealous.
What's going on?	George got into trouble anyway.
What's the problem with having a fawn as a pet?	Cause he'll eat everything. He's like a goat.
Charlie looked at the girls and purred. What's that tell us?	The girls are happy that they might have found him.
Why would termites be a worry for the owl?	Because the termites might eat the owl's home cause it's made out of wood.
What happened?	The people saw the signmaker and chased him into the woods and they thought that the signmaker did it, but the boy did.

From McKeown and Beck (2003, p. 164). Reprinted with permission.

If I told you that your teacher was going to stand on his/her head to teach you—that would be absurd. If someone told you that dogs could fly—that would be absurd.

I'll say some things, and if you think they are absurd, say: "That's absurd!" If you think they are not absurd, say: "That makes sense."

I have a singing cow for a pet. (absurd)

I saw a tall building that was made of green cheese. (absurd)

Last night I watched a movie on TV. (makes sense)

This morning I saw some birds flying around the sky. (makes sense)

If I said let's fly to the moon this afternoon, that would be absurd. Who can think of an absurd idea? (When a child answers, ask another if they think that was absurd, and if so, to tell the first child: "That's absurd!") (McKeown & Beck, 2003, p. 165)

This discussion extends the meaning of the word as encountered in the story. From a single encounter, it is unlikely that children would gain much information about the word. This Text Talk both gives the child a rough definition for the word and extends the word's use into other contexts. Including both types of information was found to be characteristic of vocabulary instruction that improved children's comprehension (Stahl & Fairbanks, 1986). In addition, the discussion requires children to not only listen, but also to generate new knowledge about the word ("Who can think of an absurd idea?"). Generating new understandings is also important in word learning. Through generation, words become more memorable. In all, this interaction, like the interactions around storybooks described earlier, leads to more vocabulary learning (McKeown & Beck, 2003).

Note that the discussion is not extensive. This may be more than a simple mention, but only a little bit. In contrast to the lessons used by Beck et al. (1982), in which up to 20 minutes were spent on each word, these are brief mentions of the word's meaning with a few examples. This sample is 195 words in length. Our estimate is that it would take between 2 and 3 minutes of class time. Even this might be a bit more than is needed.

Summary

We have given a number of examples of cognitively challenging talk about words. Many teachers do this instinctively; others need to discipline themselves to talk in this way. We find that teachers can learn to modify their talk about texts in a way that pushes children to think more deeply about the text (Beck, McKeown, Sandora, Kucan, & Worthy, 1996) and that this discussion leads to greater word learning than do more didactic approaches.

There are a number of reasons why teachers find it difficult to change their instructional patterns. First is that "they've always done it that way." Not to minimize this concern, it is difficult to change a long-time pattern. We are comfortable with ways of teaching. It is work to change to include more open-ended questions, more coaching, and less telling. However, it can be done, and it is rewarding, both in terms of more interesting classes and higher learning, when this teaching style is employed. Second, teachers are concerned about classroom control. The tight interaction pattern embodied in "telling"—in which the teacher provides some information, questions the students, and evaluates the answers—would seem to not allow students to wander offtask and create disruptions. However, we find that a more interactive class is less disrupted, because the students are more engaged. Third, many teachers do not see their students as capable of the higher-level thought required by this approach. We disagree. If children are challenged, and supported in that challenge through coaching, we find that even children from whom little is expected can rise somewhat to the challenge.

We have shown how cognitively challenging talk about words can be embedded in book introductions, as well as in talk both during and following reading. In this, we see vocabulary development as part of a larger program of using language in the classroom.

III

Independent Word Learning

In Part II of this book, we talked about various ways to teach students the meanings of specific words—"vocabulary instruction" in a narrow sense. However, teaching the meanings of specific words is not enough to ensure that students develop adequate vocabularies. Students need to become independent word learners.

The first requirement for independent word learning is that students have raw material from which to learn. Chapter 9, "Exposure to Rich Language," explains what teachers can do to make sure that their students get as much exposure to rich language as possible—both oral and written.

Chapter 10 is about *word consciousness;* a phrase used to refer to the interest in and awareness of words that support vocabulary growth. Motivation is essential for vocabulary learning, and there are numerous ways to make words interesting to students. However, beyond the desirability of making vocabulary instruction as fun as is feasible, it is important for students to develop an understanding of words and, especially, the power of word choice as a tool for effective communication in written language.

Chapters 11 through 13 talk about word learning strategies—how to help students make more effective use of word parts (chap. 11), context (chap. 12), and dictionaries (chap. 13). Each of these three sources of information about words is important, but each can be problematic, and students need to learn how to use them wisely.

9

Exposure to Rich Language

Out of the mouths of babes and sucklings hast thou ordained strength.

(Psalms, 8:2)

The Importance of Massive Exposure to Rich Language

We have suggested the vocabulary pyramid as a way of thinking about the big picture in vocabulary instruction. One of the main points of the pyramid is that there is an inverse relationship between intensity of instruction and the number of words that can be covered. At the top of the pyramid is the thorough type of instruction we discussed in chapters 5 and 6—instruction aimed at bringing students to a point of ownership; that is, being able to use the words that are taught in class in their own writing and speaking as well as reading. Relatively few words can be covered with this level of intensity. In chapter 8, we talked about the next level of the pyramid—informal talk about words that should permeate the schoolday and cover a much larger number of words. However, even this level does not cover as many words as students need to learn. Besides, for those words that are explained informally during the schoolday, students still need opportunities to gain a deeper understanding of their meanings and how they are used.

The bulk of vocabulary growth is at the lowest level of the pyramid; that is, most words are learned through context. As children repeatedly encounter words in the language they hear or read, the children gradually come to learn the meanings of those words and how they are used. This does not ignore the importance of vocabulary instruction, but it does stress the importance of exposure to words in context. At first, the context is oral, but, as children learn to read, reading becomes a more and more important source of words. The more language with which children interact, the more words they will learn.

Where the Words Are

The maximum vocabulary learning, however, comes from books. Storybook reading is the most powerful source of new vocabulary, including those academic words that are valued in school discourse. Books are literally "where the words are." Hayes and Ahrens (1988) examined the vocabulary used in a variety of sources; some of their results are given in Table 9.1.

The figures in the column labeled "Average Number of Rare Words (per 1,000)" is an index of the richness of vocabulary found in different types of language. The phrase *rare words* may be a little misleading; Hayes and Ahrens used this to describe any word not in the 10,000 most frequent words in the language. The fact that a word is not among the 10,000 most frequent words in the language certainly does not mean that it is not important—for example, the words in Table 9.2 would all be considered rare words under this definition. The most striking thing about Table 9.1 is how ordinary adult conversation compares with written language. Children's books are almost twice as rich in rare words as adult conversation; comic books are about three times as rich, as are adult books. The language of television, however, is generally not much richer than that of normal conversation.

TABLE 9.1
Vocabulary Difficulty of Various Sources of Language

	Average Number of Rare Words (per 1,000)
Newspapers	68.3
Adult books	52.7
Comic books	53.5
Children's books	30.9
Children's TV	20.2
Adult TV	22.7
Mr. Rogers	2.0
Cartoon shows	30.8
Conversation between two college-educated adults	17.3

Source: Hayes and Ahrens (1988, p. 401).

TABLE 9.2
Some "Rare" Words

banjo	fantasy	numb	reluctant
blizzard	gem	oasis	scold
boast	glossary	optional	serpent
cautious	interrupt	pantry	soar
conserve	invade	participate	stimulate
debris	logic	peer	taut
edible	luster	porous	trench
eruption	motto	pry	trigger
exceed	nasal	quaint	
exert	nudge	refrain	

Source: Carroll, Davies, & Richman (1971).

These findings suggest that children's participating in conversations with adults, although certainly quite valuable, is not necessarily sufficient to prepare them for the language they will encounter when they read. Books use more and different words. Even a book like *Curious George Gets a Job* (Rey, 1947), intended for first graders to read and younger children to listen to, contains some relatively rare words. These include not only *curious* but also *cozy, dizzy, wound, scold,* and *attention,* just from the first 20 pages. Not surprisingly, Cunningham and Stanovich (1991) and Stanovich (2000) found that exposure to books, as measured by author recognition or title recognition measures, can account for a great deal of the variation in vocabulary knowledge among children and adults.

Differences in access to books may play an important role in the differences in vocabulary size associated with family income. Neuman and Celano (2001) examined the availability of print resources in low-income and middle-income communities. They noted striking differences in the availability of print resources between these communities. For example, in one middle-class community, there were 13 venues selling children's books, with 358 titles available. In a contrasting low-income community, there were 4 venues with only 55 titles available. Thus, the gap between well off and struggling that begins with differences in the richness of language continues through differences in print resources available.

Wide Reading

For older students and more able readers, wide reading is the largest single source of vocabulary growth. Thus, encouraging wide reading is one important component of a comprehensive approach for vocabulary (Graves, 2000). Many educational researchers, ourselves included, believe that wide reading is essential for increasing students' vocabulary size. As we noted earlier in this text, 25 minutes of reading a day could lead to a gain of over 2,000 words per year. Reading has also been demonstrated to lead to a variety of cognitive benefits in addition to vocabulary growth (Cunningham & Stanovich, 1998).

However, it must also be recognized that providing more reading time does not automatically result in gains in vocabulary growth (National Reading Panel, 2000). For younger and less able readers, exposure to rich oral language and to talk about word meanings is essential (Biemiller, 1999). Learning words from context is also sometimes problematic for second-language readers, although these learners have been found to benefit from programs that stress large amounts of reading (Elley, 1991).

The National Reading Panel (NRP) discerned that sustained silent reading did not consistently result in measurable gains in vocabulary knowledge. However, there is a wealth of other evidence that vocabulary can be learned incidentally through reading—evidence reviewed by the National Reading Panel (2000), and also in a meta-analysis of word learning while reading conducted by Swanborn and de Glopper (1999). Therefore, care must be taken to ensure that the time students spend reading is used most effectively.

Effective use of reading to promote vocabulary growth requires increasing both students' volume of reading and their level of comprehension, by (a) matching students with appropriate texts—student-selected books do not always contain language rich enough to promote vocabulary growth (Carver, 1994; Carver & Leibert, 1995); (b) providing adequate time for reading; (c) employing teaching strategies that help children comprehend text better and cope with unfamiliar words; and (d) fostering a classroom environment that encourages social interactions related to reading (Guthrie, Schafer, Wang, & Afflerbach, 1995).

What kinds of reading are necessary to produce vocabulary growth? Some have argued that almost any reading will ultimately have powerful benefits for children (Krashen, 1993). Others have maintained that if students consistently select texts below their current reading level, such free reading will not result in measurable vocabulary growth (Carver, 1994; Carver & Leibert, 1995). Likewise, reading a text full of unfamiliar words is not likely to produce large gains in word knowledge (Shefelbine, 1990).

Thus, children should read books at an appropriate level of difficulty. How does a teacher decide what is an appropriate level? A few tried and true methods are the five-finger approach and the three-word approach. The five-finger approach simply involves having a child read aloud a 100-word section from a book that the child chooses. If the child makes more than five errors (counted by putting down a finger for each error) in the 100 words, then the book may be too difficult for the child. Sometimes children can learn from difficult books if their interest is high, but most of the time you should make sure that students' free reading is well within their independent reading level.

The failure to find positive effects from sustained silent reading (SSR) may be due to two factors. First, the NRP looked only at experimental evidence. In this area, the best studies are not experimental but instead are correlational (NRP, 2000). Studies such as those by Anderson, Wilson, and Fielding (1988) and Taylor et al. (1990), among many others, have found that the amount of reading that children do correlates strongly with their gains in reading ability. Correlations between variables do not imply that one variable causes the other; this is why correlational studies were not used by the National Reading Panel. This is an area, however, that is difficult to study experimentally. If one group is given a period of time for sustained silent reading and the other is not, one is not sure whether and how much the children in the SSR program are actually reading. Many SSR advocates do not allow teachers to check up on children or recommend that teachers read their own books during this time to be a model of a reader. Without teacher monitoring, it is unclear whether children were reading or not.

A series of studies by Stanovich and Cunningham (see Cunningham & Stanovich, 1998, for review) noted that the amount of reading that adults and children did contributed significantly to their vocabulary knowledge. For example, in one study, the researchers gave adults a title recognition test containing titles of real books and made-up foils. They found that the greater the number of real books that their subject identified (which should reflect the amount of reading that they had done), the greater was their vocabulary knowledge. This was found with college students, adults in an airport terminal, and children.

One set of experimental studies that do find positive effects for practice in reading are the "book flood" studies. Elley and his colleagues (2000; Elley & Mangubhai, 1983), in a series of studies, discerned that increasing the amount of reading material available to children and teaching teachers how to encourage children to use that material can dramatically improve children's reading achievement. In book floods, children were given large amounts of text and the opportunity to read them. This work was done with second-language learners, generally in the South Pacific, so it was outside of the purview of the NRP.

One failing of SSR is that teachers may not monitor their children's reading. We have observed SSR is a number of classrooms and noted that children are often not reading during that time or are reading material that is inappropriate for their level. One pair of children observed in a study (Stahl, Suttles, & Pagnucco, 1996) were taking turns talking and turning pages in a shared book, looking as if they were sharing reading. However, when one of us came close enough to listen to what the children were saying, they were talking about what they were going to do that weekend. In other observations, we have seen children read books that were very easy for them or very difficult, neither of which would aid in their reading development.

Although the research reviewed by the National Reading Panel (2000) does not support the use of sustained silent reading, common sense suggests that children should have some time during the day to read books of their own choosing, if only for motivational purposes (see Turner, 1995). However, unlike in traditional SSR, we suggest that teachers actively monitor children's reading by both going around the room to make sure that the children are on task and by asking questions about what the children are reading. We also recommend that teachers encourage children to read books of an appropriate level. Effective teachers can cajole children to read books that will engage them as well as develop their reading abilities. In short, reading practice may be useful for children, but it needs to be actively monitored and guided by the teacher and should involve reading books of an appropriate level of difficulty.

There are a number of things a teacher can do to help students get the most out of reading. One is to encourage students to read at a variety of levels: some material simply for enjoyment (which should benefit their fluency if nothing else), and some material that is more challenging. Another is to help students develop reading strategies that will allow them to read more challenging texts with lower levels of frustration. Guthrie et al. (1995) discovered that students whose teachers taught comprehension strategies tended to do more reading. Some useful resources on reading comprehension strategies are:

Block, C., Gambrell, L., & Pressley, M. (2002). *Improving comprehension instruction: Rethinking research, theory, and classroom practice*. San Francisco: Jossey-Bass.

Block, C. C., & Presley, M. (2002). *Comprehension instruction*. New York: Guilford.

Harvey, S., & Goudvis, A. (2000). *Strategies that work: Teaching comprehension to enhance understanding*. Ontario, Canada: Pembroke.

Hoyt, L. (1998). *Revisit, reflect, retell: Strategies for improving reading comprehension*. Portsmouth, NH: Heinemann.

Pressley, M., & Woloshyn, V. (1995). *Cognitive strategy instruction that really improves children's academic performance*. Cambridge, MA: Brookline Press.

Tierney, R. J., & Redence, J. (1999). *Reading strategies and practices*. Boston: Allyn & Bacon.

And the following, all published by Lawrence Erlbaum Associates, Mahwah, NJ:

Anders & Guzzetti. (2005). *Literacy development in the content areas* (2nd ed.).
Au. (2005). *Multicultural issues and literacy development*.
Valencia. (2005). *Classroom based literacy assessment* (2nd ed.).
Worl. (2003). *Interpreting literature with children*.

As is true for any method of promoting vocabulary growth, wide reading has some limitations. One is the problem facing students who are not yet able to read very much independently; we address that shortly. Another limitation is that wide reading may be effective for producing general vocabulary growth, but it is not an effective method if you have certain words in mind that the students need to master. Finally, it must be recognized that the effects of wide reading are cumulative, and will only emerge over time.

The Importance of Oral Language

For students who are becoming, or have become, fluent readers, we believe that wide reading is the single most powerful tool for developing large reading vocabularies. However, this does not mean that wide reading is the only thing, or the first thing, that can be done to help children learn words. Vocabulary growth starts at birth, and there is much that can be done during the years before children are capable of substantial reading on their own. Oral language plays a crucial role in vocabulary development.

In our discussion of Table 9.1, we made the point that normal conversation between adults—even college-educated adults—was not especially rich in vocabulary, and therefore was not a sufficient basis for helping students develop large reading vocabularies. However, this does not mean that oral language cannot contribute to vocabulary development. First of all, even normal conversation constitutes rich and challenging input for young children. Second, and more important, not all types of oral language are created equal. Everyday conversation may not be very rich in vocabulary, but everyday conversation is not the only kind of language to which children can be exposed. In an article in the *Reading Teacher* entitled "My Mother Never Read to Me" (Cline & Necochea, 2003), one of the authors attributed her later academic success to her home environment. Although her parents did not read to her, and in fact did not even speak English, she did grow up in an environment rich in storytelling. The language of storytelling is much more like the language of books than is the language of conversation.

Storytelling is, of course, only one of many ways to provide children with an experience of rich oral language. In the second half of this chapter, we talk about a variety of ways to make the most effective possible use of oral language as a way of promoting children's vocabulary growth.

Providing Students With Rich Experiences With Oral Language

Reading is important for vocabulary growth, but is not the main avenue of vocabulary growth for young children. In the early stages of reading, there are limitations on the amount and complexity of the material that children can read independently. Therefore, it is essential that oral language be used effectively in the classroom to foster growth in children's knowledge of words and concepts (Biemiller, 1999).

In the primary grades, while students are still in the process of acquiring the mechanics of reading, it is especially important that teachers make effective use of oral language to promote vocabulary growth. It is during the primary years that teachers have the opportunity to build the foundation of the vocabulary and concepts that children will need to understand the increasingly difficult texts they will encounter in fourth grade and beyond.

Talking to Children

One simple but powerful way to expand children's vocabularies is to talk to them. It is striking, as Hart and Risley's (1995, 1999) work demonstrated, how wide the variations are in how much adults talk to children. For children to develop rich vocabularies, they need to have many interactions with adults. It is from these interactions that they will develop the words they need to negotiate their world. Huttenlocher et al. (1991) found both the total amount of words and the number of different words mothers spoke to children significantly influenced the child's vocabulary learning.

"Goldilocks" Words.   It is not enough to just throw big words into conversations with children. This does not seem to be effective in improving children's vocabularies. Juel (2002) observed children in various kindergartens. She discerned that the one teacher who used the most rare words in her lessons was among the least effective in aiding children's vocabulary growth. Juel's interpretation was that the children could not understand the rare words because they did not have enough conceptual knowledge to comprehend the words' meanings. Instead, the children disregarded these words.

Beck, McKeown, and Kucan (2002) suggested teaching what they called "Tier Two" words. These are words that are in general use in written language, but are not commonly used in everyday conversation. In chapter 5, we equated Tier Two words with the words in the Academic Word List. Tier One words would be common words, such as common sight words, simple nouns, and verbs. Tier Three words are words that are rare, limited to a single context, or that represent concepts that young children might not have, such as *cogitate* or *photosynthesis*. Tier Two words could be called "Goldilocks" words—words that are not too difficult, not too easy, but just right.

There is evidence that children learn words in a similar order. Biemiller and Slonin (2001) found that the order of vocabulary acquisition seemed similar among children, with high correlations in word knowledge among children. This appears to be because words grow in complexity, and children cannot learn a more complex word without learning the simpler words. Thus, we should make sure that the words we are teaching are of appropriate complexity. This sounds harder than it is. In natural conversation, mothers and teachers seem quite able to get the right level, if they keep their ears open to how the children are responding to them.

Just talking is important. However, it is equally important to have something to talk about. This means that adults (teachers and parents) need to consciously provide experiences that expand children's horizons. These experiences might include trips around one's neighborhood, to the grocery store (to talk about all those varieties of orange juice), to the park, to the zoo, or to any other place that gives the child new experiences or a chance to expand on older experiences.

If we are to decrease the gaps among children, we should start where the gap begins, in the preschool or at least the primary grades. By addressing the gap early, we might be able to diminish some of the differences among children later on in school, allowing more children to succeed in school.

The way that teachers interact with young children has been shown to have a powerful impact on their vocabulary growth (Biemiller 1999; Dickinson & Smith, 1994; Dickinson & Tabors, 2001). The quality of the interactions between teachers and children, and the nature of the language that is used, are extremely important. In particular, the oral language of the classroom has to prepare students for the language they will encounter in text.

The Language of School

However, many teachers are not fully aware of the profound differences between the conversational register (how we usually talk to each other) and the written register (the language of text). Proficiency in conversational English is not, by itself, an adequate foundation for facing the vocabulary demands of most text (Cummins, 1994). It takes intentional and skillful use of oral language activities to support the level of vocabulary growth necessary for success in school.

Reading aloud to children can have a substantial impact on their vocabulary growth. Children can benefit from listening to stories read aloud, even when these stories are not in the language variety spoken at home (Feitelson, Goldstein, Iraqi, & Share, 1993). For example, Stahl, Richek, and Vandevier (1991) noted that sixth graders learned word meanings from listening at roughly the same rate at which children have been found to learn words from reading (e.g. Nagy et al., 1987). For children who have reading problems, reading to them could be a valuable source of vocabulary growth.

Although reading aloud to children is especially important, it is not the only way for teachers to expose children to the rich vocabulary characteristic of written language. Telling stories, engaging in pretend play, talking about words, and employing other kinds of cognitively challenging talk can make a substantial contribution to children's language development (Dickinson & Smith, 1994; Snow, Burns, & Griffin, 1998).

Like good children's authors, teachers should use words that are over their students' heads, but in a playful way that invites learning and word consciousness. Teachers should also make the discussion of new words a common and natural part of class activities. Talking about words in stories, and explanations in passing of difficult words in a story, can lead to significant increases in learning (Brabham & Lynch-Brown, 2002; Brett, Rothlein, & Hurley, 1996; Dickinson & Smith, 1994; Elley, 1989).

One of us once asked a group of teachers what they could do to use more sophisticated vocabulary in their language without intimidating or confusing their students. The first response was "Make it fun!" We definitely agree. Playing with language is an essential component to language development.

The following are some ways to increase student's exposure to rich oral language:

- Read aloud to children from text that is above their independent reading level, but at the cutting edge of their listening comprehension level.
- Read aloud a variety of text—picture books, chapter books, poetry, and especially nonfiction (because it is so rich in concepts and vocabulary). In 2000, Duke found that children in the primary grades were exposed to nonfiction only 3.6 minutes per day. In part because of Duke's research, there is more nonfiction in primary classrooms, but it is important to make sure there is a balance between genres in children's reading materials.
- Use the language of the written register with children—model the use of complete sentences with explicit referents. For example, say "Please put the marker in the box on the shelf," not "Put this over there." This forces children to use the register of school language—decontextualized language that underlies academic language.

It is important for students not only to hear, but also to use, richer oral language. Interestingly, in *Preventing Reading Difficulties in Young Children* (Snow et al., 1998), the authors reported that children's expressive vocabulary is a stronger predictor of their future success in reading than is their receptive vocabulary. Here are some ways to increase students' use of richer oral language:

- Encourage discussion around text, using tools such as journal responses, story maps, and drawings to elicit more elaborate discussion.
- Encourage children to expand their oral responses by prompting, and waiting for them to elaborate.
- Provide collaborative problem-solving tasks that require negotiation and explanation (e.g., science experiments, board games, and imaginary play).
- Provide students with opportunities to engage in talk that require more elaborate oral language—telling stories, retelling stories, or sharing ideas as a prewriting activity.

- Provide students with opportunities to teach each other or give directions (use tasks that require precise, audience-considerate talk).
- Have children work in groups or dyads.

Summary

In order for vocabulary to grow, children need to be immersed in a bath of language, both written and oral. Although children's literature and nonfiction is "where the words are," because children's books have a higher percentage of rare or academic words than do many other forms of communication to which children are exposed—children need rich diets of oral language as well.

In both interactions around print as well as oral interactions with adults, children need exposure to "nonimmediate" talk, or talk that mirrors the decontextualized language used in books and in schooltalk. This can come from parents, but it should start from the beginning of preschool and continue as the child grows. Discussion around books that extends the ideas in the books also extends children's vocabulary and prepares them for the interactions around academic concepts in school.

Wide reading is important throughout the grades as well. Although the evidence for sustained silent reading is mixed, we recommend that classrooms provide some time for children to read books of their own choosing. We do recommend that teachers monitor children's reading, so that children do not restrict themselves to only easy books or only books that are too difficult for their comfort. We use the term *"Goldilocks" words* to refer to that comfort level at which the book is not too difficult, nor too easy, but instead just right. Children do not benefit from books without words that are unknown to them; nor do they benefit from books with too many difficult words to learn. Getting children to choose the right books requires teacher monitoring, cajoling, or even explicit assistance in choosing. We think it is worthwhile to do so.

Most of the words a person learns come from seeing or hearing them in context. The more language, oral or written, to which a child is exposed, the more unknown words that child will encounter, and the more words that child will learn. Without ignoring the importance of instruction, children learn to read by reading, at school and at home. More practice in reading is a vital piece of a vocabulary program.

10

Promoting Word Consciousness

A single word even may be a spark of inextinguishable thought.
(Percy Bysshe Shelley, 1821, *A Defense of Poetry,* p. 63)

Words, when well chosen, have so great a Force in them, that a Description often gives us more lively Ideas than the Sight of Things themselves.
(Joseph Addison, 1712, "Secondary Pleasures of the Imagination: Consideration Limited to Literature," *The Spectator,* no. 416, p. 292)

Putting children in an environment rich in words is obviously essential. However, it isn't everything. Children will not necessarily notice things in their environment that aren't perceived as being interesting, useful, or valuable. We not only need to surround children with rich language; we need to create a classroom culture in which words are recognized as being interesting and valuable.

Motivation and Vocabulary Growth

Word consciousness is a phrase used to refer to the interest in and awareness of words that should be part of vocabulary instruction. In other words, motivation plays an important role in vocabulary learning, as it does in any other kind of learning.

In the field of motivation, a distinction is made between "intrinsic" and "extrinsic" motivation. Intrinsic motivation is when you do something because you feel that doing it is intrinsically valuable—it's worth doing for its own sake. Extrinsic motivation is when you do something not because you necessarily want to do it, but instead for some reward. Studies of motivation generally show that intrinsic motivation promotes learning more effectively than does extrinsic motivation. Extrinsic motivation can be used to promote learning, but it needs to be employed sparingly and carefully. (Wigfield, 1997). If children are rewarded for doing things they might have done on their own, they may cease to do these things when the rewards are withdrawn.

What does intrinsic motivation look like in the case of vocabulary learning? One part of intrinsic motivation would be recognition that the words being learned are actually used in the real world. This is one of the reasons for the word wizard activity used by Beck and her colleagues (1982). In this activity, children receive points for providing evidence that they had seen, heard, or used one of the instructed words outside of the classroom context. The points are, of course, an example of extrinsic motivation. However, experiencing the words used outside of the classroom contributes to intrinsic motivation, because the children see that the words they are learning are not simply "school" words, but instead are words used in the "real world."

Another part of intrinsic motivation is a sense of the power of words—understanding that word choice is a powerful communicative tool. Although you might need to tell this to students once in a while, it is much more important to show them. Later, we give some more specific ideas about how to show children the power of words. First, however, we want to go over a few more general principles relating to motivating children to learn words.

One part of Steven Krashen's (1987) theory of language acquisition is the "affective filter." The basic idea is that it's hard to learn a language if you don't want to learn it, and it's hard to want to learn the language if you can't identify in some way with the people who speak it. Krashen applied this notion of the affective filter to English language learners, but we find that it also applies well to native English speakers. McDermott (1987) suggested that for many children, especially those from marginalized populations, learning in school means identifying with an alien culture. For such children, school failure can become one way of expressing solidarity with their home culture. The academic words that are rewarded in school at not only outside of their experience, but are to be avoided, because using "high-falluting" words would be a rejection of their own cultural identity.

To help such children acquire the vocabulary of literate English requires sensitivity as well as skill on the part of their teachers. How can we help our students to feel like potential members of the group that uses this language, without making them feel that they must abandon their own background to do so?

There are a number of things that we need to do to help children feel like members of the culture of literate English. One, of course, is to encourage their writing. Another has to do with the attitudes we express or convey toward their own home language. Teaching effective use of literate English does not need to involve a rejection or devaluing of the students' family and culture. Most people in the world learn to successfully negotiate multiple languages, or multiple stylistic levels of the "same" language, so there is no reason to see literate English as being in competition with other languages or dialects. If the student feels that he or she is being forced to make a choice between the language of home and the language of school, the language of school is ultimately very likely to be the loser.

Language has the power to evoke strong emotional reactions. No matter how tolerant we may think we are, there are probably some dialects or accents that would create a very negative impression in our minds. Another way that language can be emotionally charged is the fear of making mistakes. For some children (and adults), making a mistake in spelling or in choice of words can feel humiliating. However, despite the emotionally loaded nature of language, teachers need to create an atmosphere in which experimenting with words and language feels safe. One way they can do this is to model being word learners, and admit freely and often when they do not know the meaning of a word.

Another important aspect of motivation is helping the student to experience a reasonably high rate of success in instructional activities. Many activities that are supposed to be vocabulary "learning" activities are actually review activities, and can only be engaged in successfully if one already has at least partial prior knowledge of the word (or else some other kind of scaffolding or support to make the task manageable). If you already know the word, you are likely to underestimate the difficulty of the task for children who do not already know it.

Vocabulary tasks can easily end up simply increasing existing differences among students. Children who know the words being taught, or at least partially know them, are able to do the activities successfully, and perhaps learn something from them. Other students may not be able to do the activities—at best, they go through the motions.

The practice of giving children a definition and asking them to write a sentence is a good example. If children already know the meaning of the word, or have at least some experience with the word, this task can be an interesting and creative challenge. However, for students who do not already know the word, the task is actually too difficult to accomplish successfully. Most children have trouble figuring out what a word means from the definition, and the definition in general provides little or no useful information about how the word is used. Under these conditions, the task is not meaningful—nor are the sentences that the children produce (Miller & Gildea, 1987).

The task of giving children the definition first and having them make up a sentence is precisely backwards, at least in terms of the way adults use dictionaries. When we use a dictionary, typically, we have encountered a word in text, and want to know what it "means." Thus, we already have a sentence context. With a sentence at hand, knowing the *genus* and *differentiae* is useful. As pointed out in chapter 13, Nist and Olejnik (1995) found that college students learned more word meanings when the dictionary was presented after they read the word in a sentence than before. This makes sense, given how we ordinarily use dictionaries. Therefore, we recommend teaching children to use dictionaries the way we adults use them, after reading, not as word learning tools.

There are a variety of things we can do, then, to make vocabulary learning in the classroom less onerous. However, to return to a point from earlier in the chapter, the main motivation for vocabulary learning must be intrinsic—that is, children must see vocabulary as being something interesting and useful. The term *word consciousness* is used for this interest in, awareness of, and appreciation of words.

Different Aspects of Word Consciousness

Word consciousness is held up as a goal by a number of educational researchers (e.g., Anderson & Nagy, 1992; Beck, McKeown, & Omanson, 1987; Blachowicz & Fisher, 2004; Graves & Watts-Taffe, 2002; Johnson, Johnson, & Schlichting, 2004; Scott & Nagy, 2004). However, it is not a simple goal. Word consciousness is a multifaceted construct, involving the following:

A Feel for How Written Language Works.   Oral language is often highly contextualized, relying on gesture, intonation, and a shared context to communicate meaning. Written language is typically decontextualized, relying heavily on word choice for communicative effect. Students need to develop a feel for how written (decontextualized) language is different from everyday conversation. Hearing text read aloud is one important way to familiarize students with the nature of decontextualized language. However, it is also valuable to draw students' attention to distinctive characteristics of written language, and to help them learn to read like a writer, and write with an audience in mind.

McKeown and Beck (2003) also discussed the care that teachers need to exercise in relating text to children's background knowledge. Conventional wisdom tells us that it is essential for students to relate to the text to their own experience. This is true; but young children have a strong tendency to override the text on the basis of their own experience. They can be very persistent in trying to apply to text various language strategies suitable for conversation, even when these are counterproductive. Thoughtful and consistent questioning is required in order to respond to the text rather than simply to recall personal anecdotes triggered by details in the text.

Sensitivity to Syntax.   To infer the meanings of new words, and to make effective use of information in definitions, students must be able to reflect on word order, and understand how the position of a word in a sentence determines how its meaning relates to the larger context.

Awareness of Word Parts.   Students' awareness of morphology (prefixes, roots, and suffixes) contributes to their vocabulary growth (Anglin, 1993), and to their reading achievement (Carlisle, 1995, 2000; Nagy et al., 2003). In chapter 11, we talk more about how to help children make use of prefixes, roots, and suffixes in their vocabulary learning.

In-Depth Knowledge of Specific Words.   To appreciate the power of words, students need to have in-depth knowledge of some specific words. For example, students cannot reflect on effects of using the word *bewildered* rather than the word *astounded* in a story if they have only superficial knowledge of these two words. Unfortunately, most traditional vocabulary instruction results at best in only a passing acquaintance with words. Hence, another motivation for intensive vocabulary instruction is to bring students to a sufficient level of knowledge such that they be able to appreciate what is conveyed by the choice of specific words.

Activities for Promoting Word Consciousness.   One specific activity for promoting word consciousness is to have students copy into their journals phrases or sentences from their reading that exemplify especially effective use of language—vivid descriptions, striking metaphors, interesting similes, plays on words, or any of the various techniques that authors use to make language more alive. These can be shared with the class or posted on the wall, and used as inspiration or models for experimentation in the students' own writing (Scott & Nagy, 2004). For younger grades, another possibility is to read two versions of the same short story—perhaps a familiar fairy tale (ideally, one with rich language and the other with plainer language)—and to ask students which they liked better, and why.

Promoting awareness of language can be done in a way that helps children become aware of differences between standard English and nonstandard varieties, without stigmatizing the latter. Shirley Brice Heath (1983a, 1983b) described classrooms in which children learned to be "language detectives," studying how people spoke differently in different groups and in different situations. She maintained that this awareness made an important contribution to these students' academic success. It can be especially important to make the differences explicit for those children who are less familiar with standard English.

Differences between home language and school language, or between informal and formal language, can be a source of embarrassment and confusion. However, a good teacher can turn these differences into an opportunity for insight.

Fun With Words

We believe that the most important part of motivation for vocabulary learning is helping children learn to value words. They need to understand that in written language, unlike in conversation, precision in word choice is one of the most powerful tools for effective communication. However, another part of motivation for vocabulary learning is simply to make working with words enjoyable. In addition, creating a classroom atmosphere in which words are fun and playing with words is encouraged can be a powerful antidote to the very natural fear of making mistakes that can so easily inhibit learning. In the following sections, we present some vocabulary activity that have worked for teachers, and proven motivating for students.

Word of the Week

In one second-grade class, Wednesday was word day and each child brought in an unfamiliar or interesting word that he or she had heard or read during the previous week. (This was optimistic. Most of the time, it was 10–15 children out of 22 in the class who brought in words, but this was enough for good discussions.) The WOW (word of the week) sheet included the interesting word, where it had been heard or seen, the meaning, and the word in a sentence. Some children's parents helped them look up the word in a dictionary and provided the definition as well as their own sentence. If the parents did not, the teacher would look the word up or give a definition. Then a few children would volunteer sentences orally. Each word was put on a piece of sentence strip and displayed on a vocabulary word wall. Throughout the week, children would use the words in their journals or conversations or note the words if they happened to come up in the children's reading. A tally was kept—checks were given to each child for words contributed, and also to each word for every time it was reported or used. Each Wednesday, both the children who had received the most checks and the children who had contributed the words with the most checks since the previous Wednesday ate lunch with the teacher in a special section of the cafeteria. Rewarding the contributors in this way resulted in a wider range of student participants receiving the special lunch. It also resulted in the selection of words that were likely to be actually used in the classroom, rather than obscure words that were difficult to apply in classroom conversations.

Word of the week could be used on a schoolwide basis. In this variation, individual children would volunteer words to be used by the entire school. Words would be broadcast during the public announcements. Turns could be given to different grades, who would take turns volunteering words. It would probably be most useful if there was a first- and second-grade word, a third- and fourth-grade word, and a fifth-grade word each week. Teachers would tally how many times the word was used in writing and reading. The person with the most uses of the word would earn a special lunch.

Word Wizard

The word wizard activity was designed by Beck et al. (1982) to sensitize children to a wide range of words and to provide encouragement and incentive for the repeated use of new vocabulary. Individual classroom teachers apply the word wizard ideas in a variety of ways.

In some classrooms, interesting words from class read-alouds are posted on a vocabulary word wall. A class poster contains the children's names along the side and the words along the top. When the children use the vocabulary in their conversations or written products, they receive a check on the poster (see Fig. 10.1). They may also receive a check for noticing the word in a new book, conversation, or elsewhere. The student with the most checks at the end of a designated time period becomes the "word wizard."

confide	flourish
enigma	lament
oblivious	perplex
shudder	beguile
thrive	persist
eradicate	surly

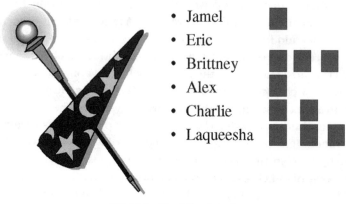

- Jamel
- Eric
- Brittney
- Alex
- Charlie
- Laqueesha

FIG. 10.1.   Word Wizard chart.

Vocabulary Self-Collection Strategy

In the vocabulary self-collection strategy (Haggard, 1986; Ruddell & Shearer, 2002), each child in a class is asked to locate one word that is "good for our class to learn." Children are asked to share (a) where they found the word, (b) the context, and (c) the importance of the word and why they selected it. The teacher nominates a word as well, and also provides a rationale for including it.

Ruddell and Shearer found that the seventh- and eighth-grade low-achieving students tended to choose words that were academic words, appropriate for school learning, such as *rendezvous, terra cotta, carbohydrate, radiation, minute,* and *nocturnal.* Generally, the words came from content areas. Students chose words from a variety of reasons. Following are some of the reasons students used to justify their choices:

- Peer group usage—"Melissa used it in another class and I just loved it."
- Strong emotion—"Justin asked me to please use it as my word this week instead of the one I planned to use.... He thought it was a beautiful word."

- Immediate usefulness—"I had to know for journal writing," "Jamie and I were talking about the Taco Bell commercial and she said the dog was a Chihuahua."
- Adultness/sound/interestingness of word—"It's a cool word with two z's," "I liked what it meant and how it sounds," "Bigger word for *often*."
- General usefulness—This included words that were found in many places or words that students felt they might need in the future: "I might need this in eighth grade." (Ruddell & Shearer, 2002, pp. 358–359).

Once the words were chosen, the class and teacher collectively refined a definition for each word, using the dictionary if necessary. Once the definitions were established, each student wrote the words and their definitions in vocabulary journals. These words were taught during the week using a variety of means, such as discussion, semantic mapping, semantic feature analysis, and other interactive word learning activities. Every 3 weeks, students reviewed past lists.

Ruddell and Shearer (2002) had students write about this activity in their journals. The self-reflection of these low-achieving children gets at what we mean by "becoming sensitive to words." The journal entries suggested that children were becoming metacognitive, strategic word learners who were increasingly aware of new words in their reading and in their environment. Their entries were categorized as follows:

- Noticing—What makes a word good? In this category, students reflected on how they chose the words for VSS. One student wrote, "I pick a word that is hard to spell and has a tricky definition—that's not too hard and not too easy and has more than one meaning."
- Choosing—What do I like about this choice? Students uniformly liked choosing their own words. One student wrote, "I think we should keep on being able to pick our own words because then we will want to study them more efficiently. If we get something handed out or picked by the teacher, we don't want to study something we don't like."
- Using metacognition—What are my strategies? In this category, students articulated the personal strategies they use to learn new words. Typical of these responses are the following: "Whenever I see or hear a new word I ask myself what it could mean.... I can say just about any words, but I have not a clue what they mean. So lately I've been paying my full attention to different or odd words." "I have been learning more and asking more about what the word is. If I find a word I don't know what it means, I ask for help or I look it up in the dictionary."

- Valuing—Why is this important? Students gave highly personal reasons why VSS was important to them. For example, one student wrote, "All that matters is if we can spell or not. All I want is to spell right."
- Learning—How am I improving? Journal entries in this category focused on self-evaluation. "I am learning that the more you look at words and the more you become familiar with them you will get better at spelling them. I think that when you pick a word that you are not very familiar with and you become familiar with it you can tell you are learning."
- Transforming—How am I changing the way in which I see the world? Student journals reflected high levels of word awareness and new-found curiosity about unknown words. "I hear words from all over the place. I mean there are millions of words just sitting out there I don't know." "I heard three of our words this week. Mr. D used the words *mortal* and *intriguing* to describe the Civil War. My pastor used *aerobic* when I was at Confirmation last night." (Ruddell & Shearer, 2002, p. 360).

We like the vocabulary self-collection strategy for several reasons. First, it does seem to promote independent word learning, through increasing word consciousness. Ruddell and Shearer (2002) noted that the students were motivated and learned the words that they had chosen more effectively than they had learned words the teacher had chosen in the past. Second, the learning activities themselves are solid activities, which have been found to promote word learning. The activities chosen to teach the words can be varied from class to class and week to week, depending on the nature of the words and the nature of the learners. Finally, the activity is adaptable to a variety of instructional settings without a significant amount of preparation.

Here are some more things you can do to help children develop an awareness of words:

- Model noticing words in text by thinking and wondering aloud about word meanings; for example, "*Fragile*: I wonder what that word means?"
- Talk about language and language forms: Incorporate linguistic terms *word, sentence, say,* and *mean* into conversations with children.

An important way to increase awareness of language is to talk with students about differences between the conversational and written registers, including generating and posting examples of both in the classroom.

Humor

Why would we include a section on humor in such a serious book on vocabulary? Partially because it is fun, and partially because humor can be a low-key way of teaching and learning words. Puns work off of multiple meanings and sound-alikes of words, often exactly what we are trying to teach. Consider the following:

> A man sits down at the bar and orders a club soda. He hears a soft voice say, "My, you are a handsome man." He looks around and does not see anyone else at the bar. He picks up his drink and hears, "That shirt is a good color on you." This time he thinks that the voice is coming from a bowl of nuts at the end of the bar. He motions the bartender over and says he thinks he is hearing voices. The bartender says, "It's the nuts. They're complimentary."

A joke like this can fix the meaning of the word *complimentary* in a student's mind better and more effectively than can a long, drawn-out lesson. Not only may the joke be more effective than a lesson, but, if the joke is any good, it will be told and retold throughout the schoolday. How many of our lessons are retold on the school bus? Furthermore, the same joke can be a reminder that words often have multiple meanings, again a curriculum objective.

Although analyzing humor can be deadly, it is obvious that the "joke" is based on the two meanings of the word *complimentary*. Could a teacher make the point about multiple-meaning words any better than the story does? Although we confess to having a weakness for puns, humor can make the point in a way that is motivating and reinforcing, because children are likely to repeat to their friends, siblings, and parents the jokes you tell during the day. The puns that follow are based on either polysemous words or sound-alikes (about a thousand versions of this list can be found on the Web):

- A bicycle can't stand alone because it is two-tired.
- What's the definition of a will? It's a dead giveaway.
- Time flies like an arrow. Fruit flies like a banana.
- A backward poet writes inverse.
- In democracy it's your vote that counts; in feudalism it's your count that votes.
- She had a boyfriend with a wooden leg, but broke it off.
- A chicken crossing the road is poultry in motion.
- If you don't pay your exorcist you get repossessed.

- With her marriage she got a new name and a dress.
- Show me a piano falling down a mineshaft and I'll show you A-flat minor.
- When a clock is hungry it goes back four seconds.
- The man who fell into an upholstery machine is fully recovered.
- A grenade thrown into a kitchen in France would result in Linoleum Blownapart.
- You feel stuck with your debt if you can't budge it.
- He often broke into song because he couldn't find the key.
- Every calendar's days are numbered.
- A lot of money is tainted. 'Taint yours and 'taint mine.
- A boiled egg in the morning is hard to beat.
- She had a photographic memory that was never developed.
- A plateau is a high form of flattery.
- The short fortune-teller who escaped from prison was a small medium at large.
- Those who get too big for their britches will be exposed in the end.
- When you've seen one shopping center you've seen a mall.
- Those who jump off a Paris bridge are in Seine.
- When an actress saw her first strands of gray hair, she thought she'd dye.
- Bakers trade bread recipes on a knead to know basis.
- Santa's helpers are subordinate clauses.
- Acupuncture is a jab well done.
- Marathon runners with bad footwear suffer the agony of defeat.

More sound-alikes, like those in the following list, can be used to point out homographs. These can help teachers make the point that English has words spelled alike with different sounds and meanings better than a worksheet or two can (the following list can now be found in at least 5,000 Web sites):

- We polish the Polish furniture.
- He could lead if he would get the lead out.
- A farm can produce produce.
- The dump was so full it had to refuse refuse.
- The soldier decided to desert in the desert.
- The present is a good time to present the present.
- At the Army base, a bass was painted on the head of a bass drum.
- The dove dove into the bushes.
- I did not object to the object.
- The insurance for the invalid was invalid.
- The bandage was wound around the wound.

- There was a row among the oarsmen about how to row.
- They were too close to the door to close it.
- The buck does funny things when the does are present.
- They sent a sewer down to stitch the tear in the sewer line.
- To help with planting, the farmer taught his sow to sow.
- The wind was too strong to wind the sail.
- After a number of Novocaine injections, my jaw got number.
- I shed a tear when I saw the tear in my clothes.
- I had to subject the subject to a series of tests.
- How can I intimate this to my most intimate friend?
- I spent last evening evening out a pile of dirt.

If effective vocabulary instruction involves a conversation about words, then humor should be part of that conversation. The use of puns, double meanings, and the like draws attention to the meanings of words. In the case of *complimentary,* it might be used to teach the two meanings. In the case of many of the puns just listed, clever word play might be used to develop word consciousness or at least consciousness of multiple meanings.

Some of the following medical terms for laymen (from Dr. Peter Gott) can be used as a springboard for discussion of what the real terms mean:

- *alimentary:* What Sherlock Holmes said to Dr. Watson.
- *aorta:* Down-east dialect for "I should."
- *apparent:* A person who changes diapers.
- *atonic:* A drink made with gin.
- *benign:* What we want when we are eight.
- *bite plate:* When a ballplayer slides home.
- *bulla:* A tough guy.
- *carcinoma:* Evil acts done in an automobile.
- *carpal tunnel syndrome:* Fear of driving through tunnels with a passenger.
- *castrate:* The fee for setting a fracture.
- *cauterize:* What a man does before winking at his date.
- *cul-de-sac:* Chilling of the bed after a romantic interlude.
- *cyst:* Half sister.
- *deficiency:* Lack of seafood.
- *denture:* Absolutely certain.
- *diagnosis:* Facial deformity.
- *duodenum:* Two types of jeans.
- *elixir:* What your dog does when your mother gives him a bone.
- *emetic:* A trained ambulance driver.

- *flatulence:* The belief that the earth is not round.
- *fluoroscope:* What you need to find a contact lens you dropped.
- *flu:* A deceased fly.
- *fundi:* What Princess Diana was before she married Prince Charles.
- *gallstone:* A French rock.
- *gout:* Instructions to an unwanted visitor.
- *herpes:* She has no problem with elimination.
- *hippocampus:* Where large African animals go for a degree.
- *inbred:* The basis of a sandwich.
- *incontinent:* A country within a country.
- *infest:* What you do in the stock market.
- *kidney:* In a child, the joint between the hip and the ankle.
- *lactose:* Deformity of the feet.
- *lung:* To thrust forward.
- *mammogram:* A message from your mammy.
- *menopause:* Frequent rest periods for males.
- *migraine:* Not your oats.
- *neurosis:* New red flowers.
- *nitrate:* AT&T's charges after 5 P.M.
- *organ:* A northwestern state.
- *paradox:* Two physicians.
- *Parkinson's disease:* A father who habitually leaves his car in his son's driveway.
- *phlebotomy:* An escape from the buttocks.
- *placenta:* A Spanish coin.
- *pneumonia:* Substitute for old monia.
- *prognosis:* Noses from Prague.
- *psoas:* In order that.
- *pyorrhea:* A disease caused by excessive use of the number 3.14.
- *scurvy:* Winding road.
- *serum:* How to cook steaks on the grill.
- *testes:* What doctors order when they're confused.
- *thrombosis:* A lip disease affecting trombone players.
- *vertigo:* How foreigners ask directions.

A teacher can use these subtly, such as putting a "groaner of the day" on the blackboard, encouraging students to contribute. Or the teacher can use humor more deliberately, incorporating puns and jokes into vocabulary discussion. Wacky definitions such as these can be a stimulus for children's own wacky definitions. These can be a spur to vocabulary learning, not only in your class but throughout the school.

Another form of humor that could be useful in developing word consciousness is "hink pinks." These are rhyming words that are synonyms for a definition. For example, "an *imitation serpent* is a *fake snake*." Other examples are:

> What do you call an *identical smile?* (a twin grin)
> What do you call a *group of boats carrying flour?* (a wheat fleet)
> What do you call a *bird's visitor?* (a nest guest)
> What do you call a *phony mollusk?* (a sham clam)

We can give more, but children have more fun making them up.

Children's Books

Certain children's books are useful in teaching different aspects of language. For example, the *Amelia Bedelia* series by Peggy Parrish highlights the (mis)adventures of a woman working as a maid who interprets everything she is told literally. Thus, when asked to "dress the chicken," she sews a pair of pants for the chicken to wear, and when asked to "put out the lights," she puts them outside. These books are powerful illustrations of idioms, intended for second graders. Fred Gwynne's picture books illustrate homonyms in a humorous way. *The King who Rained* (1970) has one illustration showing a monarch making precipitation. Other books by Gwynne include *A Little Pigeon Toed* (1988), *A Chocolate Moose for Dinner* (1976), and the *Sixteen Hand Horse* (1980). Again, these witty books can illustrate how language works as well as any teacher discussion.

Word Histories

To us, the histories of words are fascinating. To know, for example, that *ramshackle* is one of the few words of Icelandic derivation in the English language or that *jukebox* has an African origin via the Gullah peoples of coastal Georgia keeps us reading books about word origins long after we should have gone to bed. Knowing that *sanguine* (meaning "cheerful") and *sanguinary* (meaning "bloodthirsty") come from the same Latin root is memorable. This is especially so when combined with a discussion of the medieval theory of "humours" in which it was thought that different bodily fluids affected one's dispositions. Thus, a person with too much blood would be *sanguine* or cheerful, but a person with too much bile would be *bilious* or extremely angry, and a person with too much phlegm would be *phlegmatic* or excessively calm. The words *choleric* and *melancholy* have similar origins. These are word histories that one of us remembers from high school, nearly 40 years ago. Table 10.1 presents a word history of the humours.

Stories about words can be intrinsically motivating. How many students would perk up when told that *gymnasium* literally comes from the Greek meaning a "place of nudity"? In ancient Greece, the *gymnasion* was the place where youth wrestled and exercised, naked. Gymnasia were provided by the state and began to be places of not only physical education but also intellectual instruction. Because of the association with the intellectual, in Germany a *Gymnasium* is a grammar school.

Laconic, to take another example, means "brief and blunt." Its origins go back more than 2,600 years to the Greek Wars. When told by an ambassador that "if we come to your city we will raze the walls and kill everyone," the Laconians replied, "If" (Funk, 1992). One could see Gary Cooper, the laconic hero, saying that, just as one could see more contemporary movies stars as well. That level of "cool" would impress at any age.

We would not expect most children to remember many of these stories for too long. (They are not *that* interesting!) However, these stories focus the child on the word's meaning, add a little richness to their mental representation, and integrate the meaning of the word into other aspects of the curriculum. Knowing that *salary* comes from salt (in that salt was a valuable commodity in ancient times and Roman soldiers were paid in salt) not only connects to history but also reinforces the connection between *salt* and *saline* and *salinity*.

English contains quite a few words based on Greek or Roman mythology. Knowing the relevant myth again reinforces both one's knowledge of history as well as one's vocabulary. To whit:

- Vulcan was the Roman god of fire; thus, *vulcanize, volcano.*
- Mars was the Roman god of war; thus, *martial, Martian.*

TABLE 10.1
Medieval Humors

Humor	Effect	Words	Meaning
Blood (sangus)	Warm, passionate, cheerful	Sanguine	Cheerful, confident, optimistic
		Sanguinary	Bloodthirsty
Bile (choler)	Anger	Bilious	Bad-tempered and irritable
		Choleric	Showing anger or irritation
Black bile	Sadness	Melancholy	Sadness
Phlegm	Apathy, sluggishness	Phlegmatic	Sluggish, dull, apathetic

- Hypnos was the Greek god of sleep; thus, *hypnotize, hynotic.*
- Hercules was a Greek hero; thus, *Herculean.*
- Vesta was the Roman goddess of the hearth; thus, *vestal.*
- Terra was the Roman goddess of the earth; thus, *terrestrial, terrarium.*

Over our history, we have borrowed not only from German, French, Greek, and Latin, but also from every culture with which we have had contact. We have borrowed words from African languages (*cola*) to Yiddish (*bagel*) and everything in between. A small list of our borrowings is presented in Table 10.2.

It may not be as important for children to know from where each word came. (Indeed, we were surprised by many of the words on the list that we knew quite well without knowing their origins.) However, it is important that children appreciate the diversity of their language and understand how words come to it. Demystifying language is an important step in helping children make it their own.

Books on word histories continue to be popular. John Ayto's (1990) *Dictionary of word origins* is a scholarly but accessible example. There are also myriad volumes on the origins of idioms and expressions, for example, those by Charles Earle Funk—*A hog on ice and other curious expressions* (1958), *Heavens to Betsy! and other curious sayings* (1955), and *Horsefeathers and other curious words* (1958).

Or how about some eponyms? Eponyms are real or legendary people from whom a theory, idea, or object takes its name. Some of these include:

- *Sandwich:* After Fourth Earl of Sandwich (1718–1792), for whom sandwiches were made so that he could stay at the gambling table without interruptions for meals.
- *Quisling:* After Vikdun Quisling, the Norwegian Prime Minister who invited the Germans to occupy his country at the start of World War II.
- *Chauvinism:* After Nicolas Chauvin, a soldier excessively devoted to Napoleon; meaning blind allegiance. (The word has been changed recently, because *male chauvinist* appears to refer to a person expecting to receive blind allegiance rather than one giving it.)
- *Guillotine:* The inventor, a French physician, J. I. Guillotin, thought his invention was a great humanitarian contribution, because it was a speedier and more efficient method for administering the death penalty than were the drawn-out tortures that had been used previously.

We have an enjoyable book full of such words: *O Thou Improper, Thou Uncommon Noun* by Willard R. Espy (1978). Some of its entries include:

TABLE 10.2
Sources of Some Words That English Has Borrowed

Language	Sample Words
African (many languages)	aardvark, banjo, cola, gumbo, mumbo jumbo, safari, trek, voodoo, zombie
American English	cafeteria, commuter, cowboy, frontier, hijack, jackknife, maverick, mustang, O.K., patrol, pioneer, turkey, Yankee
Arabic	alcohol, algebra, apricot, assassin, magazine, zenith, zero
Australian/ New Zealand (including Aborigine)	boomerang, kangaroo, kiwi
Celtic	walnut
Chinese	tea, typhoon, wok
Czech	pistol, robot
Dutch	caboose, easel, frolic, pickle, waffle, yacht
Eskimo	igloo, kayak, mukluk, parka
Finnish	sauna
French	à la carte, ballet, beef, beige, chauffeur, chic, hors d'oeuvres, restaurant, sabotage
German	dollar, kindergarten, noodle, poodle, pretzel, waltz
Hawaiian	aloha, hula, lei, luau, ukulele
Hebrew	cherub, hallelujah, jubilee, kosher, rabbi, shibboleth
Hindi	bangle, dungaree, juggernaut, jungle, pajamas, shampoo, thug
Hungarian	goulash, paprika
Icelandic	geyser
Irish	bog, leprechaun, shamrock
Italian	carnival, extravaganza, motto, piano, pizza, solo, spaghetti, umbrella, violin
Japanese	hibachi, honcho, judo, kimono, origami
Malaysian	bamboo
Mexican Spanish	adobe, bonanza, bronco, chocolate, coyote, marijuana, ranch, tacos, tamales, tomato
Native American (many languages)	barbecue, canoe, hammock, moccasin, papoose, raccoon, skunk, tepee, tomahawk
Persian	bazaar, divan, khaki, orange, peach, shawl, sherbet, turban
Polish	mazurka, polka
Polynesian	taboo, tattoo
Portuguese	albino, cobra, coconut, molasses, piranha
Russian	czar, sputnik, steppe, tundra, vodka
Scandinavian	cozy, egg, fjord, husband, knife, outlaw, rug, skate, ski, skin, sky, ugly, window
Spanish	alligator, guitar, hurricane, lasso, mosquito, potato, vanilla

154

Language	Sample Words
Turkish	caviar, horde, khan, kiosk, yogurt
Welsh	penguin
Yiddish	bagel, chutzpah, klutz, pastrami, schmuck

Source: Adapted from Tompkins (2003, p. 231). Reprinted with permission.

Boycott—In 1880, Captain Charles Cunningham Boycott was land agent in County Mayo, Ireland, for an absentee owner, the Earl of Erne. Though the harvest had been disastrous, Captain Boycott refused to reduce rents and attempted to evict any tenants who could not pay in full. As a result, he became the object of the earliest known effort to force an alteration of policy by concerted nonintercourse. His servants departed en masse. No one would sell him food. Life became so miserable for him that at last he gave up and returned to England. To boycott is "to combine in abstaining from, or preventing dealings with, as a means of intimidation or coercion." (p. 162)

Derrick—Goodman Derrick, a Tyburn hangman, was as adept with the axe as with the noose; he cut off the head of the Earl of Essex in 1601. But it was his adeptness at gibbeting that won him vernacular immortality. Any hoisting apparatus employing a tackle rigged at the end of a spar is a derrick. (p. 170)

Charlatan—Though villainy is as ancient as man, one particular form of it was named only in the 14th century, when the sharp trading of men from Cerreto, a village about ninety miles north of Rome, made them notorious and their motives suspect. Under the influence of Italian *ciarlare*, "to chatter," a Cerretano became a *ciarlatano*, and, in English, a charlatan, "one who pretends to unheld knowledge or ability." (pp. 99–100)

Fudge—Isaac D'Israeli, father of the 19th-century British prime minister, found in a 17th-century pamphlet a curious origin of the word *fudge*, meaning "Nonsense! Humbug!" He quotes: "There was in our time one Captain Fudge, commander of a merchantman [the Black Eagle], who upon his return from a voyage, how ill fraught soever his ship was, always brought home to his owners a good crop of lies; so much that now, aboard ship, the sailors when they hear a great lie told, cry out, 'You fudge it.' " (pp. 103–104)

How do you use these word histories? Basically, you tell them. Everyone remembers the teacher with the boring stories about interesting facts, about words, about other things. Even though students rolled their eyes when they saw a story coming on (and do so this day), these are the teachers whom students remember. Be one of those teachers.

What these word histories do is let children in on language as a growing, changing entity. From understanding how English borrows from other languages, to comprehending how word parts were used to construct new meanings, to using puns and humor, to relating word histories, vocabulary is interesting. If children understand how they, too, are creating new word meanings, as those meanings had been created in the past, then English becomes a living being, not a dead mummy to be dissected.

Summary

A classroom that is effective in promoting word growth is one in which children are looking out for new words. They can find new words everywhere in such a class. Remember that an effective classroom is also a place that provides rich oral language and exposure to text through wide reading. To take advantage of that rich verbal environment, children need to want to look for words. It is not enough for children simply to encounter words; children need to actively search words out.

We believe that the kind of classroom that encourages children to be active searchers of words is a community of word learners. The activities discussed in this chapter—word of the week, word wizard, vocabulary self-collection activities—should work to create this community, in which all children are working together to use language. It is through the development of a community of learners that children will make the most growth.

Perhaps we devoted too much space to the discussion of the use of humor and word histories in vocabulary learning. In a serious vein, we see humor and word histories as being a part of word consciousness, in that children become aware of the way words work through play with words and talking about the stories of how words came into our language. This is akin to discussions about word parts. However, the reason we devoted so much space to talking about humor and word histories is simply that we enjoy them. Vocabulary learning should be enjoyable. If you enjoy words, your children should. (And if you don't, lighten up.)

11

Teaching Word Learning Strategies: Word Parts

guptopia n. the phony décor in an aquarium designed to fool fish into thinking they're in an underwater paradise.

(Hall, 1989, *When Sniglets Ruled the Earth*, p. 44)

Part of being a strategic reader is knowing how to deal with the unfamiliar vocabulary one encounters while reading. Strategic readers know how to make appropriate and flexible use of the resources available to them. Students can be taught to deal strategically with context, word parts, and definitions (Buikema & Graves, 1993; Nagy, Winsor, Osborn, & O'Flahavan, 1993; White et al., 1989).

We should not expect that students' independent word learning will lead them to complete knowledge of words, but, on their own, students can usually learn enough about a word to get the gist of the text and to keep encounters with unfamiliar words from being a disruption to their reading. Hence, we can think of independent word strategies as being on Level II of the vocabulary pyramid—a way to learn a little more about a fairly large number of words.

There are several things that teachers can do to help students become better word learners, including:

- Modeling what you do when you encounter an unfamiliar word
- Teaching about use of word parts, context clues, and definitions
- Including strategies for dealing with unfamiliar words in your comprehension strategy instruction.

Good strategy instruction also includes explicit explanations (how, when, and why to apply strategies), modeling, guided practice with authentic materials, and gradual transfer of responsibility to students (Duke & Pearson, 2002).

There are three main sources of information available for students in independent word learning: word parts, context, and definitions. As we hope to make clear in this chapter and the two that follow, each of these is a valuable source of information, but each can also be difficult to use and potentially misleading. Word learning strategy instruction should therefore include information about the limitations of context, word parts, and definitions, and should teach students to integrate information from multiple sources (e.g., does the meaning of the word parts make sense in this context?).

Good strategy instruction helps students learn *why, when,* and *how* to use individual strategies. Therefore, instruction that aims at making students better independent word learners will also include higher-level strategies that guide students' use of word parts, context, and dictionaries, causing learners to evaluate: Do I need to know this word to understand the text? Is this word worth looking up in a dictionary? Do I know enough about this word yet to go on?

In this chapter we talk about using word parts as a word-learning strategy. We go on to context and definitions in chapters 12 and 13, respectively. In all three chapters, however, we want you to keep in mind that using these three sources of information about words is a difficult and often intellectually challenging task that sometimes requires careful, reflective thinking, as well as a rich base of knowledge about one's language. Teaching word learning strategies, like the teaching of other comprehension strategies, is therefore a long-term (in fact, multiyear) proposition.

The Usefulness Of Word Parts

If you own a computer and work in any language-related field, eventually someone forwards you an e-mail about the absurdities of the English language that can be traced by to Richard Lederer's (1989) book *Crazy English* (although in the versions circulated through the Internet, the source is seldom acknowledged). In a tour de force of morphological madness, Lederer identified case after case in which the parts of a word don't lead to its meaning—grocers don't groce, hammers don't ham, fingers don't fing; you drive on a parkway, and park in the driveway, and so on. (A legitimate Internet version can be found at http://pw1.netcom.com/~rlederer/arc_ceng.htm.) There are so many such examples that some people have concluded that word parts are simply not worth one's attention.

Is the situation really so bad as to make word parts useless? Nagy and Anderson (1984) analyzed the language of printed school materials, and found that a little over 75% of prefixed, suffixed, and compound words had meanings that could be easily figured out from the meanings of their parts. In the majority of cases, then, word parts can be useful.

However, this finding is not grounds for unqualified optimism about the use of word parts. Being mislead by word parts one time out of four can still be a problem. Besides, irregular meanings are more likely to be found in more frequent words, whereas many of the nice predictable words are very rare in text. Thus, students are more certainly going to encounter misleading word parts more than 25% of the time they see a compound, prefixed, or suffixed word.

A realistic look at word parts tells us once more, as is so often the case with language and reading, that simplistic either-or approaches don't work. Word parts are too valuable a resource to ignore, but they are too inconsistent to use blindly. Students need to learn to use word parts strategically, cautiously, and thoughtfully.

Nation (1990) gave a very specific suggestion about using word parts: If you encounter a new word that can be broken into parts, first use the context to get a general idea of the meaning, and only then look to the word parts to see if they can give you further help. Nation's advice was based on much experience, so it should be given serious consideration, although we know of no research that would demonstrate the superiority of this specific approach to word parts. However, it's clear that, at very least, context needs to be consulted to see whether a meaning constructed on the basis of the parts of a word actually makes any sense for that text.

Teaching Word Parts

Teaching word parts—such as prefixes, suffixes, and roots—should be part of a comprehensive vocabulary teaching program. Although words like *misread, interdependent,* and *substandard* can often be figured out from context, decomposing such words into known parts like *mis-, read, inter-, depend,* and so on, not only makes the words themselves more memorable, but, in combination with sentence context, may be a useful strategy in determining the meaning of unknown words. This strategy may be especially important for content area reading, in which many of the words contain identifiable word parts whose meaning is the same in many different words.

Jeremy Anglin's analysis of children's vocabulary growth between first and fifth grades suggests that most children experience a substantial increase in their ability to understand prefixed and suffixed words during this period. However, not all children are proficient at using word parts. A number of studies (e.g., O'Rourke, 1979; Sternberg & Powell, 1983) have provided evidence that even many high school students are unaware that decomposing words into their parts can help with their meaning, and often these students do not know the meanings of common word parts. Morphological awareness—the ability to analyze words into prefixes, roots, and suffixes, and to recognize relationships among words based on shared word parts—is correlated with reading ability (Nagy, Diakidoy, & Anderson, 1993; Tyler & Nagy, 1990). Morphological awareness has been found to contribute to reading comprehension; that is, all other things being equal, students who are more aware of words parts are better readers (Carlisle, 1995; Nagy et al., 2003). Thus, less able readers might benefit from instruction in this area.

What Parts to Teach?

One must first decide which parts are worth teaching. One can find exhaustive lists containing hundreds of prefixes, suffixes, and Greek and Latin roots (e.g., Dale & O'Rourke, 1986; Fry, Kress, & Fountoukidis, 1993). Although such lists may be useful, it hardly seems possible or even fruitful to teach each element on each list. It would seem most useful to both directly teach the most commonly employed or important elements and teach a general strategy for decomposing words. Such a strategy would instruct a student on how to combine word part information with information from the sentence context.

Prefixes.   Only 20 prefixes account for 97% of prefixed words that appear in printed school English, excluding those that were followed by non-English roots, such as the *ad* in *adjacent* (White et al., 1989). Teaching at least the top 9 (if not all 20) to middle school students would pay dividends in increased vocabulary learning. White and his colleagues noted that third graders who were given training on these nine prefixes and a strategy for decomposing words into roots and suffixes outperformed a control group on several measures of word meaning.

Suffixes.   White and his colleagues also estimated the frequency of suffixes in printed school English. Inflectional endings such as noun endings (*-s, -es*), verb endings (*-ed, -ing, -en*), and adjective endings (*-er, -est*) were the most common. In general, these are used in even young children's oral language, and should not be a problem for middle school and older children.

Derivational suffixes appear in fewer than a quarter of all the words that contain suffixes, but they might be useful to teach. Comprehension of relatively infrequent words such as *exponential* and *unfeelingly* can be aided by knowledge of the *-ial* and *-ly* suffixes. Many children, especially poorer readers, have difficulty isolating the root word. Knowledge of which letter patterns are suffixes may also serve to help poor readers identify the root. Often, the length of words overwhelms such children. Giving them a word part reduces the size of the word and allows them to focus in on relevant information within the word (Adams, 1990). This is a natural extension to decoding instruction that teaches children to look at chunks of words. Compare/contrast decoding approaches, such as that of Cunningham (1995), have children look at words, such as *enlistment* and verbalize a strategy of comparing chunks of the words to known, shorter words. For example, *enlistment* might be decoded as "If ten is 'ten,' then en is 'en,' if fist is 'fist,' then list is 'list,' and if ten is 'ten,' then ment is 'ment.' By putting it together we get en-list-ment, enlistment." Teaching suffixes seems to be the next step beyond such a decoding strategy—first of all, because the pieces are usually larger; and second, because the pieces are meaningful.

We do have to be careful, however, not to assume too much about students' ability to understand the meanings or functions of word parts. In particular, suffixes tend to have relatively abstract meanings, to the extent that they can be said to have any meaning at all. A few suffixes, like *-less* and sometimes *-ful*, have fairly understandable meanings. In most cases, however, suffixes simply represent a change in part of speech. One can of course try to put this meaning into words; for example, the suffix *-ion* has been defined as meaning "the state, condition, or process of." Hence, the word *aggravation* would mean "the state, process, or condition of being aggravated." We don't think that this kind of definition will be especially helpful to most students. It should be explained that suffixes mark part of speech—for example, words ending in *-ly* are usually adverbs—but it is more helpful to show students, through example sentences, how a suffix changes the way a word is used.

Prefixes, on the other hand, often have fairly clear meanings. The *re -* in *reread* means "again"; the *pre-* in *preheat* means "beforehand"; the *un-* in *unhappy* means "not." However, even in the case of prefixes, one must be careful not to oversimplify. The *re-* in *report* doesn't mean "again." The *un-* in *untie* or *unload* does not mean "not" (although we have seen such an explanation in print). The *un-* in *uncle* doesn't mean anything. Thus, it is helpful to talk about the meanings of prefixes, but you shouldn't gloss over the exceptions and give students the misimpression that prefixes will always have a constant meaning.

Roots.   When children encounter unknown words like *interdependent, readable,* and *substandard,* they can analyze the words for structural elements, including prefixes, suffixes, and familiar English roots, and combine these within-word cues with conceptual information in the context. But what about content words like *biology, extraterrestrial, geologist,* and *projectile?* In addition to their prefixes or suffixes, they also contain Greek or Latin roots. Reading educators are divided as to whether to teach these roots or not. Nagy and Anderson (1984) argued that the modern meanings of words (especially the most common derived words) often do not reflect the meanings of their historical roots, and that readers might be misled by a literal translation of root to meaning. For example, knowing that *-mort* refers to "death" may help with *mortal* or *immortal,* but probably does not help a person guess the meaning of *mortgage* or *mortify.* The *Oxford English Dictionary* (available online through many libraries) gives the following quote to explain the relationship between *mort* and *mortgage:*

> 1628 Coke On Litt. 205 It seemeth that the cause why it is called mortgage is, for that it is doubtful whether the Feoffor will pay at the day limited such summe or not, & if he doth not pay, then the Land which is put in pledge vpon condition for the payment of the money, is taken from him for euer, and so dead to him vpon condition, &c. And if he doth pay the money, then the pledge is dead as to the Tenant, &c. (Volume IX, p. 1102)

Mortify has an even more interesting history, moving from "put to death" in the 14th century, to "bruise," to "destroy the vitality of or to neutralize the effect of," to "to bring into subjection the appetites of the body by self-denial," and finally "to cause a person to feel humiliated." This word, in itself, is a case study of how language changes over time. Likewise, knowing *saline* will not help with *salary,* even though they are both derived from the same root. (Salt was once so valuable that it was used to pay workers.)

On the other hand, teaching roots may make the words more memorable by adding a story to the word's definition. Research has found that having children elaborate basic information makes it more memorable (Pressley, 1988). For example, *sanguinary* and *sanguine* both derive from the Latin word meaning "blood," but *sanguinary* means "bloodthirsty" and *sanguine* (through the Middle Ages' belief that body fluids affected one's disposition) means "cheerful." One of us heard this example in high school, and has remembered both the meanings and the example since.

We would suggest that a distinction be made between using word parts as an independent reading strategy and using word parts as a word study tool. When a student encounters new words while reading, it is useful to see if one can take off prefixes or suffixes and identify a known word. Because poor readers tend to be overwhelmed by long words, they may need to be taught how to do this. For example, a teacher might instruct students to attack *inter-dependent* by teaching them to cover the prefix *inter-* to see if the rest of the word is recognizable. If not, then covering the suffix *-ent*, and leaving *depend*, might make it easier. Practice in adding and removing prefixes and suffixes might also be useful. For example, a teacher might take the base *dependent* and add prefixes such as *in-* or *non-* to make new words.

When using word parts as an independent reading strategy, however, breaking words down further into Latin roots is less likely to be helpful. We doubt, for example, that a struggling reader would be helped by breaking *depend* down further into *de-* and *pend*, even if he or she could assign these means such as "down" and "hang." For the purposes of word study, however—when the meaning of the word has been provided by the teacher or by a definition—knowing the metaphor behind the history of the word may well make the word more memorable.

A distinction should also be made between those roots, especially Greek roots used in scientific terminology, that have relatively specific meanings (*bio, hemo, meter*), and those, more often from Latin, whose meanings have come to wander all over the map (e.g., the *ceive* in *conceive, deceive, receive*).

How to Teach Word Parts

Introductory lessons in word part lessons should stress the idea that words can be composed of elements, such as prefixes, suffixes, and roots. These should be defined for the students, but the emphasis should not be on learning the specific terms as much as on learning about how parts function together to affect word meaning. For example, a lesson on *un-* might not only provide examples of words beginning with *un-*, but also ask students to generate *un-* words of their own, including silly words. The use of imaginative extensions may not only solidify the meaning of *un-*, but also may solidify the concept of *prefix* in general. Nonexamples of prefixes, such as *under* and *uncle,* also help reinforce the basic concept of prefixing.

After the basic concepts of prefix, suffix, and root are known, teaching specific word parts should be easier. This can be done within the context of other vocabulary instruction, as part of the discussion of a particular word's meaning, or using direct instruction. Such instruction would include providing a definition for the target word part, offering models of words using that word part, and reading sentences containing the target parts. For prefixes, one should attempt to extend the instruction to include as many real and silly words as possible. For *un-*, we not only have *unclean, unimaginable,* or *uninformed,* but also the *Uncola, unhamburger, unsleep,* and so on.

This strategy could be done for suffixes as well. Although prefixes should be defined, because their definition tends to be consistent over a variety of words, definitions of suffixes may confuse children. Some sources define *-ance/-ence* and *-ment* as "condition of, quality of, or state of." Adding this to the definition of a root might make understanding *amendment* or *precedence* a complicated task indeed. Instead, many examples of words containing suffixes might be given, along with the words from which they were derived. Ample experience with both the suffixed words and the original words would probably be more useful than would memorizing an abstract definition.

For roots, similar teaching procedures could be employed. It also might be useful to use a web such as that in Fig. 11.1. Such webs would introduce children to many new words while teaching a few target words. Nagy and Anderson (1984) suggested that such a strategy of discussing derivatives when introducing a new word, with or without a web, is useful and motivational. Including words that are relatively infrequent (e.g., *geocentric* or *geode*) may make target words (e.g., *geology*) more memorable.

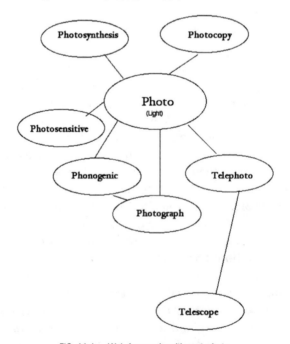

FIG. 11.1.   Web for words with root *photo*.

Clearly, there are benefits to be gained from teaching children to break words into their parts as a strategy for determining the meanings of unknown words. When combined with the use of context clues, using word parts seems to be especially fruitful, particularly in the content areas, because so many of the words encountered in content area texts contain recognizable parts.

In Tables 11.1, 11.2, 11.3, and 11.4 we have provided lists of prefixes, suffixes, and roots. There is a list of common prefixes and suffixes, a list of common number prefixes and roots, a list of common Greek and Latin word parts, and another list of word parts that we have found to be useful. These can be a start in developing a word part instructional program. Aside from the first list, they were not scientifically chosen. Feel free to add your own. Fry, Kress, and Foutoukidis (1993) provide extensive lists that should prove helpful.

In summary, teaching the use of word parts is an important part of a comprehensive approach to vocabulary-building. Children's knowledge of words parts plays an important role in vocabulary growth (Anglin, 1993), and it is strongly related to their reading ability (Nagy, Berninger, Abbott, Vermeulen, & Vaughn, 2003; Tyler & Nagy, 1990). Furthermore, there is ample evidence that children can be taught to use word parts to figure out the meanings of new words (Graves, 2004).

Though children can be introduced to basic information about word parts in the primary grades, teaching of word parts is not simple. Fortunately, the majority of prefixed, suffixed, and compound words have meanings that can be inferred from their parts (Nagy & Anderson, 1984). However, there is still a substantial remainder of words whose meanings are *not* predictable from their parts (e.g., *shiftless*). Then there are all those words whose meanings have *something* to do with their parts, but the connection is only obvious if one can fudge a little bit, and knows secondary meanings of the words. (The word *prefix* itself is good example—it makes sense if you know that *fix* can mean "attach" as well as "repair," and that *pre* can mean "in front of" as well as "before").

The craziness of the English language so well captured in Lederer's essay does not mean that we can ignore word parts. Rather, students must learn to use word parts strategically rather than mechanically. Teachers must recognize use of word parts as a complex cognitive strategy. This means taking the time to model and practice the use of word-part strategies with real words situated in real text, and taking the time for the discussion that becomes necessary when one encounters the nonexamples and gray-area examples that will arise when you do so. The same is true for the use of context—the topic of the next chapter.

TABLE 11.1
The Most Frequent Affixes in Printed School English

Rank	Prefix	Percentage of All Prefixed Words	Suffix	Percentage of All Suffixed Words
1.	un-	26	-s, -es	31
2.	re-	14	-ed	20
3.	in-, im-, il- ir- (not)	11	-ing	14
4.	dis-	7	-ly	7
5.	en-, em-	4	-er, -or (agent)	4
6.	non-	4	-ion, -tion, -ation, -ition	4
7.	in-, im- (in)	4	-able, -ible	2
8.	over-	3	-al, -ial	1
9.	mis-	3	-y	1
10.	sub-	3	-ness	1
11.	pre-	3	-ity, -ty	1
12.	inter-	3	-ment	1
13.	fore-	3	-ic	1
14.	de-	2	-ous, -eous, ious	1
15.	trans-	2	-en	1
16.	super-	1	-er (comparative)	1
17.	semi-	1	-ive, -ative, -tive	1
18.	anti-	1	-ful	1
19.	mid-	1	-less	1
20.	under- (too little)	1	-est	1
All others		3		7

Note. Percentages for suffixed words add up to more than 100% because figures for suffixes accounting for less than 1% of all suffixed words have been rounded up to 1.
Source: From White, Sowell, and Yanagihara (1989). Teaching elementary students to use word-part clues. *The Reading Teacher, 42,* 303–304. Reprinted with permission of Thomas G. White and the International Reading Association.

TABLE 11.2
Useful Prefixes and Roots Derived From Greek and Latin Number Words

Number	Greek	Latin
one		uni- *unit, unison, unicycle*
two		du- *duet, dual, duplex* bi- *bicycle, biped, biplane, bigamy, bimonthly*
three	tri- *triple, triad, triangle, tripod, triathalon*	
four	tetra- *tetrahedron*	quad- *quadrangle, quadruped*
five	pent- *pentagon*	quin- *quintuplet, quintet*
six	hex- *hexagon*	sex- *sextet*
seven		septem- *September*
eight	oct- *octagon*	octo- *October, octopus*
nine		novem- *November*
ten	deca *decagon-*	deci-, dec- *December, decimal, decade*
hundred		cent- *centimeter, century, cent, percent*
thousand	kilo- *kilogram, kilometer*	mille- *milligram, millimeter*
first	proto- *proton, protégé, protoplasm*	prim- *primary, primal, primitive*
single	mono *monotony, monarchy*	
many	poly *polygon*	multi- *multiple, multi-purpose*
half	hemi *hemisphere*	semi semicircle

TABLE 11.3
Relational Prefixes

	Greek	*Latin*
above, over	hyper *hypertension, hyperspace*	super *supersonic, superscript,* *superlative*
across, through	dia *diagonal, diagram,* *diarrhea*	trans *transparent, transmit,* *transatlantic*
after	meta *metamorphosis*	post *post-mortem, postwar*
against	anti *antibiotic, antipathy*	contra *contradict, contravene, contrary*
around	peri *perimeter, periscope,* *peripatetic*	circum *circumference, circumscribe,* *circumnavigate*
away from	apo *apostrophe, apostate*	
backwards		retro *retrospective, retrograde*
before	pro *prologue*	ante *antecedent, antebellum* pr *preposition, preface, prefix*
below, under	hypo *hypodermic, hypothermia*	sub *submarine, subterranean,* *subversive*
beside, near		proxime *approximate, proximity*
between		inter *international, interchange*
beyond		ultra *ultraviolet, ultrasuede*
down		de *descend, deposit*
in		in or im *impress, insert intra* *intravenous, intrapersonal*
on	epi *epidermis, epicenter, epilogue*	
out of	ex or ec *eccentric, export*	
outside	ectos *ectoplasm*	extra *extraordinary, extramural*

	Greek	*Latin*
self	auto *automobile, automatic,* *autobiography, autograph,* *autopsy*	
together		con, com, *congress, consent, convenient,* *compromise, commission*
with	sym, syn *syndrome, sympathy, synthesis*	
without	a or an *agnostic, anhydrous, atheism*	

TABLE 11.4
Other Prefixes and Roots

Word Part	Meaning	Examples
air, aero	air	*airplane, aeronautics*
alt	high	*altitude, altimeter, exalt*
ambl	walk	*amble, ambulance, ambulatory, perambulator*
anno, enni	year	*annual, Anno Domini, biennial, centennial, anniversary, annuity*
anthro	man	*anthropology, misanthrope*
arch	chief	*archvillain, hierarchy, archbishop*
astro	star	*astronomy, asterisk, astrology*
aud	hear	*auditory, audition, auditorium, audiophile*
bell	beautiful	*belle, embellishing*
bello	war	*bellicose, antebellum, belligerent*
bene	good	*benefit, benediction, beneficiary, benevolence*
bio	life	*biology, biochemistry, biome, biography*
chemo	chemical	*chemistry, chemotherapy*
chloro	green	*chlorine, chlorophyll*
verd	green	*verdant*
cide	kill	*homicide, suicidal, fratricide, pesticide, herbicide*
cogn	learn	*cognitive, recognize, cognizant*
cosmos	universe	*cosmopolitan, cosmic, cosmology, Cosmonaut*
crypt	hide	*crypt, cryptography, cryptic, encrypt*
dem	people	*democracy, demography, demagogue*
demos	people	*democracy, demagogue*
populo	people	*popular, population, populate*
dict	speak	*dictate, dictator, dictaphone, predict, contradict, dictum*
ego	I	*egotism, egocentric*
equi-	equal	*equilateral, equidistant, equator*
fac	make	*factory, manufacture, facilitate, artifact*
fid	faith	*fidelity, hi-fi, infidel, Fido, fiduciary*
flat	wind	*inflate, deflate, flatulence*
gen-	race (offspring)	*genetics, progeny, genocide*
geo	earth	*geology, geography, geode*
terra	earth	*terrestrial, territorial, terrarium, Mediterranean, terrain*
gyn	woman	*gynecologist, misogynist*
femina	woman	*feminine, effeminate*
helio	sun	*helium, heliotrope*
sol	sun	*solar, solarium*

Word Part	Meaning	Examples
hydro	water	*hydroelectric, dehydrate, hydrogen*
jur	law	*jury, injury, jurisdiction*
leg	law	*legal, illegal, legislate*
jur	swear	*conjure, perjury*
lat	side	*lateral, bilateral, unilateralism*
leucos	white	*leukemia, leucocyte*
albo	white	*albino, albumin*
littera	letter (alphabet)	*literacy, literary, literal*
logos	words, discourse	*logic, dialogue, monologue*
verbo	words, discourse	*verb, verbose, adverb, verbal, verbiage*
macro	large	*macro, macrocosm*
mal	bad	*malfeasance, malefactor, malnourished, malignant, malediction*
mis	bad	*mislead, mismanage, misdemeanor, misplace, misadventure, miscreant*
manu-, man	hand	*manufacture, manuscript, manual, manipulate*
matri	mother	*maternal, matriarchal, matron*
micro-	small	*microscope, microwave, Micronesia, microcosm*
min	small	*minimum, minimal, miniskirt*
mis, mit	send	*mission, missile, transmit, remit, admit, mission, emit*
mort	death	*mortuary, mortal, mortician, mortification, moribund*
nom	name	*nominate, nominal, denomination*
novus	new	*novel, novice, renovate*
ocu-	eye	*binoculars, monocle*
opt-	eye	*optometrist, optics*
opus	work	*operate, opera, operative*
ori	east	*oriental, disorient*
pax	peace	*pacify, pacific, pacification*
ped-	foot	*pedestal, pedestrian, pedal*
philo-	love	*philanthropist, philharmonic, bibliophile*
amo-	love	*amorous, amateur, amatory*
phobe	fear, fearful	*phobia, claustrophobia, xenophobe, triskaidekaphobia*
phon	sound	*phonograph, phonogram, phoneme, microphone*
son-	sound	*sonorous, dissonant*
photo	light	*photograph, photosynthesis*
lumen, luce	light	*luminescent, illuminate, lucent, translucent*
plac	please	*placate, complaisant, placid*

TABLE 11.4 (*continued*)

Word Part	Meaning	Examples
polis, polites	city, state, citizen	*metropolis, police, politics, policy, poll*
port	carry	*portable, transport, import*
pyr	fire	*pyre, pyrex, pyromaniac*
rapt	seize	*rapture, raptor, rapt*
rupt	break	*rupture, disruption, interrupt*
scribe	write	*scribble, manuscript, transcribe, inscription, scripture, script*
graph	write	*phonograph, graphics*
scope	watch	*microscope, telescope, scope*
sen	old	*senile, senior, senescent, senator*
sol	alone	*solitary, sole, solitaire, solace*
soph-	wisdom	*philosophy, sophisticated*
spec	see	*spectacles, specter, spectator*
spect	look	*spectator, inspect, respect*
struct	build	*structure, construction, destruct, instruct*
sym, syn	together	*sympathy, synthesis*
tele	far	*telescope, telephone, telemetry*
theo	God	*theology, atheist*
deo	God	*deism, deify*
therm	heat	*thermometer, thermostat*
vert	turn	*invert, convert, vertical, averted*
vest	clothes	*vestment, divest, vestry, invest*
viv	live	*vivacious, vivisection, revival, convivial*
voc	call	*vocalize, vocation, evoke, advocate*
xeno	stranger	*xenophobia*
xero	dry	*Xerox, xerography, xeroscape*

12

Teaching Word Learning Strategies: Context

So, as I heard the same words again and again properly used in different phrases, I came gradually to grasp what things they signified.

(Augustine, 386/1943, 1.8.13, p. 11)[2]

Much, if not most, of students' vocabulary knowledge is gained through encountering words in context. Children pick up information about what words mean and how the words are used as they repeatedly hear the words or see them in print. Even for those words that are explicitly taught, much of students' knowledge of them ultimately comes from further encounters with those words in text. We think it is safe to assume that most adults with large reading vocabularies acquired them primarily through reading—that is, through inferring the meanings of words from context—rather than through extensive use of dictionaries or extensive vocabulary instruction.

The fact that learning words from context is a "natural" means of vocabulary acquisition, however, does not necessarily mean that it is very efficient. We obviously think that context is important enough to devote a chapter to it, and believe that it is important to help students become more effective users of contextual information. However, to start with, we need to make it

---

[2]This quote was first brought to our attention by Judith Boettcher's 1980 dissertation *Fluent Readers' Strategies for Assigning Meaning to Unfamiliar Words in Context,* which, besides being an early and very thorough study of the use of context in learning words, should be acknowledged for having the earliest citation we have seen in a dissertation.

clear that as a source of information about word meanings, context is definitely problematic.

Problems With Context

Context contains a great deal of valuable information about a word's meaning. Children can acquire huge amounts of vocabulary knowledge "naturally," picking up the meanings of words from context as they read large amounts of appropriately challenging text. However, research has made it clear that the benefits of context are primarily long term—a matter of gradually accumulating partial information about words as one repeatedly encounters them. On the other hand, the chance of learning the meaning of any particular word from one encounter with that word in context is rather slim (Nagy, Anderson, & Herman, 1987; Schatz & Baldwin, 1986).

A number of authors have suggested categories of context clues designed to help children use context more effectively (e.g., Kuhn & Stahl, 1998; Quealy, 1969). Some of these are simple, such as a synonym used as an appositive (e.g., *"An armadillo, a small animal with scaly skin that looked like armor, crossed the road."*). Other clues involve pulling information from a number of places in the passage to infer a word's meaning. Studies have found that teaching context clues can help a child derive the meaning of a word when asked to do so, but there is no support that teaching context clues can transfer to actual reading situations, in which the reader comes across an unknown word without being explicitly told to derive its meaning (Fukkink & de Glopper, 1998; Kuhn & Stahl, 1998).

The problem with context clues is that, in real writing, authors choose the words for their appropriateness and do not stop and define them for their audience. Thus, real contexts usually provide little explicit information about a word's meaning. Appositives, although useful, are rare. The most common contexts require extensive inference and often lead to misleading guesses about the word's meaning. Consider the following contexts:

> No one would deny the _____ advantages, both cultural and civic, of such arts districts. Atlanta's Midtown Business Association of real estate interests and business-men points out that 4 million visitors flock to the district each year for arts-related events. "The arts are up on a level with religion and education," says association president Hiram Wilkinson. (Shatz & Baldwin, 1986, p. 445)

> Just about the time when the Allied troops were liberating Europe from the Nazi _____, American forces were routing the Japanese from their captured Pacific possessions. By the end of February 1945, the

Philippines were liberated by General MacArthur. (Shatz & Baldwin, 1986, p. 445)

Take a moment to try to figure out what word fits into each context. These are contexts taken from fairly conventional sources, representative of contexts that adults might read. The first is from *Newsweek,* the second from a history text, but neither are particularly obscure. Shatz and Baldwin (1986) found that few of their adult subjects could correctly guess the word that fit in the blank. When we gave these examples to students or teachers, we similarly found that few could get the exact word. Because they were competent readers and fairly intelligent, most groups came up with good choices that made sense in the context of the passage, but rarely synonyms.[3] In real-life contexts, each word amplifies the ideas in the passage rather than reiterates them, so that guessing exact words can be difficult, at least for content words. (Function words can be easier to guess because there are fewer of them and they tend to be more predictable.)

What are the chances of learning a previously unknown word from context? A meta-analysis of research on this topic (Swanborn & de Glopper, 1999) indicated that students learn about 15% of the unknown words they encounter. Whether this should be considered a high percentage or a low percentage depends on whether one is taking a long-term or short-term view of learning from context. From a long-term perspective, 15% is reasonably high. Assume, for example, that a child might read 150 words per minute, and reads 25 minutes per day for 200 days a year. This is a total of 750,000 words per year. If the child is reading text at an independent reading level (98% of the words are known), then 2% of the words, or 15,000, might be unknown. If the child learns 15% of these, that would result in an annual gain of 2,250 words, just from reading 25 minutes a day.

Although these estimates are purely speculative, none of the figures involved are unattainable. Of course, none of them are guaranteed, either. Ron Carver (1994) has argued, for example, that in much of the reading children that do, much fewer than 2% of the words children encounter are unfamiliar to them. For reading, by itself, to result in such a level of vocabulary growth might take substantial care in matching children with appropriate levels of reading materials. However, for now our point is simply that learning 15% of the unknown words one encounters can in principle lead to substantial gains in vocabulary in the long run.

In the short run, however, 15% is not such a high number. If we were to get the right answer on only 15% of the long division problems we did, we

---

[3]See endnote for original words used.

would find long division extremely frustrating. Of course, careful use of context might lead to a success rate higher than 15%. However, no matter how careful you are in your use of context, the success rate will never approach 100%. As Beck, McKeown, and McCaslin (1983) pointed out, context is sometimes uninformative, and sometimes even misleading (see Fig. 12.1). Good writers do not include an implicit definition for every hard word they use.

In fact, it is logically impossible for context to be 100% informative. Even a directive context such as the one in Fig. 12.1 requires the reader to make some inference about the word's meaning. In natural contexts, words are not explicitly defined, because that would involve providing the reader with exactly the same information twice. A word is informative only to the extent that it is not predictable. Hence, to the extent that a sentence contributes information to a text, some of the words in that sentence cannot be completely predictable from context. In fact, it is generally believed that language is about 50% redundant, so one should not expect context to work more than half of the time at best.

Our point here is not that context is useless, simply that it is problematic. Careful use of context can increase the amount of information one can gain,

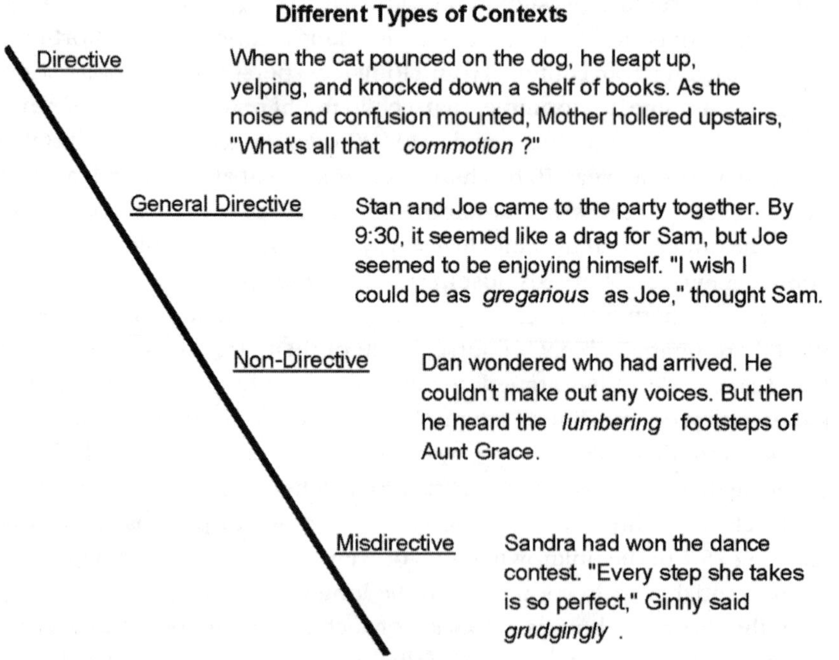

Different Types of Contexts

Directive
When the cat pounced on the dog, he leapt up, yelping, and knocked down a shelf of books. As the noise and confusion mounted, Mother hollered upstairs, "What's all that *commotion*?"

General Directive
Stan and Joe came to the party together. By 9:30, it seemed like a drag for Sam, but Joe seemed to be enjoying himself. "I wish I could be as *gregarious* as Joe," thought Sam.

Non-Directive
Dan wondered who had arrived. He couldn't make out any voices. But then he heard the *lumbering* footsteps of Aunt Grace.

Misdirective
Sandra had won the dance contest. "Every step she takes is so perfect," Ginny said *grudgingly*.

FIG. 12.1.   Different types of contexts.
Adapted from Beck, McKeown, & McCaslin, 1983, pp. 178–179. Reprinted with permission.

but it should not be expected that context will consistently give you adequate information about the meaning of a word.

Teaching Students to Use Context

Can students be taught to be more effective users of context? There is still some debate about this. Fukkink and de Glopper (1998) did a meta-analysis of 21 studies in which students were taught to use context, and concluded that such instruction had a reasonably strong and positive effect. Kuhn and Stahl's (1998) analysis of some of the same studies called into question whether teaching use of context had more of an effect than did simply having students practice using context.

Our take on this issue is that although it is worthwhile helping students become better at dealing with unfamiliar words, there are significant limitations on any attempt to do so focusing on context alone. First of all, there are the limitations stemming from the uninformative nature of many contexts. Also, we are not convinced that teaching students detailed information about types of context clues (e.g., appositives) is an effective use of instructional time.

As a model for helping students learn to cope with unfamiliar words they encounter, we would suggest approaches that focus primarily on the goal of text comprehension, rather than on context per se. Approaches such as reciprocal teaching (Palincsar & Brown, 1984) or collaborative strategic reading (Klinger & Vaughn, 1999) teach students to monitor their comprehension, and to identify words or phrases that they don't understand. In Klinger and Vaughn's collaborative strategic reading, for example, the primary focus is on collaborative discussion of text aimed at gaining an understanding of the gist of the text. One of the major tools, however, is to identify "clunks" (points at which comprehension has broken down). These breakdowns typically involve unfamiliar words. Use of context and word parts are part of the set of fix-up strategies students are taught in order to deal with the "clunks."

One specific approach for teaching children to get word meanings from context is that of Goerss, Beck, and McKeown (1999). The authors presented only qualitative data with a few children, so its effectiveness is only suggestive. However, the approach they describe is consistent with what we know about the types of cognitively challenging talk that promote vocabulary growth (e.g., Dickinson & Smith, 1993), and with others' recommendations for effective discussion about words (see chap. 8). Goerss et al. employed an interactive approach to lead children through contexts to help them use information in those contexts to infer word meanings. The goal was not necessarily to get a dictionary-perfect definition, but instead to obtain enough information to make sense of the story in which the word was found. Goerss et al.'s (1999) program has the following components (see Table 12.1). The examples that follow to illustrate this approach are from Goerss et al. (1999, pp. 155–156).

Read/reread. When the student realizes that he or she has come to an unfamiliar word, or when the teacher suspects that the meaning of the word is not clear to the student, the teacher rereads (or asks the student to reread) the relevant context—the sentence containing the word, and perhaps the sentences before and after. In this particular example, the relevant context was the following:

> As for Rusty, he scowled at Mary before stamping out of the room. "And I'm not coming back either, see!"

Discussion. The next step is to discuss the context to make sure the student understands the gist of the text:

Goerss: What is happening in these sentences?

Student: Rusty is mad at Mary about something and he stamped out of the room.

Goerss: Good. Is there anything else?

Student: Well, he yelled at her as he went out the door that he wasn't coming back.

TABLE 12.1
Goerss et al.'s (1999) Steps for Using Context

Step	Description
Read/reread	First read to introduce the context, and then reread to emphasize the role of the unfamiliar word in the context
Discussion	Focus on the clues to the word's meaning
Initial hypothesis	The child comes up with an meaning of the word with rationale for the decision
Placing constraints or developing hypothesis	Placing constraints on the original idea or developing more hypotheses
Summary	Information from the interaction is summarized

Source: Goerss et al. (1999, pp. 155–156).

Initial hypothesis.   Next, the student is asked to come up with a first guess at the word's meaning, and to identify information in the text that would support this guess. The first guess can be tentative, a starting point for further discussion. What is important at this point is not getting exactly the right meaning—as we have already pointed out, real texts seldom give sufficient information about a word to narrow the possibilities down to a single meaning. The purpose of the discussion at this point provides an opportunity for the student to practice the challenging metalinguistic task of thinking about the relationship of a word to its context, while being supported by a more knowledgeable partner.

Goerss:	What do you think *scowled* might mean?
Student:	Yelled.
Goerss:	Why do you think that?
Student:	Well, he yelled at her as he went out the door that he wasn't coming back.

If the student cannot come up with a hypothesis, the teacher can redirect him or her to look again at the context, pulling together information from the discussion. This is another student's response to the same word.

Goerss:	What do you think *scowled* means?
Student:	(No response)
Goerss:	Let's look at the sentence containing *scowled*. "As for Rusty, he scowled at Mary before stamping out of the room. 'And I'm not coming back either, see!' " When someone stamps out of a room, what do you think they are feeling?
Student:	Mad or upset
Goerss:	Right, so if Rusty is mad or upset, what are some things he might do at Mary?
Student:	Yell or throw something

Placing constraints or developing hypothesis.   The teacher can help guide the student by drawing his or her attention to ways in which the context constrains the meaning of the unfamiliar word. Note, however, that the meaning provided by the student in the preceding example, though not the actual meaning of the word used by the author, is a possible meaning for a word in this context. If a teacher were simply to dismiss the meaning "yelled" out of hand, the student could legitimately get the impression that the task required not use of context clues, but mind-reading. On the other hand, to accept "yelled" as the meaning for *scowled* is not a desirable option. We have to get back to the purpose of this activity, which is not just to get the "right" meaning—which is not always possible, since context does not always uniquely determine the meaning of an unfamiliar word. The student should understand that the first guess is not always correct and that the context should be re-examined. The student should also understand that it is often not possible to get an accurate meaning for a word from a single encounter in context. Probing for additional possible meanings helps the student see this:

Goerss: Can you think of some other possible meanings?
Student: Make faces at her
Goerss: Why did you say "make faces at her"?
Student: If you are mad at someone, you might make a face at them before you stamp out of the room.
Goerss: Can you think of anything else *scowled* might mean?
Student: Shake his fist.
Goerss: What made you say that?
Student: I shake my fist when I am mad at my sister.

Summary.   Finally, the teacher should help the student review what can be determined (and what cannot be determined) about the meaning of the word.

Goerss: What do we know about *scowled?*
Student: It is something that Rusty did to Mary. He was mad because he stomped out of the room telling her he wasn't coming back. It could be *yelled* or *shook his fist* or *made an angry face at her.*
Goerss: Any one of those might be possible meanings for *scowled* based on the sentences we read.

In this lesson, the teacher and student engaged in thoughtful analysis of the text. Such lessons could be conducted with small groups of students as well as in a tutorial setting. What is important is that the student put together the information from the context to create a reasonable hypothesis about its meaning. In this case, only one of the possible explanations was correct—that *scowled* means "make a face at"—but the teacher was not as interested in the student getting the right answer as she was in having the student think about words that were encountered in text. With additional exposure, the student was likely to fix on the correct meaning. At this point, however, it was sufficient for the student to understand that you *scowl* when you are mad.

We like the emphasis on process in these lessons. The point should be that children are sensitized to word meanings, that they think about the information in the context in relation to unknown words, and that they realize that one cannot usually get the meaning of a word from a single exposure in context. This approach, rather than lists of context clues that are rarely found, is more likely to be profitable.

Summary

In the last two chapters, we reviewed two approaches to learning about words: using word parts and using context clues. Neither of these approaches are foolproof ways of determining the meaning of an unknown word. We would be cheating our students if we told them that they are. However, used in conjunction, each can make up in part for some of the weaknesses of the other.

The existing research shows positive, although limited, benefits of teaching students to use word parts and context clues (e.g., Baumann et al., 2003). We believe that the success of such instruction depends in part on integrating word learning strategies into a comprehensive approach to vocabulary growth that also includes wide reading, teaching individual words, and promoting word consciousness. Word learning strategies must also be integrated into reading comprehension strategies. Although word parts and context seldom tell you all you might want to know about the meaning of a word, they often tell you enough to continue reading with an adequate level of comprehension, rather than being stopped cold by an unfamiliar word. It is important to remember that word learning strategies constitute what we have labeled "Level II" vocabulary instruction—a way to take one step forward on the journey to knowing a word.

Note

In the first passage, the deleted word was *pragmatic;* in the second passage, it was *yoke.*

13

Teaching Word Learning Strategies: Definitions

As sheer casual reading matter, I still find the English dictionary the most interesting book in our language.

(Albert Jay Nock, 1943, *Memoirs of a Superfluous Man*, p. 15)

This is the third of three chapters about word learning strategies—how to help students make more effective use of word parts, context, and definitions. In one sense, definitions are certainly the most reliable of the three. We have gone to some length to explain how word parts and context supply only partial, and sometimes even misleading, information about the meanings of words. Definitions, on the other hand, are explicitly designed to give the most accurate and complete information possible about the meaning of a word. Both in and out of school, dictionaries are generally regarded as an authoritative source of information about word meanings.

As we have done in the preceding two chapters, however, we want to start by making as clear as possible the limitations of definitions as a source of information about word meanings. There are at least three main problems with dictionary definitions as a tool for students:

- The meaning of a word is always dependent to some extent on the context in which it occurs.
- Definitions do not convey information about how a word is used.

- Children have trouble understanding the (often convoluted) language of definitions.

Just as was the case with word parts and context, we don't see these limitations as reasons to give up the use of dictionaries. However, using dictionaries is far more difficult for students than is commonly recognized. Dictionary use must be seen as a complex cognitive strategy that takes years to develop. After we discuss the limitations of definitions, we go on to give some suggestions for instructional activities that should help students learn to use definitions more effectively.

The Meaning of a Word Depends on the Context in Which it Occurs

It's fairly obvious that words have multiple meanings and shades of meaning that differ from one context to another. To some extent, dictionaries try to accommodate this fact by listing multiple meanings for words. The fact that a verb like *give* may have 50 or more different meanings listed in a larger dictionary is evidence that an attempt has been made to reflect such variations in the definitions. Ultimately, however, contextual variation in meaning is more pervasive, more far reaching, and more productive than can possibly be represented in a dictionary. Words continually shift their meanings to adjust to context. The word *large* means something different in the phrase *a large galaxy* than it does in the phrase *a large strawberry*. Or consider the common word *smoke*. The *Encarta* dictionary gives the definition "to inhale the smoke of any substance that can burn and be inhaled." Regardless of how helpful this definition is (and it probably would not be helpful), it is necessarily incomplete. The meaning of the word *smoke* and every other word (see Anderson & Nagy, 1991) changes in subtle ways in every sentence in which the word appears. Consider the meaning of this word in the following examples:

1. The man smoked the cigarette.
2. Humphrey Bogart smoked the cigarette.
3. The 13-year-old boy smoked the cigarette.
4. The psychologist smoked his pipe.
5. The hippie smoked the marijuana cigarette.

In the first sentence, the action may be considered as "typical," in that the person took a slow inhale and then exhaled. In the second sentence, given what we know of Humphrey Bogart, we might envision the cigarette hanging off his lip, his face half-covered with smoke. In the third sentence, the slow inhaling might be followed by a cough. The psychologist might puff on his pipe, rather than inhale. And the hippie would take a longer drag, hold it in, and then slowly exhale.

In all of these cases, the verb *smoke* has the meaning in the definition; the subject is inhaling a substance that can be burned. However, the context, and the readers' knowledge about the context, changes that meaning in subtle ways. If a person does not know who Humphrey Bogart is, then sentence 2 might be perceived similarly to sentence 1, for example. One's knowledge of Humphrey Bogart adds to the meaning of the sentence. The meaning of the word *smoke* is not its definition, nor is it the meaning of each individual context. Instead, the word's meaning is built up over a great many exposures to the word in different contexts. Over time, the person develops a sense of how *smoke* relates logically to other words, or some sort of definition. But the "meaning" of *smoke* is more than that definition.

How does this relate to students' use of dictionary definitions? One point is that using definitions—for example, combining the information from a dictionary with the information in a sentence containing the word you are looking up—is a complex and sophisticated process. If the dictionary lists multiple meanings for a word, there is always the task of figuring out which one fits a particular context. But even if there is only one meaning listed, or if a person is able to find the appropriate meaning, there is still the task of creating the meaning for that particular context; this involves a synthesis of the information in the dictionary, the context sentence, and the readers' knowledge of the topic or situation that the text describes.

A related point is that word knowledge as it exists in a person's head is not very much like a definition. Dictionary definitions, even when they represent different shades of meaning found in different contexts, are primarily an attempt to abstract the meaning from the context, and to state it in as general a form as possible. However word meanings are stored in human memory, they are far more connected to the contexts in which words have been experienced than are the abstract definitions found in dictionaries.

One evidence of the difference between our internal knowledge of words and how this knowledge is represented in dictionaries is the amount of time and effort that it can take to come up with a definition for a word, even if one knows its meaning well.

If you see a word in print—say, *embarrass*, or *exquisite*, or *strategic*—the meaning comes to mind in only a fraction of a second. It could take quite a few seconds, or even minutes, on the other hand, to actually produce a definition for some of the words that you intuitively understand almost instantaneously.

Dictionaries Do Not Convey How Words Are Used

One of the reasons is that definitions do not give (and were not designed to give) information about how words are actually used. Another reason, of course, is that children have trouble understanding definitions at all—a point we return to in the next section.

One type of evidence that definitions don't give much information about how words are used is the generally poor quality of the sentences that children produce when given a definition for a new word and asked to use it in a sentence. Miller and Gildea (1987) examined 2,000 sentences written by children who had been given a definition of a new word and asked to write a sentence. Miller and Gildea concluded from the children's performance that this task is "a waste of time" (p. 97). One of the examples they cited is a sentence a student wrote when given the following definition of *redress*:

1. set right; repair, remedy; *when King Arthur tried to redress wrongs in his kingdom.*

The student wrote:

The *redress* for getting well (when) you're sick is to stay in bed. (p. 99)

Another student, given the word *erode* defined as "to eat out," produced the sentence:

My family *erodes* often. (p. 98)

There are a number of factors contributing to the poor quality of these sentences, one of them being that many definitions are written in a way that makes them difficult for children to understand correctly. However, even well-written definitions do not always give adequate information about how words are to be used.

McKeown (1993) tried rewriting traditional definitions to make them more helpful to children, and found that her improved definitions were in fact substantially better at conveying the meanings of the words to children. However, even the revised definitions were far from perfect when it came to students generating sentences with the words. For the original dictionary definitions, only 25% of the sentences generated by students were rated as acceptable. For the revised definitions, 50% of the sentences generated by students were acceptable. This is a striking improvement, but the level of performance even for the revised definitions is not adequate. It is apparent that even the best of definitions do not give students enough information about how words are used.

In chapter 5, we talked about the fact that definitions alone are not enough for students to learn words to the point of ownership, and we described the type of instruction that is necessary if you really want students to be able to use in their own writing the words they are learning. Because we covered this point fairly thoroughly in chapter 5, and are going to talk more about related problems with definitions in a moment, we won't say more about this particular limitation here, other than to repeat that if you want students to know how a word is used, you'll have to give them examples— ideally, a number of examples—that show how the words are employed.

Children Have Trouble Understanding the Language of Definitions

The language of definitions is (in most dictionaries, at least) quite different from the language of conversation, and even from the language of most school texts. One of the forces that has contributed to the often-convoluted language of definitions is the need to save space. Use of very compressed language in definitions, although motivated by necessity, has become a tradition. (In McKeown's 1993 study, rewritten definitions, which were much more easily understood by children, were often twice as long as the originals from a dictionary.)

Another problem with definitions for students is the fact that the words being defined are already often fairly common words. Dictionaries for adults, which include familiar words more out of a compulsive need for completeness than anything else, can afford the absurdity of defining an easy word in terms of harder ones. If student dictionaries try to avoid this problem, they are likely to run afoul of restrictions on length. And if there is an attempt to make the definitions short, and to use easy words, it is unlikely that they will portray the intended meanings very accurately.

The traditional form of the definition itself may be a problem for some children. The standard form for a definition, dating back to Aristotle, first identifies a superordinate, or the class (genus) to which the word belongs, and then specifies how that word differs from other members of its class (*differentia*). For example, the *Random House Dictionary* (1987) defines a *fissure* as "a narrow opening (genus) produced by cleavage (differentia)" (p. 725).

Children only gradually become able to produce definitions in this form as they become more familiar with the particular conventions of definitions (Watson, 1985). Their ability to produce superordinate terms depends heavily on their vocabulary (Ordóñez, Carlo, Snow, & McLaughlin, 2002), because superordinate terms tend to be more abstract and learned later. In other words, it is likely that students with smaller vocabularies, who have all the more need for definitions, are less likely to be able to understand the definitions.

Research shows that children often have difficulty using conventional definitions to learn words. Scott and Nagy (1997) reported a study in which fourth- and sixth-grade children were given definitions of new words, and asked to decide whether a sentence containing that word made sense, given that definition. Some of the sentences were clearly appropriate, or clearly inappropriate, for the definition. However, Scott and Nagy included a particular type of sentence that would make sense if the child arbitrarily chose one word from the definition as representing the whole meaning. For example, they presented students with the following definition for the nonsense word *brange* (this definition was based on a definition for the word *trickle* in a real children's dictionary):

brange: to flow in a small stream

The children then had to judge whether the following sentence made sense, given that definition:

There are many fish in that brange.

Children who said that this sentence made sense for this definition would presumably have seen the word *stream* in the definition, and taken that to be the meaning of *brange*. It turns out that the children accepted such sentences about 50% of the time. In other words, their performance on this particular task had the same success rate one could achieve on this task by flipping a coin.

Scott and Nagy examined other forms of definitions to see if they would improve performance on the task. Giving definitions in what was supposed to be a more user-friendly format (similar to that of the Collins COBUILD Dictionary,[4] and some other children's dictionaries) did not lead to significant gains. Providing children with an example sentence in addition to the

---

[4]One commercially available dictionary that does not use the Aristotelian form of definitions is the COBUILD dictionary. The COBUILD approach is to explain the meaning of a word, as someone might in response to a question about the word's meaning. The definitions are in sentence form. For example, the entry for *fissure* is "A *fissure* is a deep crack in something, especially in rock or in the ground" (p. 635). Other entries have longer explanations. For example, the entry for "plunge" is "If something or someone *plunges* in a particular direction, especially into water, they fall, rush, or throw themselves in that direction. *At least 50 people died when a bus plunged into a river.... He ran down the steps to the pool terrace and plunged in*" (p. 1266). Although the COBUILD includes examples from American English, it is a British dictionary and the usages and spellings do differ from those in the United States. McKeown (1993) found that children could understand COBUILD-style definitions somewhat better than conventional definitions. It is a resource that should be considered.

traditional definition produced a gain in accuracy that was statistically significant, but not all that large. These results suggest that, at least when truly unfamiliar words are involved, elementary students have trouble understanding the structure of even relatively simple definitions.

In the previous two chapters, we discussed some of the limitations of word parts and context as potential sources of information about the meanings of new words. You might have hoped that, however misleading word parts and context might be, you could always rely on the dictionary to give you reliable information about a word. Unfortunately, as we have seen, dictionary definitions also have serious limitations.

What can we do? We are certainly not suggesting that these sources of information about words should be neglected; they are just about all we have. However, it is absolutely essential that teachers not have unrealistic expectations about them. Definitions, context, and word parts are essential tools for word learning, but to use these tools effectively requires awareness of words and flexible thinking—metacognitive and metalinguistic sophistication that you cannot necessarily take for granted on the part of your students. Furthermore, the students who need the most vocabulary growth are likely to be the least effective at using these sources of information.

One obvious response to the limitations of each of these sources of information is to use them together. For example, although word parts may be deceptive, context should let you know whether the meaning you have put together from the parts makes sense. Likewise, context supplies valuable information about how a word is used, which is the type of information that definitions are the weakest at conveying. Thus, students should be taught to triangulate across these three potential sources of information.

However, it must be understood that such triangulation is neither automatic nor easy. Students cannot always easily integrate information about words gained from two or more sources. For example, Mori (2002; see also Mori & Nagy, 1999) found that some students tend to overrely on word parts, and ignore information from context; others overrely on context, and tend to ignore information provided by word parts. Using a dictionary also involves integrating the information from the definition with the text in which the word occurs, also a very demanding task (Miller & Gildea, 1986).

Using Dictionaries

Teaching children to use dictionaries is a worthwhile goal, but using a dictionary is far harder than teachers realize. When you've taught students alphabetical order and guidewords, so they can find the word in the dictionary, you're not done—you've just gotten to the hard part. Taking the information in the definition and using it to interpret a text is a very complex and difficult cognitive strategy. Teachers need to recognize it as such, and teach it accordingly.

Teaching Dictionary Use

How Are Definitions Constructed?   As noted earlier, a dictionary definition follows a particular pattern. One part of the definition, usually the first part, is the *genus* or the category to which the word belongs. A definition also describes how this word is different than other words in the category (*differentiae*). With the exception of the COBUILD dictionary, virtually every dictionary definition follows this pattern. Yet, children are rarely taught about the structure of definitions.

Concept of definition maps (see chap. 6) are one approach to definition study. These were originally proposed as an approach to teaching definitions (Schwartz & Raphael, 1985), but had evolved beyond that point. A simplified concept word, such as that in Fig. 13.1, might be useful to sensitize children to the different information in a definition.

For *dilemma,* defined in the *Encarta* dictionary (Microsoft, 1999) as "a situation in which somebody must choose one of two or more unsatisfactory alternatives," this might look like Fig. 13.2.

Notice that we put the definition in simpler words, rather than just copying (or "cutting and pasting") the words in the boxes. It is important that stu-

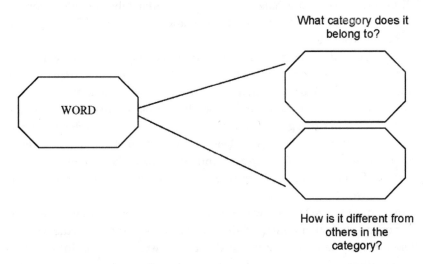

FIG. 13.1.   Basic concept of definition map.

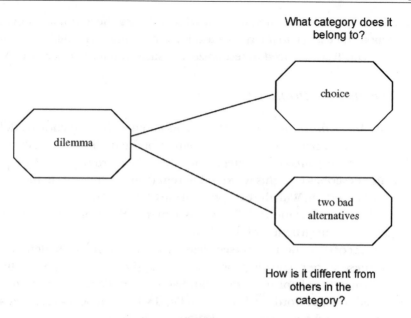

What category does it
belong to?

choice

dilemma

two bad
alternatives

How is it different from
others in the
category?

FIG. 13.2.   Concept of definition map for the word *dilemma*.

dents translate the definition into their own words; otherwise, this becomes
a mechanical exercise rather than one based on the meanings of the words.

For a simpler word, such as *lecture* from a fourth-grade basal reader, the
definition is "an educational speech on a particular subject made before an
audience." Simplifying the definition a bit and putting the definition in our
diagram it would look like Fig. 13.3.

We propose that this type of instruction begin with words for which the
children have some idea of what they mean, in order to familiarize the children with the two parts of a definition. This can be done first as a whole-
class discussion activity and later in small groups. We like the discussion
that can occur in small groups and feel that they are a more effective venue
for this kind of studying than is individual work. We feel that when students
use a concept of definition map as an individual worksheet, they tend to apply the definitions mechanically, to get the job done, rather than thinking
about the word and its meaning.

After students are familiar with definitions, we recommend that the activity be used to help them learn words. Because of the results from the Nist and
Olejnik (1995) study showing that definitions were more useful for word
learning *after* children had read the word in context, we recommend using
this activity as a postreading activity rather than as a prereading activity.

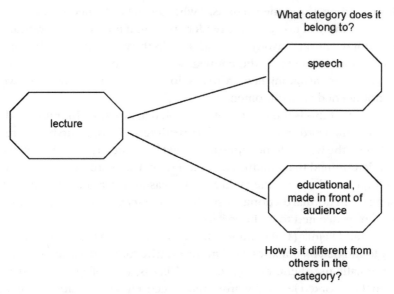

FIG. 13.3. Concept of definition map for the word *lecture*.

With time, the use of diagrams can be phased out. However, we do find that a graphic organizer such as this can be useful for a while. Concept of definition maps can be integrated into vocabulary notebooks as a useful shorthand way of capturing definitions. Slightly more complex definition maps can also serve as a framework for note taking.

Using Dictionaries During Reading. The traditional way of using definitions—indeed, the traditional approach to teaching vocabulary—was to give children a list of words, have them look the words up in the dictionary, perhaps write an example sentence for each word, and then test the children on Friday. If the test was given on Friday morning, odds were good that the children would forget most of the words by Friday lunchtime. Aside from the fact that such instruction is not particularly effective (see Stahl & Fairbanks, 1986), it brings back such bad memories that it may have been an act of courage for many of the readers of this book to pick up a book on teaching word meanings in the first place.

Contrast this traditional instruction with how real people use real dictionaries. Over years of talking with students, we find that a certain percentage of them keep a dictionary by their side during reading, especially when reading college textbooks, and the remainder of students have a dictionary somewhere in the house, at the ready. If a reader finds an unknown word during reading, the reader firsts asks whether she or he needs to know the word's meaning. If not, then the reader goes on. If the word is important to know (for whatever reason), the reader looks the word up in the dictionary, compares its meaning to the context, and goes on. Sometimes a reader would note an intriguing new word and look it up after reading, if the word was not needed at that moment.

Notice that this is the reverse of traditional instruction. In traditional instruction, the words are chosen before reading and looked up before reading. Often, the words do not appear in a text but instead just in a list that has been determined that children need to know. The words are then studied and forgotten, because the child had no reason to learn the words in the first place. In normal dictionary use, the dictionary is used during reading, if the word is deemed to be important.

Nist and Olejnik (1995) studied these two approaches to dictionary use. They found that dictionaries were more effective for word learning if used as we normally use them, during reading. That is, the college students with whom they worked learned words more effectively if dictionaries were used at the point where needed, rather than before reading.

This finding needs to be tested with younger children, of course. However, it makes sense that children will process the information in the dictionary definition in a meaningful manner if it helps them solve a problem in the comprehension of a text. That is, if the definition helps students understand, the information in the definition will become part of their long-term memory. In traditional dictionary instruction, the information in the definition is treated as random bits of information, similar to a phone number. If you look up a number in the phone book, ordinarily you will remember it only as long as you need to place the call, and forget it immediately afterward. This is because the numbers in the phone number are just random, having no particular meaning. Students tend to treat dictionary definitions just this way—as random items to memorize—and memorize them just long enough to spit them out and forget them. Because students are not putting that information in long-term memory (Craik & Lockhart, 1972), they are remembering those words by rehearsing the definitions over and over, like you would rehearse that phone number until you dial it. This is not an effective way to learn anything over the long term.[5]

---

[5]An alert reader might have noted a contradiction here, because we provided extensive word lists in an earlier chapter—word lists that would lend themselves to traditional dictionary study. We are tempted to quote Emerson that "A foolish consistency is the hobgoblin of little minds," but that would not honor our alert reader. Instead, we would say that we are *not* recommending that the word lists be given to students in isolation to be memorized. These lists in question were developed for ESL college students to help them master English academic vocabulary. They can be used for self-study in that way, by ESL students or others. They also can be used to guide students in word learning. However, we do *not* recommend that they be used to generate the kinds of lists that students, past and future, find onerous, and that we know are ineffective in helping children learn word meanings.

Vocabulary Notebooks.   One way of using dictionaries effectively in-volves vocabulary notebooks. These are personalized notebooks in which children note words they encounter during reading. Words that the child feels are interesting, important to know, or otherwise useful can be written in such notebooks. These words would be looked up in the dictionary. Chil-dren should be taught a number of different approaches to noting informa-tion about word meanings. These could include concept of definition maps (as described earlier; see Schwartz & Raphael, 1985), the use of example sentences from the text, making up new example sentences, using semantic maps (see chap. 6), and so on.

Words from vocabulary notebooks can be used in a number of different ways. For example, they can be used for vocabulary tests, similar to the tra-ditional dictionary study. Children can select their own words to study, or a group of students could select words from each other's notebooks to gen-erate a study list. Although we use the term *notebook,* words do not have to be recorded in a traditional notebook, but instead could be put on 5" × 8" cards or a computer database. These alternative forms have particular ad-vantages. For example, words in a computer database could be combined by groups or the whole class and used to develop class dictionaries or word walls. Class dictionaries could be used as a reference during reading and writing. These ideas represent alternatives to traditional dictionary study that would accommodate the teacher's need for grades.

Summary

We started this chapter with by discussing some of the limitations of dictio-nary definitions. Dictionary definitions contain limited information and are difficult for many children to understand. Definitions are a particular lin-guistic form for which children need specific instruction in order to master. If students do not understand the form of a definition, it is unlikely that they will be able to gain information from it.

Furthermore, dictionary definitions are more helpful when used as we use them—during reading to understand the meaning of an unknown word. Dictionaries are less effective when used before reading to generate lists of definitions that can be looked up.

In addition, as we have discussed, the "meaning" of a word is *not* its defi-nition. Instead, a word's meaning changes in every context in which it ap-pears. Thus, one needs to see how the word is used in context to fully understand its meaning. What one knows about words is the result of expo-sure to each word in a variety of contexts. Ordinarily, our definitional knowledge arises out of our experience with the word in context, rather than the other way around.

As we discussed at length in part II of this book, definitions are only a starting point for word learning. If the goal is to bring students to the point where they can actually use a word, we have to be prepared to provide them with a variety of opportunities to learn and practice aspects of word knowledge that definitions convey only poorly at best. Effective vocabulary instruction requires repeated encounters with words in which students must exercise creativity and deep processing, and make multiple connections among the word being learned and concepts and experiences already familiar to them.

For all their limitations, dictionaries are a powerful tool for word learning, and students must become adept at using them. However, to reach that point is no easy task. Dictionary use is a complex, cognitively challenging strategy that takes thoughtful and long-term instruction.

14

Conclusion: Matching Instructional Approaches to Students and Words

Words can give everybody wings.

(Aristophanes, 1978, *The Birds and Other Plays*
[D. Barrett & A. H. Sommerstein, Trans.], p. 202)

The message of this book can be summed up in terms of three main points: Promoting vocabulary growth is important, absolutely essential for students' success; promoting vocabulary growth is also a difficult goal, with a variety of obstacles to be overcome; and therefore, promoting vocabulary growth requires a multifaceted and long-term approach.

Among the obstacles to promoting vocabulary growth is the fact that there are so very many words that children need to learn—more than we can teach them. There are also different kinds of words, and different purposes for learning them. Therefore, it is essential for teachers to be strategic in vocabulary instruction—to know which words to teach, and what kinds of instruction are appropriate for different kinds of words.

Table 14.1 gives a summary of guidelines for choosing specific types of instruction for different types of words. Remember that which type of instruction you use depends not only on the words, but also on the knowledge, and needs, of your students.

TABLE 14.1
Categories of Words and How to Teach Them

Type of Word	How to Identify Words in This Category	How to Teach Words in This Category
1. High-frequency words	• Words that are among the most frequent in the language. • They are used in all genres and stylistic levels. • Their basic meanings are likely to be familiar to most students whose home language is English.	• Find out whether or not your students already know them. • Teach for fluency. • Provide many opportunities for students to see and use the words in context. (chap. 7)
2. High-utility general vocabulary	• Students are likely to encounter this word frequently in their reading. • This is a word you would like students to be able to use in their writing. • This is a word they are not likely to be familiar with from their oral language experience. • The meaning of this word can be explained in terms of concepts already familiar to them.	• Explain the meaning of the word. • Give examples of how the word is used. • Use multiple activities that require students to use the word and think about its meaning, while giving them enough support to do so successfully. • Use the word when you're talking with students. • Create an atmosphere in which students feel safe to experiment with using new words. • Ask students to use the word, and to report instances of seeing, hearing, or using the word outside of class. • Review words periodically. (chap. 4)
3. Important content-area vocabulary	• This word refers to a new and difficult concept. • This concept is important for them to learn.	• Activate relevant background knowledge—find out what students already know about the concept, and remind them of related concepts they have already learned. • Explain the concept and its relationship to other concepts. • Use graphic organizers, charts, or diagrams as needed to portray relationships among concepts. • Discuss examples and nonexamples. (chap. 5)

4. Words requiring some explanation	• Students probably need to know this word in order to understand the text. • This word can be explained in terms of words and concepts already familiar to the students. • This is not a word that students need to use in their own writing.	• Provide an explanation of the word when needed. • Encourage students to ask questions about words, and don't always send them to the dictionary. (chap. 8)
5. Words that provide opportunities to demonstrate or practice word learning strategies	• This word gives an opportunity to show students how context or word parts (prefixes, suffixes, roots) can help them figure out the meaning of a word.	• Using a think-aloud, model how you would figure out the meaning of this word. • Explain the strategies you use. • Practice using these strategies in small groups. • Prompt students to use strategies—remind them when these strategies might be helpful. (chaps. 11–13)
6. Words that illustrate the power and beauty of effective word choice in writing	• This word is an example of effective, vivid, or otherwise powerful writing. • Students are likely to know this word well enough to appreciate what the author is doing.	• Model an appreciation of effective writing—when you find an example of colorful or vivid writing in your own reading, tell students about it. • Have students take note of instances in which authors make effective use of language, and share these in class. • Post examples of well-crafted phrases around the classroom. • Encourage students to use these examples as models for their own writing. (chap. 10)
7. Words that don't need to be taught	• Students can probably understand the meaning of the text without knowing this word. • Students are not likely to see this word very often in their reading. • Or, students already know the meaning of this word.	• Use the word when talking with students. • Give students opportunities to read. • Help students select books for independent reading that are at an appropriate level for them. (chap. 9)

References

Adams, M. J. (1990). *Beginning to read: Thinking and learning about print*. Cambridge, MA: MIT Press.

Addison, J. (1712/1963). Secondary pleasures of the imagination: Consideration limited to literature. In G. Smith (Ed.), *The spectator* (Vol. 3). London, England: J. M. Dent & Sons Ltd.

Alighieri, D. (1314/1960). *The Divine Comedy of Dante Alighieri* (H. F. Cary, Trans.). New York: Collier & Son.

Anderson, R. C., & Davison, A. (1988). Conceptual and empirical bases of readability formulas. In A. Davison & G. Green (Eds.), *Linguistic complexity and text comprehension* (pp. 23–51). Hillsdale, NJ: Lawrence Erlbaum Associates.

Anderson, R. C., & Freebody, P. (1981). Vocabulary knowledge. In J. Guthrie (Ed.), *Comprehension and teaching: Research reviews* (pp. 77–117). Newark, DE: International Reading Association.

Anderson, R. C., & Nagy, W. (1991). Word meanings. In R. Barr, M. Kamil, P. Mosenthal, & P. D. Pearson (Eds.), *The Handbook of Reading Research: Volume II*, 690–724.

Anderson, R. C., & Nagy, W. (1992). The vocabulary conundrum. *American Educator, 16*(4), 14–18, 44–47.

Anderson, R. C., Wilson, P., & Fielding, L. (1988). Growth in reading and how children spend their time outside of school. *Reading Research Quarterly, 23*(3), 285–303.

Anglin, J. M. (1993). Vocabulary development: A morphological analysis. *Monographs of the Society of Research in Child Development, 58*. (Serial #238).

Aristophanes. (1978). The birds and other plays (D. Barrett & A. H. Sommerstein, Trans.). New York: Penguin. (Original work published 414)

Augustine. (1943). Confessions (F. J. Sheed, Trans.). New York: Sheed & Ward. (Original work published 386)

Ayto, J. (1990). *Dictionary of word origins: The histories of more than 8,000 English-language words*. New York: Arcade Publishing.

Baumann, J. F., Edwards., E. C., Boland, E. M., Olejnik, S., & Kame'enui, E. (2003). Vocabulary tricks: Effects of instruction in morphology and context on fifth-grade students' ability to derive and infer word meanings. *American Educational Research Journal, 40*(2), 447–494.

Bear, D. R., Invernizzi, M., Templeton, S., & Johnston, F. (2004). *Words their way: Word study for phonics, vocabulary, and spelling instruction* (3rd ed.). Upper Saddle River, NJ: Merrill.

Beck, I. L., & McKeown, M. G. (1991a). Social studies texts are hard to understand: Mediating some of the difficulties. *Language Arts, 68*, 482–490.

Beck, I. L., & McKeown, M. G. (1991b). Conditions of vocabulary acquisition. In R. Barr, M. Kamil, P. Mosenthal, & P. D. Pearson (Eds.), *Handbook of reading research* (Vol. II, pp. 789–814). New York: Longman.

Beck, I. L., & McKeown, M. G. (2001). Text Talk: Capturing the benefits of read-aloud experiences for young children. *The Reading Teacher, 55*(1), 10–20.

Beck, I. L., McKeown, M. G., & Kucan, L. (2002). *Bringing words to life.* New York: Guilford.

Beck, I. L., McKeown, M. G., & Kucan, L. (2003). Taking delight in words: Using oral language to build young children's vocabularies. *American Educator, 27*(1), 36–41, 45–46.

Beck, I. L., McKeown, M. G., & McCaslin, E. S. (1983). All contexts are not created equal. *Elementary School Journal, 83,* 177–181.

Beck, I. L., McKeown, M. G., & Omanson, R. C. (1987). The effects and uses of diverse vocabulary instructional techniques. In M. G. McKeown & M. E. Curtis (Eds.), *The nature of vocabulary acquisition* (pp. 147–163). Mahwah, NJ: Lawrence Erlbaum Associates.

Beck, I. L., McKeown, M. G., Worthy, J., Sandora, C., & Kucan, L. (1996). Questioning the author: A year-long classroom implementation to engage students with text. *Elementary School Journal, 96*(4), 385–414.

Beck, I. L., Perfetti, C., & McKeown, M. (1982). Effects of long-term vocabulary instruction on lexical access and reading comprehension. *Journal of Educational Psychology, 74*(4), 506–521.

Biemiller, A. (1999). *Language and reading success.* Cambridge, MA: Brookline Books.

Biemiller, A., & Slonim, N. (2001). Estimating root word vocabulary growth in normative and advantaged populations: Evidence for a common sequence of vocabulary acquisition. *Journal of Educational Psychology, 93,* 498–520.

Blachowicz, C. L., & Fisher, P. (2004). Keeping the "fun" in fundamental: Encouraging word awareness and incidental word learning in the classroom through word play. In J. F. Baumann & E. J. Kame'enui (Eds.), *Vocabulary instruction: Research to practice* (pp. 218–237). New York: Guilford.

Boettcher, J. A. (1980). Fluent readers' strategies for assigning meaning to unfamiliar words in context. *Dissertation Abstracts International, 41*(3), 1001A. (UMI No. 8019516)

Brabham, E., & Lynch-Brown, C. (2002). Effects of teachers' reading-aloud styles on vocabulary acquisition and comprehension of students in the early elementary grades. *Journal of Educational Psychology, 94*(3), 465–473.

Brautigan, R. (1967). *Trout Fishing in America.* Boston: Houghton Mifflin.

Brett, A., Rothlein, L., & Hurley, M. (1996). Vocabulary acquisition from listening to stories and explanation of target words. *The Elementary School Journal, 96*(4), 415–422.

Brice Heath, S. (1983a). A lot of talk about nothing. *Language Arts, 60,* 39–48.

Brice Heath, S. (1983b). *Ways with words: Language, life and work in communities and classrooms.* New York: Cambridge University Press.

Bridge, C., Winograd, P., & Haley, D. (1983). Using predictable materials vs. preprimers to teach beginning sight words. *The Reading Teacher, 36,* 884–891.

Buckingham, B. R., & Dolch, E. W. (1936). *A combined word list.* Boston: Ginn.

Burgess, A. (1992). *A mouthful of air.* New York: Morrow.

Buikema, J., & Graves, M. (1993). Teaching students to use context cues to infer word meanings. *Journal of Reading, 36,* 450–457.

Cantalini, M. (1987). *The effects of age and gender on school readiness and school success.* Unpublished doctoral dissertation. Toronto, Canada: Ontario Institute for Studies in Education.

Carlisle, J. F. (1995). Morphological awareness and early reading achievement. In L. Feldman (Ed.), *Morphological aspects of language processing* (pp. 189–209). Hillsdale, NJ: Lawrence Erlbaum Associates.

Carlisle, J. F. (2000). Awareness of the structure and meaning of morphologically complex words: Impact on reading. *Reading and Writing: An Interdisciplinary Journal, 12,* 169–190.

Carlo, M., August, D., McLaughlin, B., Snow, C., Dressler, C., Lippman, D., Lively, T., & White, C. (2004). Closing the gap: Addressing the vocabulary needs of English-language learners in bilingual and mainstream classrooms. *Reading Research Quarterly, 39*(2), 188–215.

Carroll, J. B., Davies, P., & Richman, B. (1971). *The American heritage word frequency book.* Boston: Houghton Mifflin.

Carver, R. P. (1992). What do standardized tests of reading comprehension measure in terms of efficiency, accuracy, and rate? *Reading Research Quarterly, 27*(4), 346–359.

Carver, R. P. (1994). Percentage of unknown vocabulary words in text as a function of the relative difficulty of the text: Implications for instruction. *Journal of Reading Behavior, 26*(4), 413–437.

Carver, R. P. (2003). The highly lawful relationships among pseudoword decoding, word identification, spelling, listening, and reading. *Scientific Studies of Reading, 7*(2), 127–154.

Carver, R. P., & Leibert, R. E. (1995). The effect of reading library books at different levels of difficulty upon gain in reading ability. *Reading Research Quarterly, 30*(1), 26–48.

Cassidy, J., & Cassidy, D. (2002, December/2003, January). What's hot, what's not for 2003. *Reading Today, 20*(3), 1–2.

Cassidy, J., & Cassidy, D. (2003, December/2004, January). What's hot, what's not for 2004. *Reading Today, 21*(3), 3.

Chall, J., & Dale, E. (1995). *Readability revisited: The new Dale-Chall readability formula.* Cambridge, MA: Brookline Books.

Chall, J. S. (1958). *Readability: An appraisal of research and application.* Columbus: Ohio State University.

Clay, M. M. (1991). Introducing a new storybook to young readers. *The Reading Teacher, 45*(4), 264–273.

Clay, M. M. (1993). *An observation survey of early literacy achievement.* Portsmouth, NH: Heinemann.

Cline, Z., & Necochea, J. (2003). My mother never read to me. *Journal of Adolescent & Adult Literacy, 47*(2), 122–128.

Coady, J., Magoto, J., Hubbard, P., Graney, J., & Mokhtari, K. (1993). High frequency vocabulary and reading proficiency in ESL readers. In T. Huckin, M. Haynes, & J. Coady (Eds.), *Second Language Reading and Vocabulary Learning* (pp. 217–228). Norwood, NJ: Ablex.

Collier, V. P. (1989). How long? A synthesis of research on academic achievement in a second language. *TESOL Quarterly, 23,* 509–631.

Coxhead, A. (2000). A new academic word list. *TESOL Quarterly, 34*(2), 213–238.

Craik, F., & Lockhart, R. (1972). Levels of processing: A framework for memory research. *Journal of Verbal Learning & Verbal Behavior, 11,* 671–684.

Cummins, J. (1994). The acquisition of English as a second language. In K. Spangenberg-Urbschat & R. Pritchard (Eds.), *Kids come in all languages: Reading instruction for ESL students* (pp. 36–62). Newark, DE: International Reading Association.

Cunningham, A. E., & Stanovich, K. E. (1991). Tracking the unique effects of print exposure in children: Associations with vocabulary, general knowledge, and spelling. *Journal of Educational Psychology, 83,* 264–274.

Cunningham, A. E., & Stanovich, K. (1998). What reading does for the mind. *American Educator, 22,* 8–15.

Cunningham, P. M. (1995). *Phonics they use: Words for reading and writing* (2nd ed.). New York: HarperCollins.

Curtis, M. E. (1987). Vocabulary testing and vocabulary instruction. In M. G. McKeown & M. E. Curtis (Eds.), *The nature of vocabulary acquisition* (pp. 37–51). Hillsdale, NJ: Lawrence Erlbaum Associates.

D'Anna, C. A., Zechmeister, E. B., & Hall, J. W. (1991). Toward a meaningful definition of vocabulary size. *Journal of Reading Behavior, 23,* 109–122.

Dale, E., & O'Rourke, J. (1986). *Vocabulary building.* Columbus, OH: Zaner-Bloser.

Davidson, A., & Green, G. M. (Eds.). (1988). *Linguistic complexity and text comprehension: Readability issues reconsidered.* Hillsdale, NJ: Lawrence Erlbaum Associates.

Davis, F. B. (1944). Fundamental factors of comprehension in reading. *Psychometrika, 9,* 185–197.

Davison, A., & Kantor, R. N. (1982). On the failure of readability formulas to define readable texts: A case study from adaptations. *Reading Research Quarterly, 17*(2), 187–209.

De Temple, J. M. (1994). *Book reading styles of low-income mothers with preschoolers and children's later literacy skills.* Unpublished doctoral dissertation, Harvard University, Cambridge, MA.

De Temple, J. M., & Snow, C. (2003). Learning words from books. In A. van Kleeck, S. Stahl, & E. Bauer (Eds.), *On reading books to children: Parents and teachers.* Mahwah, NJ: Lawrence Erlbaum Associates.

Dickinson, D., McCabe, A., Anastopoulos, L., Peisner-Feinberg, E., & Poe, M. (2003). The comprehensive language approach to early literacy: The interrelationships among vocabulary, phonological sensitivity, and print knowledge among preschool-aged children. *Journal of Educational Psychology, 95,* 465–481.

Dickinson, D., & Smith, M. (1994). Long-term effects of preschool teachers' book readings on low-income children's vocabulary and story comprehension. *Reading Research Quarterly, 29*(2), 104–122.

Dickinson, D., & Tabors, P. (2001). *Beginning literacy with language.* Baltimore: Paul H. Brookes.

Duke, N., & Pearson, P. D. (2002). Effective practices for developing reading comprehension. In A. E. Farstrup & S. J. Samuels (Eds.), *What research has to say about reading instruction* (3rd ed., pp. 205–242). Newark, DE: International Reading Association.

Duke, N. K. (2000). 3.6 minutes per day: The scarcity of informational texts in first grade. *Reading Research Quarterly, 35,* 202–224.

Dupuy, H. P. (1974). *The rationale, development and standardization of a basic word vocabulary test.* Washington, DC: U.S. government Printing Office. (DHEW Publication No. HRA 74-1334)

Durkin, D. (1978/1979). What classroom observations reveal about reading comprehension instruction. *Reading Research Quarterly, 14,* 481–533.

Eeds, M., & Cockrum, W. (1985). Teaching word meanings by expanding schemata vs. dictionary work vs. reading in context. *Journal of Reading, 28*(6), 492–497.

Egan, T. (1997). *Burnt toast on Davenport Street.* New York: Houghton Mifflin.

Ehri, L. C., Nunes, S. R., Willows, D. M., Schuster, B. V., Yoghoub-Zadeh, Z., & Shanahan, T. (2001). Phonemic awareness instruction helps children learn to read: Evidence from the National Reading Panel's meta-analysis. *Reading Research Quarterly, 36*(3), 250–287.

Elley, W. (1989). Vocabulary acquisition from listening to stories. *Reading Research Quarterly, 24,* 174–187.

Elley, W. B. (1991). Acquiring literacy in a second language: The effect of book-based programs. *Language Learning, 41*(3), 375–411.

Elley, W. B. (2000). The potential of book floods for raising literacy levels. *International Review of Education, 46,* 233–255.

Elley, W. B., & Mangubhai, F. (1983). The impact of reading on second language learning. *Reading Research Quarterly, 19,* 53–67.

Espy, W. R. (1978). *O thou improper, thou uncommon noun: A bobtailed, generally chronological listing of proper names that have become improper and uncommonly common, together with a smattering of proper names commonly used ... and certain other diversions.* New York: Potter.

Feitelson, D., Goldstein, Z., Iraqi, J., & Share, D. (1993). Effects of listening to story reading on aspects of literacy acquisition in a diglossic situation. *Reading Research Quarterly, 28,* 70–79.

Flexner, S. B. (1987). *The Random House dictionary of the English language,* 2nd ed., unabridged. New York: Random House.

Foil, C. R., & Alber, S. R. (2002). Fun and effective ways to build your students' vocabulary. *Intervention in School and Clinic, 37*(3), 131–139.

Foorman, B. R., Francis, D. J., Davidson, K. C., Harm, M. W., & Griffin, J. (2004). Variability in text features in six grade-1 basal reading programs. *Scientific Studies of Reading, 8*(2), 167–197.

Fountas, I. C., & Pinnell, G. S. (1996). *Guided reading: Good first teaching for all children.* Portsmouth, NH: Heinemann.

Fowler, A. E. (1991). How early phonological development might set the stage for phonological awareness. In S. Brady & D. Shankweiler (Eds.), *Phonological processes in literacy: A tribute to Isabelle Y. Liberman* (pp. 97–117). Hillsdale, NJ: Lawrence Erlbaum Associates.

Freebody, P., & Anderson, R. C. (1983). Effects on text comprehension of differing proportions and locations of difficult vocabulary. *Journal of Reading Behavior, 15*(3), 19–39.

Freeman, C. (1987). A study of the Degrees of Reading Power test. In R. O. Freedle & R. P. Duran (Eds.), *Cognitive and linguistic analyses of test performance* (pp. 245–297). Westport, CT: Ablex.

Fry, E. B. (1977). Fry's readability graph: Clarification, validity and extension to level 17. *Journal of Reading, 20,* 242–252.

Fry, E. B., Kress, J. E., & Fountoukidis, D. L. (1993). *The reading teacher's book of lists* (3rd ed.). Englewood Cliffs, NJ: Prentice-Hall.

Fukkink, R. G., & de Glopper, K. (1998). Effects of instruction in deriving word meaning from context: A meta-analysis. *Review of Educational Research, 68*(4), 450–469.

Funk, C. E. (1948). *A hog on ice and other curious expressions.* New York: Harper & Row.

Funk, C. E. (1955). *Heavens to Betsy! and other curious sayings.* New York: HarperCollins.

Funk, C. E. (1958). *Horsefeathers and other curious words.* New York: HarperCollins.

Garner, R., Gillingham, M., & White, C. (1989). Effects of "seductive details" on macroprocessing and microprocessing in adults and children. *Cognition and Instruction, 6,* 41–57.

Glick, A., & Olson, R. (1998). Company touts system to match students and books. *School Library Journal, 44*(9), 94.

Goerss, B., Beck, I., & McKeown, M. (1999). Increasing remedial students' ability to derive word meaning from context. *Reading Psychology, 20,* 151–175.

Goodman, K. S. (1965). A linguistic study of cues and miscues in reading. *Elementary English, 42,* 639–643.

Goulden, R., Nation, P., & Read, J. (1990). How large can a receptive vocabulary be? *Applied Linguistics, 11,* 341–363.

Graves, M. F. (1986). Vocabulary learning and instruction. In E. Z. Rothkopf & L. C. Ehri (Eds.), *Review of research in education* (Vol. 13, pp. 49–89). Washington, DC: American Educational Research Association.

Graves, M. (2000). A vocabulary program to complement and bolster a middle-grade comprehension program. In B. Taylor, M. Graves, & P. van den Broek (Eds.), *Reading for meaning: Fostering comprehension in the middle grades* (pp. 116–135). Newark, DE: International Reading Association.

Graves, M. F., & Watts-Taffe, S. M. (2002). The place of word consciousness in a research-based vocabulary program. In A. E. Farstrup & S. J. Samuels (Eds.), *What research has to say about reading instruction* (3rd ed., pp. 140–165). Newark, DE: International Reading Association.

Green, G. M. (1984). *Some remarks on how words mean* (Technical Report No. 307). University of Illinois at Urbana Champaign: Center for the Study of Reading.

Guthrie, J. T., Schafer, W. D., & Hutchinson, S. R. (1991). Relations of document literacy and prose literacy to occupational and societal characteristics of young black and white adults. *Reading Research Quarterly, 26*(1), 30–48.

Guthrie, J. T., Schafer, W. D., Wang, Y. Y., & Afflerbach, P. (1995). Relationships of instruction of reading: An exploration of social, cognitive, and instructional connections. *Reading Research Quarterly, 30*(1), 8–25.

Gwynne, F. (1970). *The king who rained*. New York: Simon & Schuster.

Gwynne, F. (1976). *A chocolate moose for dinner*. New York: Simon & Schuster.

Gwynne, F. (1980). *The sixteen hand horse*. New York: Simon & Schuster.

Gwynne, F. (1988). *Little pigeon toad*. New York: Simon & Schuster.

Haggard, M. R. '(1986). The vocabulary self-collection strategy: Using student interest and world knowledge to enhance vocabulary growth. *Journal of Reading, 29*, 634–642.

Hall, R. (1989). *When sniglets ruled the earth*. New York: Collier Books.

Harrison, C. (1980). *Readability in the classroom*. Cambridge: Cambridge University Press.

Hart, B., & Risley, T. (1995). *Meaningful differences in the everyday lives of young American children*. Baltimore: Paul H. Brookes.

Hart, B., & Risley, T. (1999). *The social world of children learning to talk*. Baltimore: Brookes.

Hayes, D. P., & Ahrens, M. G. (1988). Vocabulary simplification for children: A special case of "motherese"? *Journal of Child Language, 15*(2), 395–410.

Heimlich, J. E., & Pittelman, S. D. (1986). *Semantic Mapping: Classroom Applications*. Newark, DE: International Reading Association.

Hiebert, E. H. (1999). Text matters in learning to read (Distinguished Educators Series). *The Reading Teacher, 52*, 552–568.

Higa, M. (1963). Interference effects of intralist word relationships in verbal learning. *Journal of Verbal Learning and Verbal Behavior, 2*, 170–175.

Hsueh-chao, M., & Nation, P. (2000). Unknown vocabulary density and reading comprehension. *Reading in a Foreign Language, 13*(1), 403–430.

Jenkins, J. R., Pany, D., & Schreck, J. (1978, August). *Vocabulary and reading comprehension: Instructional effects* (Technical Report No. 100). Champaign: University of Illinois, Center for the Study of Reading. (ERIC Document Reproduction Service No. ED 160 999)

Johnson, D. D., Johnson, B., & Schlichting, K. (2004). Logology: Word and language play. In J. F. Baumann & E. J. Kame'enui (Eds.), *Vocabulary instruction: Research to practice* (pp. 179–200). New York: Guilford.

Kaplan, J. (Ed.). (2002). *Bartlett's familiar quotations: A collection of passages, phrases, and proverbs traced to their sources in ancient and modern literature* (17th ed.). Boston: Little Brown.

Klausmeier, H. J., Ghatala, E. S., & Frayer, D. A. (1974). *Conceptual learning and development: A cognitive view*. New York: Academic Press.

Klingner, J., & Vaughn, S. (1999). Promoting reading comprehension, content learning, and English acquisition through Collaborative Strategic Reading (CSR). *The Reading Teacher, 52*(7), 738–747.

Koskinen, P. S., Wilson, R., & Jensema, C. J. (1986). Closed-captioned television: A new tool for reading instruction. *Reading World, 24*(4), 1–7.

Krashen, S. (1993). *The power of reading: Insights from the research*. Englewood, CO: Libraries Unlimited.

Krashen, S. (2001, October). More smoke and mirrors: A critique of the National Reading Panel report on fluency. *Phi Delta Kappan, 83*(2), 119–123.

Krashen, S. D. (1987). *Principles and practices in second language acquisition*. New York: Prentice-Hall.

Kuhn, M. R., & Stahl, S. (1998). Teaching children to learn word meanings from context: A synthesis and some questions. *Journal of Literacy Research, 30*(1), 119–138.

Kuhn, M. R., & Stahl, S. A. (2003). Fluency: A review of developmental and remedial practices. *Journal of Educational Psychology, 95*(1), 3–21.

LaBerge, D., & Samuels, S. J. (1974). Toward a theory of automatic information processing in reading. *Cognitive Psychology, 6*, 293–323.

Laufer, B. (1989). What percentage of lexis is essential for comprehension? In C. Lauren & M. Nordman (Eds.), *Special language: From humans thinking to thinking machine* (pp. 69–75). Clevedon, England: Multilingual Matters.

Laufer, B. (1997). The lexical plight in second language reading: Words you don't know, words you think you know, and words you can't guess. In J. Coady & T. Huckin (Eds.), *Second Language Vocabulary Acquisition* (pp. 20–34). Cambridge: Cambridge University Press.

Lederer, R. (1989). *Crazy English*. New York: Simon & Schuster.

Lee, H. (1960). *To Kill a Mockingbird*. Philadelphia, PA: Lippincott.

McDermott, R. P. (1987). The explanation of minority school failure, again. *Anthropology and Education Quarterly, 18*, 361–364.

McGinley, W. J., & Denner, P. R. (1987). Story impressions: A prereading/writing activity. *Journal of Reading, 31*(3), 248–253.

McKeown, M. (1993). Creating definitions for young word learners. *Reading Research Quarterly, 28*(1), 16–33.

McKeown, M., & Beck, I. (2003). Taking advantage of read-alouds to help children make sense of decontextualized language. In A. van Kleeck, S. Stahl, & E. Bauer (Eds.), *On reading books to children* (pp. 159–176). Mahwah, NJ: Lawrence Erlbaum Associates.

McKeown, M., Beck, I., Omanson, R., & Perfetti, C. (1983). The effects of long-term vocabulary instruction on reading comprehension: A replication. *Journal of Reading Behavior, 15*(1), 3–18.

McKeown, M. G., Beck, I. L., Omanson, R. C., & Pople, M. T. (1985). Some effects of the nature and frequency of vocabulary instruction on the knowledge and use of words. *Reading Research Quarterly, 20*, 522–535.

Metsala, J. L. (1999). Young children's phonological awareness and nonword repetition as a function of vocabulary development. *Journal of Educational Psychology, 91*, 3–19.

Metsala, J. L., & Walley, A. C. (1998). Spoken vocabulary growth and the segmental restructuring of lexical representations: Precursors to phonemic awareness and early reading ability. In J. L. Metsala & L. C. Ehri (Eds.), *Word recognition in beginning literacy* (pp. 89–120). Mahwah, NJ: Lawrence Erlbaum Associates.

Mezinski, K. (1983). Issues concerning the acquisition of knowledge: Effects of vocabulary training on reading comprehension. *Review of Educational Research, 53*(2), 253–279.

Microsoft. (1999). *Encarta Reference Suite 99*. Seattle, WA: Microsoft.

Miller, G., & Gildea, P. (1987). How children learn words. *Scientific American, 257*(3), 94–99.

Moll, L. C., Amanti, C., Neff, D., & Gonzalez, N. (1992). Funds of knowledge for teaching: Using a qualitative approach to connect homes and classrooms. *Theory into Practice, 31*(2), 132–140.

Moll, L., & Greenberg, J. (1991). Creating zones of possibilities: Combining social contexts for instruction. In L. Moll (Ed.), *Vygotsky and education* (pp. 319–348). Cambridge, UK: Cambridge University Press.

Mori, Y. (2002). Individual differences in the integration of information from context and word parts in interpreting unknown kanji words. *Applied Psycholinguistics, 23*, 375–397.

Mori, Y., & Nagy, W. (1999). Integration of information from context and word elements in interpreting novel kanji compounds. *Reading Research Quarterly, 34*, 80–101.

Morris, D., Bloodgood, J., Lomax, R., & Perney, J. (2003). Developmental steps in learning to read: A longitudinal study in kindergarten and first grade. *Reading Research Quarterly, 38*(3), 302–328.

Morrison, F. J., Williams, M., & Massetti, G. (1998, April). *The contributions of IQ and schooling to academic achievement*. Paper presented at the Annual Meeting of the Society for the Scientific Study of Reading, San Diego, CA.

Nagy, W. E., & Anderson, R. C. (1984). How many words are there in printed school English? *Reading Research Quarterly, 19*, 304–330.

Nagy, W. E., Anderson, R. C., & Herman, P. (1987). Learning word meanings from context during normal reading. *American Educational Research Journal, 24*, 237–270.

Nagy, W. E., Berninger, V., Abbott, R., Vaughan, K., & Vermeulen, K. (2003). Relationship of morphology and other language skills to literacy skills in at-risk second grade readers and at-risk fourth grade writers. *Journal of Educational Psychology, 95*, 730–742.

Nagy, W. E., Diakidoy, I., & Anderson, R. C. (1993). The acquisition of morphology: Learning the contribution of suffixes to the meanings of derivatives. *Journal of Reading Behavior, 25*, 155–170.

Nagy, W. E., & Herman, P. A. (1987). Breadth and depth of vocabulary knowledge: Implications for acquisition and instruction. In M. McKeown & M. Curtis (Eds.), *The nature of vocabulary acquisition* (pp. 19–35). Hillsdale, NJ: Lawrence Erlbaum Associates.

Nagy, W. E., Herman, P., & Anderson, R. (1985). Learning words from context. *Reading Research Quarterly, 19*, 304–330.

Nagy, W. E., & Scott, J. A. (2000). Vocabulary processes. In M. L. Kamil, P. B. Mosenthal, P. D. Pearson, & R. Barr (Eds.), *Handbook of Reading Research* (Vol., pp. 269–284). Mahwah, NJ: Lawrence Erlbaum Associates.

Nagy, W. E., Winsor, P., Osborn, J., & O'Flahavan, J. (1993). Structural analysis: Guidelines for instruction. In F. Lehr & J. Osborn (Eds.), *Reading, language, and literacy: Instruction for the twenty-first century* (pp. 45–58). Hillsdale, NJ: Lawrence Erlbaum Associates.

Nation, I. S. P. (1990). *Teaching and learning vocabulary.* Florence, KY: Heinle & Heinle.

Nation, I. S. P. (2001). *Learning vocabulary in another language.* Cambridge, UK: Cambridge University Press.

Nation, P. (1994). *New ways in teaching vocabulary.* Alexandria, VA: Teachers of English to Speakers of Other Languages, Inc.

National Reading Panel. (2000). *Teaching children to read: An evidence-based assessment of the scientific research literature on reading and its implications for reading instruction.* Washington, DC: National Institute of Child Health and Human Development.

Neuman, S. B., & Celano, D. (2001). Access to print in low-income and middle-income communities: An ecological study of four neighborhoods. *Reading Research Quarterly, 36*(1), 8–26.

Neuman, S. B., & Koskinen, P. (1992). Captioned television as comprehensible input: Effects of incidental word learning from context for language minority students. *Reading Research Quarterly, 27*(1), 94–106.

Newman, J. M. (1991). *Interwoven conversations: Learning and teaching through critical reflection.* Toronto: OISE Press.

Nicholson, T. (1991). Do children read words better in context or in lists: A classic study revisited. *Journal of Educational Psychology, 83*(4), 444–450.

Nist, S. L., & Olejnik, S. (1995). The role of context and dictionary definitions on varying levels of word knowledge. *Reading Research Quarter, 30*, 172–193.

Nock, A. J. (1943). *Memoirs of a superfluous man.* New York: Harper.

O'Rourke, J. (1979). *Prefixes, roots, and suffixes: Their testing and usage.* Paper presented at the annual meeting of the International Reading Association, Atlanta, GA.

Ordóñez, C. L., Carlo, M. S., Snow, C. E., & McLaughlin, B. (2002). Depth and breadth of vocabulary in two languages: Which vocabulary skills transfer? *Journal of Educational Psychology, 94*(4), 719–728.

Palincsar, A. S., & Brown, A. L. (1984). Reciprocal teaching of comprehension-fostering and comprehension-monitoring activities. *Cognition and Instruction, 1*, 117–175.

Penno, J. F., Wilkinson, I. A. G., & Moore, D. W. (2002). Vocabulary acquisition from teacher explanation and repeated listening to stories: Do they overcome the Matthew effect? *Journal of Educational Psychology, 94*(1), 23–33.

Person, N. K., & Graesser, A. G. (1999). Evolution of discourse during cross-age tutoring. In A. O'Donnell & A. King (Eds.), *Cognitive perspectives on peer learning* (pp. 69–86). Mahwah, NJ: Lawrence Erlbaum Associates.

Peterson, B. (2001). *Literary pathways: Selecting books to support new readers.* Portsmouth, NH: Heinemann.

Pressley, M. (1988). *Elaborate interrogation.* Paper presented at the annual meeting of the International Reading Association, New Orleans, LA.

Qian, D. D. (1999). Assessing the roles of depth and breadth of vocabulary knowledge in reading comprehension. *Canadian Modern Language Review, 26*(2), 282–307.

Quealy, R. J. (1969). Senior high school students use of contextual aids in reading. *Reading Research Quarterly, 4*(4), 512–533.

Richek, M. A. (in press). Words are wonderful! Interactive time-efficient strategies to teach meaning vocabulary. *The Reading Teacher.*

Rowling, J. K. (1998). *Harry Potter and the sorcerer's stone.* New York, NY: Scholastic Inc.

Ruddell, M., & Shearer, B. (2002). "Extraordinary," "tremendous," "exhilarating," "magnificent": Middle school at-risk students become avid word learners with the vocabulary self-collection strategy (VSS). *Journal of Adolescent and Adult Literacy, 45*(4), 352–363.

Samuels, S. J. (2002). Reading fluency: Its development and assessment. In A. E. Farstrup & S. J. Samuels (Eds.), *What research has to say about reading instruction* (3rd ed., pp. 166–183). Newark, DE: International Reading Association.

San Souci, R. D. (1988). *The talking eggs: A folktale from the American South.* New York: Dial Books for Young Readers.

San Souci, R. D., & Pinkney, J. (1989). *The talking eggs: A folktale from the American South.* New York: Dial Books for Young Readers.

Schatz, E. K., & Baldwin, R. S. (1986). Context clues are unreliable predictors of word meanings. *Reading Research Quarterly, 21*(4), 439–453.

Schwanenflugel, P., Stahl, S., & McFalls, E. (1997). Partial word knowledge and vocabulary growth during reading comprehension. *Journal of Literacy Research, 29*(4), 531–553.

Schwartz, R. M., & Raphael, T. E. (1985). Concept of definition: A key to improving students' vocabulary. *The Reading Teacher, 39*(2), 198–205.

Scott, J., Jamieson-Noel, D., & Asselin, M. (2003). Vocabulary instruction throughout the school day in 23 Canadian upper-elementary classrooms. *The Elementary School Journal, 103*(3), 269–286.

Scott, J. A., & Nagy, W. E. (1997). Understanding the definitions of unfamiliar words. *Reading Research Quarterly, 32,* 184–200.

Scott, J. A., & Nagy, W. E. (2004). Developing word consciousness. In J. Baumann & E. Kame'enui (Eds.), *Vocabulary instruction: Research to practice* (pp. 201–217). New York: Guilford.

Shefelbine, J. (1990). Student factors related to variability in learning word meanings from context. *Journal of Reading Behavior, 22,* 71–97.

Shelley, P. B. (1821/1965). *A defense of poetry.* New York: Bobbs-Merrill.

Simpson, J. A., & Weiner, E. S. C. (1989). *The Oxford English dictionary* (2nd ed.). Oxford: Clarendon Press.

Sinclair, J. (1995). *Collins COBUILD English Dictionary.* London: HarperCollins.

Smith, M. K. (1941). Measurement of the size of general English vocabulary through the elementary grades and high school. *Genetic Psychology Monographs, 24,* 311–345.

Smith, R. R. (2000). How the Lexile framework operates. *Popular Measurement, 3*(1), 18–19.

Snow, C. E., Barnes, W., Chandler, J., Goodman, I., & Hemphill, L. (1992). *Unfulfilled expectations: Home and school influences on literacy.* Cambridge, MA: Harvard University Press.

Snow, C., Burns, M. S., & Griffin, P. (1998). *Preventing reading difficulties in young children.* Washington, DC: National Academy Press.

Spiro, R. J., Coulson, R. L., Feltovich, P. J., & Anderson, D. K. (1988). *Cognitive flexibility theory: Advanced knowledge acquisition in ill-structured domains* (Technical Report No. 441). Urbana, IL: University of Illinois, Center for the Study of Reading. (ERIC Document Reproduction Service No. ED302821)

Spiro, R. J., Coulson, R. L., Feltovich, P. J., & Anderson, D. K. (2004). Cognitive flexibility theory: Advanced knowledge acquisition in ill-structured domains. In R. Ruddell & N. J. Unrau (Eds.), *Theoretical models and processes of reading* (5th ed., pp. 640–653). Newark, DE: International Reading Association.

Spiro, R. J., & Jehng, J. (1990). Cognitive flexibility and hypertext: Theory and technology for the non-linear and multidimensional traversal of complex subject matter. In D. Nix & R. Spiro (Eds.), *Cognition, education, and multimedia* (pp. 163–205). Hillsdale, NJ: Lawrence Erlbaum Associates.

Stahl, S. A. (1986). Three principles of effective vocabulary instruction. *Journal of Reading 29*(7), 662–668.

Stahl, S. A. (1999). *Vocabulary development*. Cambridge, MA: Brookline Books.

Stahl, S. A., Burdge, J., Machuga, M., & Stecyk, S. (1992). The effects of semantic grouping on learning word meaning. *Reading Psychology, 13*(1), 19–35.

Stahl, S. A., & Clark, C. H. (1987). The effects of participatory expectations in classroom discussion on the learning of science vocabulary. *American Educational Research Journal, 24,* 541–556.

Stahl, S. A., & Fairbanks, M. (1986). The effects of vocabulary instruction: A model-based meta-analysis. *Review of Educational Research, 56,* 72–110.

Stahl, S. A., & Jacobson, M. G. (1986). Vocabulary difficulty, prior knowledge, and text comprehension. *Journal of Reading Behavior, 18*(4), 309–323.

Stahl, S. A., Jacobson, M. G., Davis, C. E., & Davis, R. L. (1989). Prior knowledge and difficult vocabulary in the comprehension of unfamiliar text. *Reading Research Quarterly, 24*(1), 27–43.

Stahl, S. A., & Kapinus, B. A. (1991). Possible sentences: Predicting word meanings to teach content area vocabulary. *The Reading Teacher, 45,* 36–43.

Stahl, S. A., Richek, M. G., & Vandevier, R. (1991). Learning word meanings through listening: A sixth grade replication. In J. Zutell & S. McCormick (Eds.), *Learning factors/teacher factors: Issues in literacy research. Fortieth yearbook of the National Reading Conference* (pp. 185–192). Chicago: National Reading Conference.

Stahl, S. A., Suttles, W., & Pagnucco, J. R. (1996). The effects of traditional and process literacy instruction on first graders' reading and writing achievement and orientation toward reading. *Journal of Educational Research, 89,* 131–144.

Stahl, S. A., & Vancil, S. J. (1986). Discussion is what makes semantic maps work. *The Reading Teacher, 40,* 62–67.

Stanovich, K. E. (1986). Matthew effects in reading: Some consequences of individual differences in the acquisition of literacy. *Reading Research Quarterly, 21,* 360–407.

Stanovich, K. E. (1993). Does reading make you smarter? Literacy and the development of verbal intelligence. In H. Reese (Ed.), *Advances in child development and behavior* (Vol. 24, pp. 133–180). San Diego, CA: Academic Press.

Stanovich, K. E. (2000). *Progress in understanding reading: Scientific foundations and new frontiers*. New York: Guilford.

Stanovich, K. E., & Cunningham, A. E. (1993). Where does knowledge come from? Specific associations between print exposure and information acquisition. *Journal of Educational Psychology, 85,* 211–229.

Sternberg, R., & Powell, J. (1983). Comprehending verbal comprehension. *American Psychologist, 38,* 878–893.

Sticht, T., & James, J. (1984). Listening and reading. In R. Barr, M. Kamil, & P. Mosenthal (Eds.), *Handbook of Reading Research* (Vol. 1, pp. 293–317). White Plains, NY: Longman.

Swanborn, M. S. L., & de Glopper, K. (1999). Incidental word learning while reading: A meta-analysis. *Review of Educational Research, 69*(3), 261–285.

Tagliabue, J. (2003, July 5). In Portugal, cork makers just say não to screwcap. *The New York Times,* p. B1.

Tan, A., & Nicholson, T. (1997). Flashcards revisited: Training poor readers to read words faster improves their comprehension of text. *Journal of Educational Psychology, 69*(2), 276–288.

Taylor, B. M., Frye, B. J., & Maruyama, G. M. (1990). Time spent reading and reading growth. *American Educational Research Journal, 27*(2), 351–362.

Taylor, B. M., Pressley, M. P., & Pearson, P. D. (2000). *Research-supported characteristics of teachers and schools that promote reading achievement*. Washington, DC: National Education Association, Reading Matters Research Report.

Thorndike, E. L. (1917). Reading as reasoning: A study of mistakes in paragraph meaning. *Journal of Educational Psychology, 8,* 323–332.

Thorndike, R. L. (1974). Reading as reasoning. *Reading Research Quarterly, 9,* 137–147.

Tinkham, T. (1993). The effect of semantic clustering on the learning of second language vocabulary. *System, 21*(3), 371–380.

Tompkins, G. E. (2003). *Literacy for the 21st century* (3rd ed.). Upper Saddle River, NJ: Merrill Prentice-Hall.

Tovani, C. (2000). *I read it, but I don't get it: Comprehension strategies for adolescent readers.* Portland, ME: Stenhouse.

Turner, J. C. (1995). The influence of classroom contexts on young children's motivation for literacy. *Reading Research Quarterly, 30,* 10–41.

Tyler, A., & Nagy, W. (1990). Use of derivational morphology during reading. *Cognition, 36,* 17–34.

Van Allsburg, C. (1983). *The Wreck of the Zephyr.* Boston: Houghton Mifflin.

van Kleeck, A., Stahl, S., & Bauer, E. (Eds.). (2003). *On reading books to children.* Mahwah, NJ: Lawrence Erlbaum Associates.

Vermeer, A. (2001). Breadth and depth of vocabulary in relation to L1/L2 acquisition and frequency of input. *Applied Psycholinguistics, 22*(2), 217–234.

Waring, R. (1997). The negative effects of learning words in semantic sets: A replication. *System, 25*(2), 261–274.

Watson, R. (1985). Towards a theory of definition. *Journal of Child Language, 12,* 181–197.

Watts, S. M. (1995). Vocabulary instruction during reading lessons in six classrooms. *Journal of Reading Behavior, 27*(3), 399–424.

Wells, G. (1986). *The meaning makers: Children learning language and using language to learn.* Portsmouth, NH: Heinemann.

West, M. (1953). *A general service list of English words.* London: Longman.

White, E. B. (1952). *Charlotte's web.* New York: Harper & Row.

White, T., Graves, M., & Slater, W. (1990). Growth of reading vocabulary in diverse elementary schools: Decoding and word meaning. *Journal of Educational Psychology, 82,* 281–290.

White, T., Power, M., & White, S. (1989). Morphological analysis: Implications for teaching and understanding vocabulary growth. *Reading Research Quarterly, 24,* 283–304.

White, T., Sowell, J., & Yanagihara, A. (1989). Teaching elementary students to use word-part clues. *The Reading Teacher, 42,* 302–308.

Wigfield, A. (1997). Children's motivations for reading and reading engagement. In J. T. Guthrie & A. Wigfield (Eds.), *Reading engagement: Motivating readers through integrated instruction* (pp. 14–33). Newark, DE: International Reading Association.

Willingham, D. T. (2002). Allocating student study time: "Massed" versus "distributed" practice. *American Educator, 26*(2), 37–39, 47.

Willingham, D. T. (2003). Ask the cognitive scientist. Inflexible knowledge: The first step to expertise. *American Educator, 26*(4), 31–33.

Wixson, K. K. (1986). Vocabulary instruction and children's comprehension of basal stories. *Reading Research Quarterly, 21*(3), 317–329.

Wood, P. H., Nemeth, J. S., & Brooks, C. C. (1985). Criterion-related validity of the Degrees of Reading Power Test (Form CP-1a). *Educational & Psychological Measurement, 45*(4), 965–969.

Zakaluk, B. L., & Samuels, S. J. (Eds.). (1988). *Readability: Its past, present and future.* Newark, DE: International Reading Association.

Zechmeister, E., Chronis, A., Cull, W., D'Anna, C., & Healy, N. (1995). Growth of a functionally important lexicon. *Journal of Reading Behavior, 27*(2), 201–212.

Zeno, S. M., Ivens, S. H., Millard, R. T., & Duvvuri, R. (1995). *The educator's word frequency guide.* Brewster, NY: Touchstone Applied Science Associates, Inc.

Author Index

A

Abbott, R., 12, 141, 160, 165
Adams, M. J., 161
Addison, J., 137
Afflerbach, P., 128, 130
Ahrens, M. G., 40, 126
Alber, S. R., 70
Alighieri, D., 47
Amanti, C., 6
Anderson, D. K., 43, 80, 91
Anderson, R. C., 4, 5, 9, 10, 14, 27, 28, 29, 32,
        42, 62, 129, 134, 140, 159, 160,
        162, 164, 174, 183
Anglin, J. M., 21, 27, 28, 32, 141, 165
Asselin, M., 7
Augustine, 173
Ayto, J., 153

B

Baldwin, R. S., 174, 175
Barnes, W., 5
Baumann, J. F., 16, 181
Bear, D. R., 54
Beck, I. L., 15, 27, 29, 44, 66, 68, 102, 111,
        115, 119, 120, 121, 122, 133, 138,
        140, 141, 143, 176, 177, 178
Berninger, V., 12, 141, 160, 165
Biemiller, A., 20, 27, 53, 57, 128, 132, 133, 134
Blachowicz, C. L., 140
Bloodgood, J., 12
Boettcher, J. A., 173
Boland, E. M., 16, 181
Brabham, E., 134

Brautigan, R., 39, 40
Brett, A., 134
Bridge, C., 103
Brooks, C. C., 20
Brown, A. L., 177
Buckingham, B. R., 98
Buikema, J., 157
Burgess, A., 61
Burns, M. S., 134, 135

C

Cantalini, M., 5, 27
Carlisle, J. F., 141, 160
Carlo, M. S., 186
Carroll, J. B., 50, 127
Carver, R. P., 4, 20, 128, 175
Cassidy, D., 7
Cassidy, J., 7
Celano, D., 127
Chall, J., 18, 19, 23, 24
Chandler, J., 5
Chronis, A., 30
Clark, C. H., 70, 87, 88
Clay, M. M., 112
Cline, Z., 132
Coady, J., 33
Cockrum, W., 81
Collier, V. P., 6, 40
Coulson, R. L., 43, 80, 91
Coxhead, A., 102
Craik, F., 192
Cull, W., 30
Cummins, J., 6, 40, 134
Cunningham, A. E., 14, 40, 127, 128, 129

Cunningham, P. M., 161
Curtis, M. E., 103

D

D'Anna, C. A., 29, 30, 32
Dale, E., 19, 23, 160
Davidson, A., 24
Davidson, K. C., 19
Davies, P., 50, 127
Davis, C. E., 111
Davis, R. B., 9
Davis, R. L., 111
Davison, A., 24
de Glopper, K., 174, 177
De Temple, J. M., 116, 118
Denner, P. R., 71, 72
Diakidoy, I., 160
Dickinson, D., 6, 26, 134, 177
Dolch, E. W., 98
Duke, N., 134, 158
Dupuy, H. P., 29
Durkin, D., 7

E

Edwards, E. C., 16, 181
Egan, T., 120
Ehri. L. C., 12
Elley, W. B., 54, 128, 129
Espy, W. R., 153

F

Fairbanks, M., 15, 121, 191
Feitelson, D., 134
Feltovich, P., 80
Fielding, L., 129
Fisher, P., 140
Foil, C. R., 70
Foorman, B. R., 19
Fountas, I. C., 112
Fountoukidis, D. L., 98, 99, 160, 165
Fowler, A. E., 12
Francis, D. J., 19
Frayer, D. A., 79
Freebody, P., 4, 5, 9, 10, 14, 62
Freeman, C., 20
Fry, E. B., 18, 98, 99, 160, 165
Frye, B. J., 129
Fukkink, R. G., 174, 177
Funk, C. E., 152, 153

G

Garner, R., 56
Ghatala, E. S., 79
Gillingham, M., 56
Glick, A., 29

Goerss, B., 177, 178
Goldstein, Z., 134
Gonzalez, N., 6
Goodman, I., 5
Goodman, K. S., 103
Goulden, R., 29, 30, 32
Graesser, A. G., 119
Graney, J., 33
Graves, M. F., 14, 27, 36, 43, 48, 63, 128, 140, 157, 165
Green, G. M., 13, 24
Griffin, J., 19
Griffin, P., 134, 135
Guthrie, J. T., 4, 128, 130
Gwynne, F., 151

H

Haggard, M. R., 144
Haley, D., 103
Hall, J. W., 29, 30, 32
Harm, M. W., 19
Harrison, C., 18, 19, 22
Hart, B., 5, 116, 118, 132
Hayes, D. P., 40, 126
Healy, N., 30
Heimlich, J. E., 83, 84
Hemphill, L., 5
Herman, P. A., 27, 28, 29, 32, 134, 174
Hiebert, E. H., 21
Higa, M., 64
Hsueh-chao, M., 62
Hubbard, P., 33
Hurley, M., 134
Hutchinson, S. R., 4

I

Invernizzi, M., 54
Iraqi, J., 134

J

Jacobson, M. G., 11, 111
James, J., 53
Jamieson-Noel, D., 7
Jehng, J., 64
Jenkins, J. R., 62
Jensema, C. J., 106
Johnson, B., 140
Johnson, D. D., 140
Johnston, F., 54

K

Kame'enui, E., 16, 181
Kantor, R. N., 24
Kapinus, B. A., 94
Klausmeier, H. J., 79

Klingner, J., 16, 177
Koskinen, P. S., 106
Krashen, S., 128, 138
Kress, J. E., 98, 99, 160, 165
Kucan, L., 15, 102, 122, 133
Kuhn, M. R., 106, 174, 177

L

LaBerge, D., 13
Laufer, B., 19, 62
Lederer, R., 158
Lee, H., 56
Leibert, R. E., 128
Lockhart, R., 192
Lomax, R., 12
Lynch-Brown, C., 134

M

Magoto, J., 33
Makhtari, K., 33
Mangubhai, F., 129
Maruyama, G. M., 129
Massetti, G., 0
McCaslin, E. S., 176
McDermott, R. P., 138
McFalls, E., 44
McGinley, W. J., 71, 72
McKeown, M. G., 15, 27, 29, 44, 66, 68, 102,
        111, 115, 119, 120, 121, 122, 133,
        138, 140, 141, 143, 176, 177, 178,
        185, 186, 187
McLaughlin, B., 186
Metsala, J. L., 12
Mezynski, K., 13
Microsoft, 189
Miller, G., 140, 185, 188
Moll, L. C., 6
Moore, D. W., 54
Mori, Y., 188
Morris, D., 12
Morrison, F. J., 5, 27

N

Nagy, W. E., 12, 27, 28, 29, 32, 34, 42, 44, 134,
        140, 141, 157, 159, 160, 162, 164,
        165, 174, 183, 188
Nation, I. S. P., 50, 101, 107, 159
Nation, P., 29, 30, 32, 62
National Reading Panel, 15, 128, 129, 130
Necochea, J., 132
Neff, D., 6
Nemeth, J. S., 20
Neuman, S. B., 106, 127
Nicholson, T., 103
Nist, S. L., 140, 190, 192

Nock, A. J., 182
Nunes, S. R., 12

O

O'Flahavan, J., 157
O'Rourke, J., 160
Olejnik, S., 16, 140, 181, 190, 192
Olson, R., 29
Omanson, R. C., 68, 140
Ordóñez, C. L., 186
Osborn, J., 157

P

Pagnucco, J. R., 130
Palincsar, A. S., 177
Pany, D., 62
Pearson, P. D., 118, 134, 158
Penno, J. F., 54
Perfetti, C., 44, 66, 67, 68, 122, 138, 143
Perney, J., 12
Person, N. K., 119
Peterson, B., 21
Pinnell, G. S., 112
Pittelman, S. D., 83, 84
Pople, M. T., 68
Powell, J., 11, 16, 160
Pressley, M. P., 162

Q

Qian, D. D., 13
Quealy, R. J., 174

R

Read, J., 29, 30, 32
Reltovich, P. J., 43, 80, 91
Richek, M. G., 49, 134
Richman, B., 50, 127
Risley, T., 5, 116, 118, 132
Rothlein, L., 134
Rowling, J. K., 26
Ruddell, M., 144, 145, 146

S

Samuels, S. J., 13, 21, 105
San Souci, R. C., 74
Sandora, C., 122
Schafer, W. D., 4, 128, 130
Schatz, E. K., 174, 175
Schlichting, K., 140
Schreck, J., 62
Schuster, B. V., 12
Schwanenflugel, P., 44
Schwartz, R. M., 80, 189, 193

Scott, J. A., 7, 34, 44, 65, 140, 142, 187
Shanahan, T., 12
Share, D., 134
Shearer, B., 144, 145, 146
Shefelbine, J., 6, 128
Shelley, P. B., 137
Slater, W., 27
Slonim, N., 20, 57, 133
Smith, M., 6, 26, 134, 177
Smith, R. R., 20
Snow, C. E., 5, 116, 118, 134, 135, 186
Sowell, J., 21, 157, 160, 166
Spiro, R. J., 43, 64, 80, 91
Stahl, S. A., 11, 15, 44, 49, 62, 70, 74, 87, 88, 94, 106, 111, 112, 121, 130, 134, 174, 177, 191
Stanovich, K. E., 6, 13, 14, 40, 127, 128, 129
Sternberg, R., 11, 16, 160
Sticht, T., 53
Suttles, W., 130
Swanborn, M. S. L., 128, 175

T

Tabors, P., 134
Tagliabue, J., 110
Tan, A., 103
Taylor, B. M., 118, 129
Templeton, S., 54
Thorndike, E. L., 18
Thorndike, R. L., 4
Tinkham, T., 64
Tompkins, G. E., 155
Turner, J. C., 130
Tyler, A., 160, 165

V

Van Allsburg, C, 72, 73
Vancil, S. J., 87

Vandevier, R., 49, 134
Vaughan, K., 12, 141, 160, 165
Vaughn, S., 16, 177
Vermeer, A., 13, 31
Vermeulen, K., 12, 141, 160, 165

W

Walley, A. C., 12
Wang, Y. Y., 128, 130
Waring, R., 64
Watson, R., 186
Watts-Taffe, S. M., 140
Wells, G., 39, 119
West, M., 101
White, C., 56
White, E. B., 44
White, T., 21, 27, 157, 160, 166
Wigfield, A., 138
Wilkinson, I. A. G., 54
Williams, M., 5, 27
Willingham, D. T., 79
Willows, D. M., 12
Wilson, P., 129
Wilson, R., 106
Winograd, P., 103
Winsor, P., 157
Wixson, K. K., 74, 79
Wood, P. H., 20
Worthy, J., 122

Y

Yanagihara, A., 21, 157, 160, 166
Yoghoub-Zadeh, Z., 12

Z

Zakaluk, B. L., 23
Zechmeister, E. B., 29, 30, 32

Subject Index

A

Academic language, *see* Literate English
"Academic vocabulary," 108
Academic Word List, 57, 102
Access hypothesis, 13, 15
"Affective filter," 138
Affixes, *see also* Prefixes; Suffixes; Word parts
    absolute vocabulary size and, 30–31
    most frequent in printed English, 166
    word frequency and, 20–21
Amelia Bedelia (Parrish), 151
Antonyms
    in teaching words, 64
    using in concept development, 79–80
Aptitude hypothesis, 13
    in classroom teaching, 16
    overview of, 11–12
Automaticity, 13

B

Bingo, 74, 104–105
"Bird-walking," 111
"Book flood" studies, 129–130
Books/stories
    oral introductions to, 111–116
    significance to vocabulary learning, 126–127
    word consciousness and, 151
Burnt Toast on Davenport Street (Egan),
    120–121

C

Charades, 70
Charlotte's Web (White), 44

"Cleveland Wrecking Yard, The" (Brautigan),
    39–40
Closed-captioned television, 106
"Clunks," 177
Coaching, 119
COBUILD Dictionary, 187
Collaborative strategic reading, 177
Complex concepts, 77
Concept development
    categorization of concepts, 91
    comparing and contrasting concepts,
        88–91
    "criss-crossing" concepts, 96
    "four square" vocabulary learning, 81–82,
        83
    general principles in, 77–80
    possible sentences activity, 94–95
    semantic feature analysis, 91–94
    semantic mapping, 83–88
    word maps, 80, 81
"Concept of definition" map, 80, 82
Concepts
    complex, 77
Content words, 98, 99
Context
    different types of, 176
    problems with, 174–177
    teaching high-frequency words, 105–106
    teaching students to use, 177–181
    using the Internet for, 66–67
    using with word parts and definitions, 188
    vocabulary instruction and, 62–64, 65–67
    word learning and, 173–174
    word meaning and, 183–184, 193
Contextualized language, 37–41

Conversational language, *see also* Oral language; Talking about words
  contextualized/decontextualized qualities, 37–38
  English Language Learners and, 40
  tools to distinguish from written language, 146
  vocabulary growth and, 131–132
  vocabulary richness of, 126
Core vocabulary, 34–36, *see also* High-frequency words
Crazy English (Lederer), 158
Curious George Gets a Job (Rey), 127

D

Decontextualized language, 38–41
  becoming familiar with, 140–141
Definition maps, 189–191
Definitions
  construction of, 189–191
  difficulties in using, 184
  difficulty children have in understanding, 186–188
  failure to convey how words are used, 185–186
  having students re-write, 64–65
  limitations of, 182–183, 193
  standard form for, 186
  using with word parts and context, 188
  vocabulary instruction and, 62, 64–56
  weakness in teaching high-frequency words, 107
  word knowledge and, 42, 44
Derived words
  absolute vocabulary size and, 30–31
  word frequency and, 20–21
Dictionaries
  difficulty children have in understanding, 186–188
  failure to convey how words are used, 185–186
  limitations of, 193
  multiple word meanings in, 183
  "proper names" in, 30
  using, 188–189
Dictionary of word origins (Ayto), 153
Discussions
  used in semantic mapping, 87–88
  used to teach word meanings, 69–74
Dolch Word List, 100
Dramas, 70–71

E

Echo reading, 106
Encarta dictionary, 183, 189
English language

vocabulary size and, 4
word histories, 151–156
words borrowed by, 154–155
English Language Learners
  learning conversational and written English, 40
  problems in teaching high-frequency words, 107
Eponyms, 153, 155
Expressions
  books on, 153
Extrinsic motivation, 138

F

Flashcards, 103–104
Flesch Reading Formula, 23
"Four square" vocabulary learning, 81–82, 83
Function words, 98–99

G

Games
  used in teaching high-frequency words, 104–105
  used in vocabulary instruction, 70, 71, 74
General Service List, 101
Generative word knowledge, 49–50
"Goldilocks" words, 133–134, 136
Greek
  number words, 167
  relational prefixes from, 168–169
Greek mythology, 152–153

H

High-frequency words
  categories of, 97–98, 108
  core vocabulary, 34–36
  lists of, 101–103
  overview of, 98
  problems in teaching, 107
  teaching, 103–106
  very high-frequency, 98–100
High-utility words, 57
"Hink pinks," 151
"Hip pocket" vocabulary learning, 82, 83
Holmes, Oliver Wendell, 78
Homographs, 148–149
Homonyms, 151
Humor, 147–151
Humours, 151, 152

I

Idioms
  books on, 153
  word frequency and, 19–20

Inferences, 16
aptitude hypothesis and, 11–12
Instrumental hypothesis
in classroom teaching, 15
overview of, 10
Intelligence
vocabulary size and, 5
Internet
using to develop word contexts, 66–67
Intrinsic motivation, 138, 140

K

King who Rained, The (Gwynne), 151
Knowledge
readability and, 21–23
vocabulary size and, 5
Knowledge hypothesis
in classroom teaching, 15–16
core vocabulary and, 34, 36
overview of, 10–11
readability and, 22

L

Language
emotional reactions to, 139
rich, importance of exposure to, 125–126
Latin
number words, 167
relational prefixes from, 168–169
Literacy
information culture and, 6
Literate English, *see also* Written language
marginalized children and, 138–139
vocabulary growth and, 36–42, 45–46

M

Matthew effect, 6
Memory game, 74
Metacognition, 145
Metalinguistic awareness
classroom instruction and, 16–17
derived words and, 21
reading comprehension and, 12–13
Metalinguistic hypothesis
in classroom teaching, 16–17
overview of, 12–13
Morphological awareness, 12, 160
Morphology, 141, *see also* Word parts
"Motherese," 116–118
Motivation
fun with words, 142–146
types of, 138
vocabulary growth and, 137–140
Multiple meanings
absolute vocabulary size and, 31–32

metalinguistic awareness and, 12–13
word frequency and, 19
"My Mother Never Read to Me" (Cline and
Necochea), 132

N

"Nonimmediate" talk, 116–118, 136

O

O Thou Improper, Thou Uncommon Noun
(Espy), 153, 155
Open-ended questions, 118
in Text Talk, 119–121
Oral language, *see also* Conversational language; Talking about words
contextualized/decontextualized qualities,
37–38
importance to vocabulary growth, 131–132
language used at school, 134–136
talking to children, 132–134
in the vocabulary growth pyramid, 53–54
vocabulary learning and, 49
Oral reading, *see* Reading aloud
Oxford English Dictionary, 162

P

Pantomimes, 70
Parents
talk around words, 116–118
Phonemic awareness, 12
Picture walking, 112–116
Polysemy, *see* Multiple meanings
Possible sentences activity, 94–95
Prefixes, *see also* Affixes; Word parts
absolute vocabulary size and, 31
derived from Greek and Latin number
words, 167
ease of understanding, 161
examples of, 170–172
how to teach, 163–164
ones most relevant to teach, 160
relational, 168–169
word frequency and, 20–21
*Preventing Reading Difficulties in Young Chil-
dren* (Snow et al.), 135
Proper names/nouns
absolute vocabulary size and, 30
word frequency and, 20
"Psychologically basic words," 32
Puns, 147–148

R

Random House Dictionary, 186
Rare words, 126

Readability
    defined, 18
    knowledge and, 21–23
    vocabulary and, 17–21
    vocabulary-comprehension connection,
        23–24
    word difficulty and, 18–21
    younger children and, 22–23
Readability formulas
    affixes and, 1
    problems with, 23, 24
    reader's knowledge and, 22
    vocabulary knowledge in, 24
    word frequency and, 19
Reading
    collaborative strategic reading, 177
    context and word learning, 173–181
    effective use of, 128
    strategies in, 128–129
    talking about words during, 116–118
    use of dictionaries during, 191–192
    vocabulary growth and, 127–131, 136
    vocabulary learning and, 49
Reading aloud
    impact on vocabulary growth, 134
    introductions to books, 111–116
    in teaching high-frequency words, 105–106
    Text Talk, 119–122
    vocabulary growth and, 49, 53
Reading comprehension
    "book flood" studies, 129–130
    importance of vocabulary knowledge to, 4
    morphological awareness and, 160
    readability and, 23–24
    relationship to vocabulary knowledge, 9–10
        access hypothesis, 13, 15
        aptitude hypothesis, 11–12, 13, 16
        in the classroom, 14–17
        complexity of, 14, 17–18, 24–25
        instrumental hypothesis, 10, 15
        knowledge hypothesis, 10–11, 15–16
        metalinguistic hypothesis, 12–13,
            16–17
        reciprocal hypothesis, 13–14, 17
    resources, 130–131
Reading Recovery, 22
Reading Today (newspaper), 6–7
Reciprocal hypothesis
    in classroom teaching, 17
    overview of, 13–14
Repeated reading, 106
Rich language
    books and, 126–127
    importance of exposure to, 125–126
    oral language and, 131–136
    vocabulary learning and, 48–49
    wide reading and, 127–131
Roman mythology, 152–153

Roots, *see also* Word parts
    derived from Greek and Latin number
        words, 167
    examples of, 170–172
    how to teach, 164
    most relevant to be taught, 162–163

S

Semantic feature analysis, 91–94
Semantic mapping/networks
    description of, 83–85
    example of, 85–88
    for teaching roots, 164
    vocabulary growth and, 34–36
    word meaning in, 11
Sight vocabulary, 3, 108
Skits, 70–71
Socioeconomic status
    "affective filter" concept, 138
    book availability and, 127
    exposure to language and, 118
    learning of literate English and, 139
    vocabulary size and, 5
Spoken language, *see* Conversational lan-
        guage; Oral language
Story Impression, 71–72
Storytelling, 132
Stuart Little (White), 44
Suffixes, *see also* Affixes; Word parts
    absolute vocabulary size and, 31
    how to teach, 164
    most relevant to teach, 160–161
    word frequency and, 20–21
Sustained silent reading, 128, 129, 130, 136
Syllable counting, 18–19, 20
Synonyms
    "hink pinks," 151
    in teaching words, 64
Syntax, 141

T

Talking about words, *see also* Conversational
        language; Oral language
    cognitively challenging, 118–122
    introducing a book, 111–116
    during reading, 116–118
    story reading context, 110
    teacher instructional patterns and, 122
    vs. teaching about words, 109–110
Talking Egg, The (San Souci), 74
Teachers
    assistance with student reading, 130–131
    calling on children, 70
    changing of instructional patterns, 122
    helping students be better word learners,
        157–158

language used at school, 134–136
objections to intensive vocabulary instruction, 68–69
oral book introductions and, 115
strategies for talking about words, 118–119
Text Talk, 119–122
"Three Strikes" activity, 104
"Tier One" words, 133
"Tier Three" words, 133
"Tier Two" words, 102, 133
To Kill a Mockingbird (Lee), 56

V

Venn diagrams, 88–91
Very high-frequency words, 98–100
Very Hungry Caterpillar, The, 116
Vocabulary
    categories of, 97–98, 108
    defined, 3
    estimating absolute size in children, 29–32, 45
    intelligence and, 5
    knowledge and, 5
    lack of academic interest in, 6–7
    readability and, 17–21
Vocabulary growth
    classroom as a community of word learners, 156
    classroom teaching and, 32–33
    core vocabulary knowledge and, 34–36
    difficulties of, 26–27
    education and, 5–6
    generative word knowledge, 49–50
    importance of oral language to, 131–132
    motivation and, 137–140
    promoting, 195
    rates of, 27–29, 30, 32–33, 36
    vocabulary growth pyramid, 50–58, 125–126
    wide reading and, 127–131, 136
    word knowledge complexity and, 42–45, 46
    word volume and, 27–36
    written language and, 36–42
Vocabulary growth pyramid
    levels in, 52–57
    overview of, 50–52, 57–58, 125–126
Vocabulary instruction, *see also* Concept development; Talking about words
    approaches and principles, 48–50, 62–76
    child involvement in processing word meanings, 67–68
    choosing words to teach, 55–57
    high-frequency words, 103–108
    including definitional and contextual information, 62–67
    providing multiple exposure to words, 68–69

rates of vocabulary growth and, 27–29, 30, 32–33, 36
relationship between vocabulary knowledge and reading comprehension, 14–17
sample lesson, 74–75
teaching word parts, 159–165
unpopularity of, 7
using discussions, 69–74
vocabulary growth pyramid, 50–58, 125–126
word categories and how to teach them, 196–197
word consciousness and, 50
word knowledge complexity and, 44–45
word utility and, 57
Vocabulary knowledge, *see also* Word knowledge
    cumulative nature of, 6
    importance to reading comprehension, 4
    reading comprehension and, 9–10
    in the classroom, 14–17
    hypotheses relating, 10–17
    readability, 17–24
    wide reading and, 128, 129
Vocabulary learning, *see also* Word learning strategies
    fun with words, 142–146
    humor, 147–151
    immersion in rich language, 48–49
    significance of books to, 126–127
    vocabulary growth pyramid, 50–58
    word context and, 173–174
    word histories, 151–156
Vocabulary notebooks, 193
Vocabulary self-collection strategy, 144–146
Vocabulary size, 4–5
    estimating in children, 29–32, 45
    wide reading and 128

W

Webster's Third International Dictionary, 30
Wide reading, *see* Reading
Word consciousness, 50
    activities for promoting, 141–142
    children's books and, 151
    classroom as a community of word learners, 156
    defined, 137
    different aspects of, 140–142
    fun with words, 142–146
    metalinguistic awareness and, 16
    motivation and, 137–140
    using humor, 147–151
    in the vocabulary growth pyramid, 53–54
    word histories, 151–156
Word context, *see* Context

Word frequency
  readability and, 19–21
Word Guess game, 71
Word histories, 151–156
Word knowledge, *see also* Vocabulary knowledge
  complexity of, 42–45, 46
  generative, 49–50
  in the vocabulary growth pyramid, 54–55
Word learning strategies, *see also* Vocabulary learning
  definitions and dictionaries, 182–194
  teacher instruction and, 157–158
  word context, 173–181
  word part lists, 166–172
  word parts and, 158–165
Word maps, 80, 81
Word meaning, 3, *see also* entries at Vocabulary
  context and, 183–184, 193
  in semantic networks, 11
Word of the Week, 142–143
Word parts, *see also* Morphology

how to teach, 163–165
  lists of, 166–172
  ones most relevant to teach, 160–163
  relevance of teaching, 159–160
  student awareness of, 141
  usefulness of, 158–159
  using with context and definitions, 188
Word recognition, 3
Word volume
  vocabulary growth and, 27–36
Word wizard activity, 143, 144
Wreck of the Zephyr, The (Van Allsburg), 72, 73
Written language, *see also* Literate English
  becoming familiar with, 140–141
  contextualized/decontextualized qualities, 38–40
  English Language Learners and, 40
  tools to distinguish from conversational language, 146
  vocabulary growth and, 36–42, 45–46
  in the vocabulary growth pyramid, 53–54